YO-ASQ-443

The
Americas in
Italian Literature
and Culture,
1700-1825

To my mother

Stefania Buccini

The Americas in Italian Literature and Culture

1700-1825

Translated by
Rosanna Giammanco

Foreword by Franco Fido

The Pennsylvania State University Press
University Park, Pennsylvania

First published in Italy as *Il Dilemma della Grande Atlantide* in 1990

Library of Congress Cataloging-in-Publication Data

Buccini, Stefania, 1959-
 [Dilemma della Grande Atlantide. English]
 The Americas in Italian literature and culture, 1700-1825 / Stefania Buccini ; translated by Rosanna Giammanco ; foreword by Franco Fido.
    p.   cm.
 Includes bibliographical references and index.
 ISBN 0-271-01418-0
 1. Italian literature—18th century—History and criticism. 2. Italian literature—19th century—History and criticism. 3. North America—In literature. 4. South America—In literature. I. Title.
 PQ4084.B8313 1997
 850.9'327—dc20   95-8913
                                                                                        CIP

Copyright © 1997 The Pennsylvania State University
All rights reserved
Printed in the United States of America
Published by The Pennsylvania State University Press,
University Park, PA 16802-1003

It is the policy of The Pennsylvania State University Press to used acid-free paper for the first printing of all clothbound books. Publications on uncoated stock satisfy the minimum requirements of American National Standard for Information Sciences—Permanence of Paper for Printed Library Materials, ANSI Z39.48-1992.

Contents

List of Illustrations	vii
Foreword by Franco Fido	ix
Author's Note	xiv
1. Christian America and "Savage" America	1
1. Travelers and Explorers Between Two Centuries	12
2. The Comparative Approach: Lafitau, Vico, and Boturini Benaduci	24
2. The Alibis of Exoticism: Myth, Parody, Utopia	39
1. The Italian Enlightenment and the Denunciation of the Return "To All Fours"	39
2. The American Indian in Eighteenth-Century Social Debates	46
3. Carlo Goldoni's "American" Tragicomedies	51
4. The Parody of the "State of Nature": Francesco Cerlone and Ferdinando Degli Obizzi	59
5. Pietro Chiari's Primitivism	63
6. The Utopia of Peru	68

7. Gian Rinaldo Carli's *Lettere americane* and the
   Apotheosis of Utopia 77

3. Tradition and Revision in Eighteenth-Century Histories of
   the New World 85

4. Italy and the New America 107
   1. The Quakers and the Myth of Pennsylvania 107
   2. Benjamin Franklin's Image 118
   3. Revolution and Vittorio Alfieri's *America libera* 123
   4. Filippo Mazzei, Witness to Revolution 136
   5. Luigi Castiglioni's *Travels in the United States of North
      America* 149

5. Epilogue: Nineteenth-Century Developments 161
   1. Lorenzo Da Ponte's America 161
   2. Carlo Botta's *History of the War of the Independence of
      the United States of America* 170
   3. Giacomo Leopardi and the New World 189

Select Bibliography 207

Index 219

List of Illustrations

The illustrations are reproduced courtesy of the John Carter Brown Library, Brown University.

1. Title page of Ludovico Antonio Muratori's *Il Cristianesimo felice nelle Missioni dei Padri della Compagnia di Gesù nel Paraguai.*   6

2. Geographical map of North America, from Louis Hennepin's *Description of Louisiana.*   13

3. Title page of *Il genio vagante.*   16

4. Geographical map of California from Francisco Eusebio Kino's *Passaggio per terra alla California.*   23

5. Title page of Joseph François Lafitau's *Moeurs des sauvages amériquains comparées aux moeurs des premiers temps.*   25

6. Iroquois dances in Lafitau's *Moeurs des sauvages amériquains comparées aux moeurs des premiers temps.*   26

7. Canadian Indians in Lafitau's *Moeurs des sauvages amériquains comparées aux moeurs des premiers temps.*   27

8. Title page of Lorenzo Boturini Benaduci's *Idea de una nueva historia general de l'America septentrional.* 33

9. Title page of the *Museo Historico Indiano* catalogue in Benaduci's *Idea de una nueva historia general de l'America septentrional.* 34

10. Portrait of Lorenzo Boturini Benaduci in *Idea de una nueva historia general de l'America septentrional.* 35

11. Frontispiece of the Prince of San Severo's *Lettera Apologetica.* 71

12. Title page of Gian Rinaldo Carli's *Delle Lettere Americane.* 80

13. Title page of the Burkes' *Storia degli stabilimenti europei in America.* 88

14. Reproduction of Benjamin West's painting in the Burkes' *Storia degli stabilimenti Europi in America.* 89

15. Title page of *Il gazzettiere americano.* 91

16. Geographical map of the Americas in *Il gazzettiere americano.* 92

17. Engraving of Niagara Falls in *Il gazzettiere americano.* 93

18. Title page of Carlo Botta's *Storia della guerra dell'indipendenza degli Stati Uniti d'America.* 172

Foreword

I see a Serpent in Canada who courts me to his love,
In Mexico an Eagle, and a Lion in Peru;
I see a Whale in the South-sea, drinking my soul away.
　　　　—William Blake, "America: A Prophecy"

America qua, America là,
dov'è più l'America
del padre mio?
　　　　—Rocco Scotellaro, "È fatto giorno"

The ambivalence of the reactions that America evoked in European culture was hardly a novelty in the eighteenth century; nor was it particular to the civilization of the Enlightenment.

From the first decades after their discovery, the new Indies seemed the seat of contradictory truths and myths, eliciting both enthusiasm and perplexity. Were they a fabulous reserve of precious raw materials and an inexhaustible source of wealth? Or were they an unhealthy land of punishment and exile? Was this a world inhabited by innocent, happy creatures, a Golden Age that had suddenly materialized before the eyes of the conquistadors as if prehistory had joined history in one bound? Or was it the theater of atrocious and bloody rites such as cannibalism? There seemed to be only two ways to interpret such rites: either the Amerinds were not human beings (in which case scruples about massacring them and sacking their villages were inappropriate), or they were a disquieting mirror of our past and a sad remembrance of a common primordial wild state.

As early as the sixteenth century, there had of course been acute minds capable of drawing a lesson of tolerance and an incentive for self-criticism from the trauma of the suddenly enlarged planet figured in sketchy maps. Guicciardini, for example, in the same passage in which he praised Columbus and stressed the epoch-making importance of the recent discoveries, deplored that the voyages had been motivated by an "immoderate lust for gold and riches," and he sympathized with the natives for being "not unlike tractable and mild animals, easy prey for whoever attacks them" (*History of Italy*, trans. Alexander, 182, 179). Montaigne, for his part, took the commonplace of the "barbarism" of the savages as an occasion to denounce *our* barbarity.

The fact remained that the very existence of the New World implied a denial (or at least called for a revision) of all Christian and humanistic tradition. As Guicciardini noted, the voyages of discovery had "given some cause for alarm to interpreters of the Holy Scriptures, who were accustomed to interpret those verses of the Psalms which declare that the sound of their songs had gone over all the earth and their words spread to the edges of the world, as meaning that faith in Christ had spread over the entire earth through the mouths of the Apostles; an interpretation contrary to the truth since no "signs or relics of our faith [have] been found there" (ibid., 182). In like fashion, the arts and the constructions of the Maya, the Aztecs, and the Incas, which rivaled those of the Romans in magnificence and expertise, undermined the absolutely normative nature of classicism and the certainty of a Eurocentric consciousness.

What changes did the eighteenth century bring to this picture? First, as time passed, although for Europeans America remained the target of expansionist expeditions and colonial ambitions, it was no longer the automatic bargain that it had once been. For nearly two centuries, the wealth of the West Indies had poured into Spain and Portugal and, to a lesser extent, into England and France. Now, however, with the Iberian monarchies in full political decline, England drew from the real Indies—the eastern ones—much greater and more easily won profits. And, at the end of the Seven Years' War, France could lose Canada with the Peace of Paris in 1763 without irremediably compromising its economy and, thirty years later, long managed to oppose all Europe.

If the questions of what America was worth and whom it served became less pressing or led to less peremptory answers, it should have been easier to agree on a definition of what America was and who were its inhabitants. Unfortunately, the philosophes and scholars of the eighteenth century were no less divided on the matter than the theologians and humanists of the sixteenth century had been.

On the one hand, the last voyagers (from Cook to Bougainville) were seeking, along with other, more practical, things, the mirage of an Eden found, so to speak, in symbiosis or in a relationship of mutual support with myth of the noble savage that preceded, but above all followed, Rousseau. On the other hand, a horror of anything different still led Europeans to pick out extreme manifestations of American "barbarity" and to exaggerate them to a paroxysmal extent. One example of this is the episodes of child cannibalism reported in Pedro de Cieça's *Crónica del Perú* in the sixteenth century and repeated by William Robertson in his *History of America* and later by Leopardi in his "Scomessa di Prometeo."

This is the background for Stefania Buccini's precise and intelligent study of the Italian contribution to the eighteenth-century debate on America, in which she follows the path blazed by the few but excellent studies published in Italy on the myth of the noble savage and on the new Indies from Rosario Romeo, Antonello Gerbi, and Ernesto Sestan to Sergio Landucci, Lionello Sozzi, and Piero Del Negro. From them and from other masters Stefania Buccini has learned (among other things) not to impose a linear logic, a coherence, or a philosophical significance on the texts she explores, even if we would find them a convenience. In this sense her work clearly differs, for example, from Tzvetan Todorov's study of the conquest of Mexico, a work that brilliantly put painstaking documentation to the service of ideological and anthropological theses similar to those that so suggestively dramatized the ancient world in Georges Dumézil's *esquisses de mythologie*. Once this is said, however, I must add that out of the imposing mass of memoirs, reports, treatises, histories, plays, and poems that Buccini passes in review, several traits of an Italian approach to the problem emerge, chief among them, little sympathy for the idealizations and the nostalgia for the primitive that were so strong in more industrialized and technologically more advanced countries like England and, above all, France. In the early eighteenth century, even Vico's *Patacones* (like—and the similarity is significant—the exactly contemporary *sauvages amériquains* of the Jesuit Father Lafitau) fascinated their historian as reincarnations of Homeric heroes more than as natural beings or (literally) prehistoric men.

In the debate that divided eighteenth-century students of the Americas—the cultists of nature and primitive innocence on one side and, on the other, the supporters of progress who saw in the Indians excellent disciples to be brought to civilization by more rapid and rational means than the arduous ones hitherto used, amid backsliding and errors, by Europeans—most Italian thinkers were in the latter camp. Not surprisingly, the people most admired by Italian writers from Francesco Algarotti to Giuseppe Parini and Gian Rinaldo Carli were the Incas.

In the second part of her book Buccini continues her account of discussions and myths regarding the Americas in light of the new cultural realities—above all, the political realities—of the late eighteenth and early nineteenth centuries: the rebellion of England's American colonies and the birth of the United States; the first manifestations of a civic and national awareness in Italy.

The American Revolution and the subsequent advent of a democracy of farmers, businessmen, and soldiers who all became laborious and equal citizens were a powerful innovation that inspired the enthusiasm of both a libertarian aristocrat like Vittorio Alfieri and a middle-class "moderate Jacobin" like Carlo Botta. Voltaire's model of the *ingénu*, the Huron who arrives in Europe bringing with him the healthy outlook and the frankness of the state of nature, had been accepted in Italy above all thanks to his difficult but inevitable conversion to civilized society when, "avec l'approbation de tous les honnêtes gens," he became "un guerrier et un philosophe intrépide." A few decades later, Benjamin Franklin, the peaceable but patriotic ambassador of the colonists in arms, seemed to have been born to embody the transition from the old myths of an Indian and wild America to the new myths of a Puritan and "Quaker" America. The former printer from Philadelphia had the simple manners and the modest but convenient dress of the real Quakers without their sectarian severity. Moreover, Franklin was a man of science and a philanthropist, an inventor and a philosopher, a disciple of the *encyclopédistes* sent to us from the New World to show us the ways of progress and the future.

If for more than two centuries the European mind viewed America with the fascination and the anxiety of one who meditates on his own remote past, now the free nation of Washington and Jefferson clearly represented, in the eyes of the subjects of divine-right monarchies, a hope and a possible future. As Leopardi said of pleasure, then, America was in a certain sense "always past or future and never present, just as happiness is always someone else's and never one's own." Not surprisingly, Leopardi himself, in his profound mistrust of magnificent and progressive destinies, located in California his nostalgic hypostasis of a condition that was as blessed as it was still untouched by the evils of civilization and even by thought. At the same time that he seemed to cling tenaciously to the past like a last follower of an outworn and not very "Italian" primitivism, then, Leopardi intuits the ambiguous nature of the myth that interests him, and he incorporates it in a polemical statement that was just as up to date politically as it was a glorification of the upstanding Americans.

Stefania Buccini follows with precision and efficacy the sinuous progress of Italy's "rediscovery" of America as it stood on the threshold of becoming a modern country. The voyage is full of encounters with texts of surprising interest—Muratori's *Il Cristianesimo felice* and the exotic dramas of Francesco Cerlone, Carli's *Lettere americane* and Luigi Castiglioni's *Viaggio negli Stati Uniti*, and many more—and although her book provides a wealth of information, it reads like a story.

As with all self-respecting tales, we can find a moral to this one. On the one hand, Europeans, and among them, cautiously, Italians, had long viewed America as an "elsewhere," the site of a raw young world in which it was possible for both individuals and institutions to enjoy a second chance, starting over from zero. Europeans went there, in their imaginations or on ships, on their own initiative or deported, to make their fortunes like Moll Flanders or to hide their own weakness like Des Grieux, to take on new and adventurous careers like Lorenzo Da Ponte or to search for themselves like René. On the other hand, there was the more modest and more solid reality of the New World, which was to be understood as it really was, which (before Tocqueville, with dubious success) invited firsthand knowledge, and which sent representatives to Europe that ranged from the Polynesian king Omai to the wise jack-of-all-trades from Pennsylvania. Between the ever-approaching poles of an America of the mind and a much more contradictory and uncomfortable America of fact there flourished and faded the versatile myth, long to die, that Stefania Buccini so suggestively reconstructs for us in this book.

Franco Fido

Author's Note

I remind the reader that the term *savage* is used here without any negative or disparaging intent, such intent having already been challenged by the eighteenth-century scholars.

1

Christian America and "Savage" America

Tzvetan Todorov's declaration that "Christopher Columbus has discovered America but not the Americans" serves as a point of departure for an investigation of the myth of the New World in the century of the Enlightenment.[1] Indeed, it was above all in the general context of verifications and revisions in the seventeenth and the eighteenth centuries that the Americans, lost on an immense continent discovered only two hundred years earlier, thrust themselves as exotic symbols on the attention of an intellectual generation curious to know their history. At that time, the questions of their origin and their character exerted a fascination over a European society engaged in a debate that has been summarized in exemplary fashion, in both its secular and religious aspects, by Antonello

1. Tzvetan Todorov, *The Conquest of America: The Question of the Other*, trans. Richard Howard (New York, Harper and Row, 1984), 60. On Todorov's book, see Giuliano Gliozzi, "Tre studi sulla scoperta culturale del Nuovo Mondo," *Rivista storica italiana* 98 (1985): 161.

Gerbi.[2] It should be stressed, however, that although intellectuals and missionaries started from different perspectives, they joined company to share the conviction that the Indian was a savage—a noble savage or a wicked savage—and was thus a "different" subject who did not enjoy the same rights as themselves. "American" was thus equivalent to "savage," and we need to wait until the late eighteenth century to see the term "Americans" applied to "the colonists of the United States" and "the natives" called "savages," as in the Milanese botanist Luigi Castiglioni.[3]

During the eighteenth century, the New World continued to be understood, in substance, according to two dominant but merging and complimentary *Weltanschauungen*. The first was a hispanocentric perspective that ignored the English possessions and divided "the entire great continent . . . into Mexican, or northern, America and Peruvian, or southern, America";[4] the second was a religious conception that lent legitimacy to identifying "American" with "non-Christian" and "savage" and "European" with "Christian" and "civilized." Thus two different conceptions met in "America" and "Americas." However, the two conceptions worked to give the measure of and define one another, as confirmed by the Jesuit Filippo Salvatore Gilij in his *Saggio di storia americana*: "America must be considered in various forms and from various points of view. There is the savage one; there is the civilized one. The first is the one in which only the Americans live. The other is the one that, by means of wise laws and fine and Christian customs introduced there, the Spanish occupy along with the Indians there reduced."[5] This reflection is founded not only on a geographical distinction but also on a religious presupposition that the two Americas corresponded to two distinct existential phases in the indigenous population: an earlier prehistoric phase and a

---

2. Antonello Gerbi, *The Dispute of the New World: The History of a Polemic, 1750-1900*, trans. Jeremy Moyle, rev. enl. edition (Pittsburgh: University of Pittsburgh Press, 1973).

3. Luigi Castiglioni, *Travels in the United States of North America, 1785-87. With Natural History Commentary and Botanical Observations*, translated and edited by Antonio Pace (Syracuse: Syracuse University Press, 1983), 273 n. 16. For seventeenth-eighteenth century meanings of *America* and *Americas*, see Harold Jantz, "The Myths about America: Origins and Extension," in *Jahrbuch für Amerikastudien*, 15 (1962): 6-18.

4. Vincenzo Coronelli, *Biblioteca universale sacro-profana o sia gran dizionario* (Venice: Tivani, 1703), 3:entry 109.

5. Filippo Salvatore Gilij, *Saggio di storia americana o sia naturale, civile, e sacra de' regni, e delle province spagnuole di terra-ferma nell'America meridionale* (Rome: Luigi Perego erede Salvioni, 1780) 1:xxi.

later historical phase that coincided with conversion and that changed them "from uncouth to civilized; from shameless to shameful; from those savage beasts to reasonable men."[6] Thus evangelization had the absolute merit of prompting in the savages a beneficent "crisis of presence" that determined their miraculous absorption into the rhythm of history and the process of civilization.[7]

Even at its first appearance in the sixteenth century, the debate on the nature of the Americans was flawed by this dual framework of "before" and "after" their conversion.[8] Indeed, missionaries' reports contain both the traditional negative portrait of the Indian obstinately confined within the irreversible barbarity of primordial times and a more positive image of the native as a potentially novice and disciplined Christian. As Rosario Romeo states, it was precisely "the religious fervor of the evangelizers that acted as a corrective and pushed them to seeing in the Americans brothers and creatures of God"[9] and that persuaded the Catholic church to reconcile the populations of the New World with the monogenetic postulate of the Scriptures and the dogma of original sin. Thus the Indians ceased to be lost sheep and could finally redeem their wildness by becoming an integral part of the great body of Christianity.

The missionaries, who became "ethnologists" more out of necessity than by vocation,[10] often conducted systematic inquiries into the customs of the indigenous populations, thus making the effort to recognize, beyond the natives' apparent diversity, an incipient identity between those new populations and those of the old continents. This explains why the

6. Ibid.
7. We take as starting point Ernesto De Martino and his *Il mondo magico: Prolegomeni a una storia del magismo* (Turin: Einaudi, 1948) and his essay "Crisi della presenza e reintegrazione religiosa," in *Aut Aut* 6 (1956): 17-38. According to De Martino, the crises of presence provoked by an individual's participation in magic rites and religious feasts are to be interpreted as indices of evolutionary stages, therefore as indices of the passage from unconsciousness to a conscious presence in history.
8. For a synthesis of the debate about the nature of the American Indian between the sixteenth and seventeenth centuries, see Antonello Gerbi, *La natura delle Indie Nove: Da Cristoforo Colombo a Gonzalo Fernandez de Oviedo* (Milan: Ricciardi, 1975); Federica Ambrosini, *Paesi e mari ignoti: America e colonialismo europeo nella cultura veneziana (secoli XVI-XVII)* (Venice: Deputazione Editrice, 1982); Anthony Pagden, *The Fall of Natural Man: The American Indian and the Origins of Comparative Ethnology* (Cambridge: Cambridge University Press, 1982); Rosario Romeo, *Le scoperte americane nella coscienza italiana del Cinquecento* (Bari: Laterza, 1989).
9. Rosario Romeo, *Le scoperte americane*, 79.
10. See Michèle Duchet, *Anthropologie et histoire au siècle des lumières* (Paris: François Maspero, 1971), 10.

Jesuits so often reached the conclusion in the reports they sent back from the Americas—contributions of highest importance for a knowledge of the New World—that the savages were docile, basically good, and endowed with qualities that, if cultivated, could make them into excellent Christians.[11] Better still, they enjoyed natural virtues that suggested a revival of the authentic spirit of primitive Christianity and led to the founding of a model society such as the one the Jesuits established in Paraguay.

Nonetheless, we must admit that if, on the one hand, the indigenous populations acquired positive traits because they were receptive to the word of God and permitted the missionaries who landed in the New World full of a crusading spirit to enlarge the boundaries of Christianity, on the other hand their original modus vivendi, without laws, governance, or conventions, confirmed for secular-minded intellectuals the existence of a natural morality. Both points of view idealized a "savage" world that was invented before it was discovered and that had been seen from the start through the distorting lenses of myth.[12]

The traditional legend of the Golden Age, of a precivilized, metahistorical time, thus found a historical and geographical referent in the primitive

---

11. See *Lettres édifiantes et curieuses, écrites des missions étrangères par quelques missionaires de la Compagnie de Jésus*, 34 volumes (Paris: Nicolas Le Clerc, 1702-76).

12. See Giuseppe Cocchiara, *Il mito del buon selvaggio: Introduzione alla storia delle teorie etnologiche* (Messina: D'Anna, 1948): "The so-called savage, before being discovered was invented. In good part it was invented by ethnography itself. But undoubtedly, it was the philosophy of the eighteenth century that invented it more richly and successfully" (7). Gliozzi summarizes the possible causes of idealization of the savage man (*Adamo e il Nuovo Mondo: La nascita dell'antropologia come ideologia coloniale: dalle genealogie bibliche alle teorie razziali [1500-1700]* [Florence: La Nuova Italia, 1977]): "Some wanted to attribute the idealization of the 'savage' to a fascination with tropical climes; others, noting blacks also originate from tropical regions yet were not idealized, preferred to believe that idealization was proportional to the distance traveled by the observer. Still others believed they could surmount the contradictions of geographic determinism by turning idealization into an inversely proportional factor of direct acquaintance with the natives; finally, still others resolved their predicament by constructing an idyllic image of primitive people or a kind of psychological archetype which, as such, no longer required historical explanation" (2-3). For a historical analysis of the fetishist implications of the noble savage, see Hayden White, *The Noble Savage Theme as Fetish*, in *First Images of America: The Impact of the New World on the Old*, ed. Fredi Chiappelli (Berkeley and Los Angeles: University of California Press, 1976): "The idea of the Noble Savage represents the ironic stage in the evolution of the wild man motif in European thought. It is an 'absurd' idea, the fetishistic nature of which is obvious; for its true referent is not the savage of the new or any other world, but humanity in general in relation to which the very notion of 'nobility' is a contradiction" (1:129).

state of the Americans, and the Age of Gold of the New World became a polemical antidote to civilization's social and moral failings. Montaigne, in his essay "Of Cannibals," had already taken as a point of departure the presupposition that certain peoples are judged to be savage because "each man calls barbarism whatever is not his own practice," and he concluded that "we may well call these people barbarians, in respect to the rules of reason, but not in respect to ourselves, who surpass them in every kind of barbarity."[13] This thought led Montaigne much further than one might imagine, since he discerned in the psyche of *l'homme policé* the presence of a latent savagery; an atavistic tendency coinciding with original sin. The paradox that cannibals are less barbarous than so-called civilized peoples who brutalize their enemies is thus meant as a provocative declaration that not only denounces the conquests of civilization but also reverses the traditional equations of civilized = Christian; savage = non-Christian to offer a heretical alternative: brutal because Christian; good because non-Christian and wild.[14]

Implicit in the mythologizing of the natural state that was to culminate in a primitivism à la Rousseau was a condemnation of the European conquistadors as profaners of the American Age of Gold. For example, Muratori, agreeing with Las Casas on European barbarianism, made the dissolution of the American Eden coincide with the Conquest and declared with indignation that "at the time of the Spaniards' arrival, all those mainland Islands and Provinces were filled with people, as peopled a land as any in the world; those people were for the most part simple, without malice, patient and peaceful, and they even welcomed the European strangers."[15] Muratori, for whom Las Casas's apostolate represents a precedent of the "Happy Christianity" of Paraguay, went on to deplore the unheard-of violence of the conquistadors who strode into the New World "totally oblivious not only to the Gospel, but also to being human . . . , raging like wolves among docile sheep, continuously finding pretexts and

---

13. *Of the Caniballes*, in *Montaigne's Essays*, 2 vols., trans. John Florio, ed. J. M. Stewart (London: Nonesuch, 1931), 1:209, 214. Montaigne's famous observation recalls a passage by Franklin; see *Remarks Concerning the Savages of North-America* in Benjamin Franklin, *Writings from Poor Richard's Almanac* (New York: Library of America, 1987): "Savages we call them, because their manners differ from ours, which we think the Perfection of Civility" (969).

14. See Piero Del Negro, *Il mito americano nella Venezia del Settecento* (Padua: Liviana, 1986), 58.

15. Ludovico Antonio Muratori, *Il Cristianesimo felice nelle Missioni dei Padri della Compagnia di Gesù nel Paraguai* (Venice: Pasquali, 1743), 1:8.

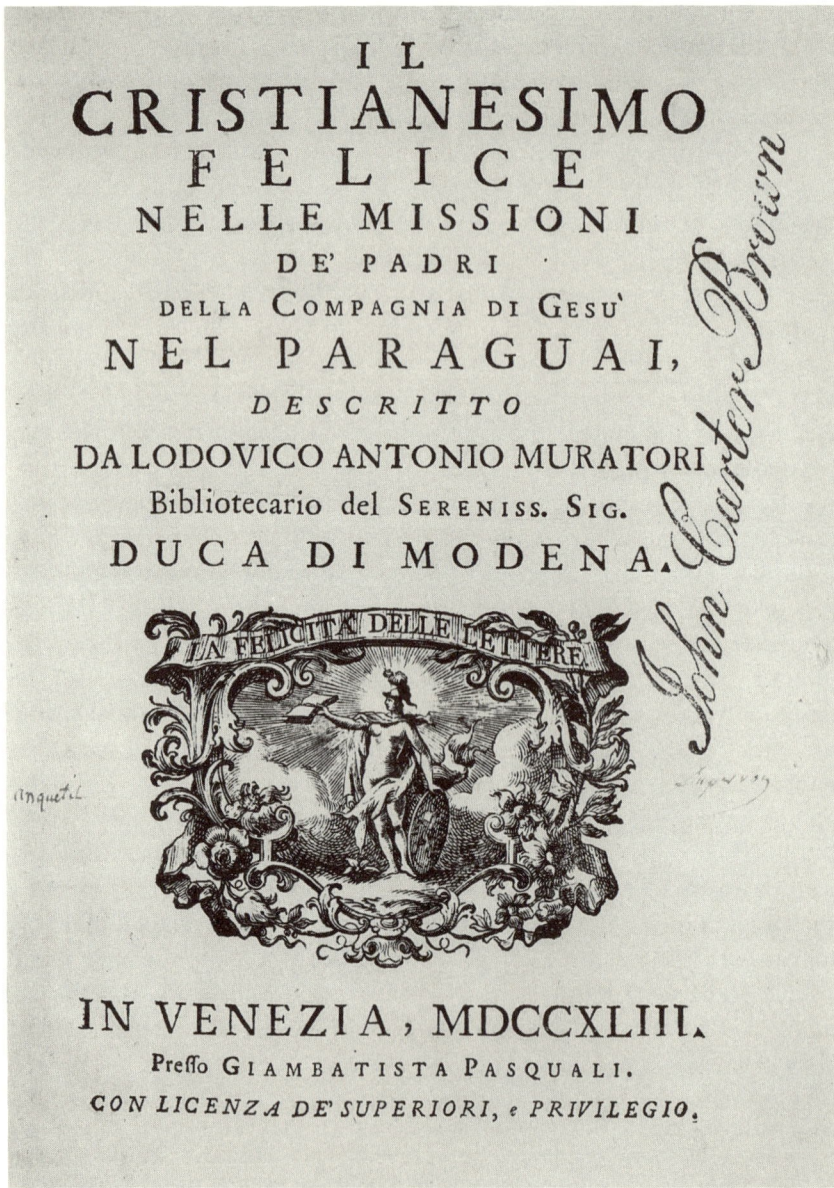

Fig. 1. Title page of Ludovico Antonio Muratori's *Il Cristianesimo felice nelle Missioni dei Padri della Compagnia di Gesù nel Paraguai*.

new cruelties to despoil so many American populations of their riches and goods."[16] Nothing remained except trying to restore to the American peoples the legendary golden ages by inducing them to profess a primitive and innocent Christianity as in the "famous Jesuit empire in Paraguay, where a partisan spirit makes the first golden age come alive again."[17] In his monumental *Il Cristianesimo felice delle Missioni dei Padri della Compagnia di Gesù nel Paraguai* (1743), Muratori illustrated to eighteenth-century society this painful yet glorious conquest of the Jesuits in South America. Most eighteenth-century intellectuals erroneously interpreted *Il Cristianesimo felice* within a Jesuit context and even believed it had been commissioned by the Society of Jesus. However, an examination of the author's correspondence and notes reveals that his idea of writing a work on the missions in South America arose freely, outside any manipulation by that religious order; and furthermore, that several attempts made by Muratori to obtain information from the Jesuits went unanswered. For example, a letter to Cassiodoro Montagioli reads: "A few days ago I thought about writing a short piece to be entitled more or less, *Il Cristianesimo felicissimo nelle Missioni della Compagnia di Gesù al Paraguai.* I have sufficient material for this. Nevertheless I wrote to the Jesuit Father Contuccio Contucci who is there, informing him of my plan and asking him to furnish whatever special records of those South American countries they may have there, for I would never make anything public unless reviewed

16. Ibid. Guicciardini also had the dissolution of the American "Garden of Eden" coincide with the Conquest. He did recognize the blessed innocence of the Americans who are "happie for the sweetnesse of the aire . . . , being most simple in their manners, and contented with that which the liberalitie of nature brought forth for them," but believed the newly discovered populations are "most unhappie, in that [they have] no certaine religion, no knowledge in learning, no science in negociations or handy crafts, and [are] without the art of warre, and without knowledge or experience in anything, be as it were no other than tractable and meeke creatures, and a prey most easie to whomsoever would assaile them"; *The Historie of Guicciardin*, trans. Geffray Fenton (London: Richard Field, 1618), book 6, 242.

17. *Il costume antico e moderno di tutti i popoli*, ed. Giulio Ferrario (Florence: Vincenzo Batelli, 1826-28), 3:228. However, some reservations are raised about the Jesuit paradise: "In Europe such a system of government appeared so laudable that the beautiful destiny of these Indians was almost envied. . . . It seems however clear that they were not so childlike as one would have wanted them to be. Supposing, however, it had been true, if after over a century and a half the Jesuit experience had not sufficed to correct their imbecility, shouldn't one of the two following deductions be true? Either the Jesuit governance was against their becoming civilized, or there was no design to keep them enslaved so as to release them from a state of infancy that was inherent in their very nature" (270).

by them first. Several weeks have gone by and I have received no reply; I cannot fathom why, since such a work would add to their glory and they should be only pleased to have a disinterested pen praise their labors."[18]

Encouraged by both the erudite reawakening of the times and the correspondence between the Jesuit Giuseppe Cattaneo (1696-1733), missionary in Paraguay, and his brother, Muratori "confined in Modena ... without having ever set foot outside Italy", with "the feet and eyes of others"[19] "traveled" to the holy lands of Paraguay in order to write the history of the Jesuit *riduzioni*. Desiring to provide a reconstruction that would differ from one written "by those who mix in adventure and romance," Muratori based his work on several Italian and foreign Jesuit sources.

The Indians of the *riduzioni* enjoyed greater freedom than all the other subjects of the kingdom of Spain, as they had no obligations other than a small tax to which men only were subjected, and military duties in case of need. In any case, although Muratori praised the institution of collective property and the limitation of currency as guarantees of equality, he never went so far as to fantasize utopias, such as proposing the "Christian communistic" system of Paraguay as a possible model for European society. He confessed to "having fallen in love" with those missions insofar as they reminded him of "the primitive Church" and praised the admirable example of the missionaries who carried the cross among barbarians:

> Looking at these apostolic workers is thus a wonderful spectacle for mankind, which could, in a manner of saying, move the angel saints in Heaven to envy. They are all afire, panting to reach such a beautiful

---

18. Letter to Cassiodoro Montagioli, May 1742, in *Opere di Ludovico Antonio Muratori*, in *Dal Muratori al Baretti*, ed. Giorgio Falco and Fiorenzo Forti (Milan: Ricciardi, 1967), 2:1963.

19. Ludovico Antonio Muratori, *Il Cristianesimo felice*, 1:ii. [Translator's note: The citation is at p. xii of the author's preface in the English translation, *A Relation of the Missions of Paraguay*, translated into English from the 1754 French translation of Félix Esprit de Lourmel of Muratori's *The happy state of Christianity in the Missions of the Fathers of the Society of Jesus in Paraguay* (London: J. Marmaduke, 1759): "But how is it possible I should write on so distant a part of the world, who never stept out of Italy, and hardly ever out of Modena? I have conveyed myself in thought into Paraguay." Based on the French text, the English version bears little resemblance to the original, the French translator having, by his own admittance, "reduced the author's account to half the length of the first chapters ..., taken a greater liberty in cutting off some things, suppressed repetitions, transposed from one chapter to another some facts that seemed to be misplaced, ... retrenched [Muratori's] diffuse style, lopping off everything that favoured to panegyric" (vi, vii, viii of the Translator's Preface).]

goal. Tell them that they will suffer immensely, constrained together in a ship's hole, among innumerable hardships, navigating four, six or eight thousand miles, experiencing the dangers of fierce storms, of pirates, of the sorrowful stillness of the equinox line: they are just not afraid. Add that they will go to live in proximity of, or amidst barbarians, or at least amidst poor country people; that they will no longer enjoy beautiful Europe and its abundant comforts; that they will see again neither relatives nor friends; and that there will be the frequent danger of losing one's life to the arrows and clubs of those inhuman populations. Nothing restrains them; on the contrary, it makes them bolder, in as much as they would call themselves quite fortunate if they were to crown the course of their sacred ministry with such a blessed death.[20]

Preaching the Gospel was therefore a modern crusade that turned savages away from "unrestrained liberty" and onto the path of honesty, probity, and truth. Several letters included in the second part of *Cristianesimo felice* document the sacrifices and discomforts borne by these "apostolic workers." Among these is a 1719 letter from Father Gervasoni to his brother Angelino that describes an unusual "land navigation" from Buenos Aires to Cordova in Tucuman:

I said navigation mainly for two reasons: first, because throughout the whole journey, which lasted one month, we not only never found a small mountain or a hill, but we also never detected from afar any mountainous swell. . . . Second, I said navigation because before starting on a journey, one must stock up on supplies just as if one were putting out to sea.[21]

---

20. Muratori, *Il Cristianesimo felice*, 2:3. "Besides planting and establishing the religion of Christ among barbarians, it is usually impossible to reach results other than those reached in the first three centuries when the religion was planted and it expanded to the three parts of the known world. In ancient times, the earth watered with the Martyrs' blood bore great fruits" (ibid., 2:179). Moved by the fervor of neophytes, Muratori writes: "It is a joy to see in those sacred temples, not precious marbles, gems, gold and silver, but the composure, devotion and fervor of these new Christians, especially as they approach the holy Sacraments or hear the word of God from the mouth of the Parish Priest. At the end of every Sermon it is customary to have them recite the Act of Contrition. You then see them full of compunction, break down in tears, denounce with a holy rage all sins, especially drunkenness, their innate vice which with God's help has finally been uprooted from those peoples" (2:58).

21. Ibid., 2:67. This page recalls a passage in which Father Gilij describes the "apostolic journey" in the Orinoco forest (*Saggio di storia americana*): "Journeying to the forest takes

The difficulty in locating water, the cold and the hostility of the *mestizos* (crossbreeds between Indians and Spaniards) did not prevent the Jesuit from reaching the mission in Cordova, and for him the fact of having reached it alive and in good health was a "special grace from God who, seeing the great scarcity of workers among these plentiful people, almost miraculously keeps those few who are already there."[22] The stories of these Jesuit adventures are found in the second volume of the work, which contains several documents on the *riduzioni* in Guyana, Sinaloa, and Sonora and the wild Californian peninsula. The accounts from California written by the Milanese Father Salvaterra confirmed that to the "Californese" [*sic*] "the most flavorful dish was human flesh" and that "their preferred forms of entertainment were dancing and getting drunk," until the time when the Jesuit fathers "came to spread the light of the Gospel in those idolatrous places" and removed Satan from his "centuries-old peaceful possessions."[23] Although Muratori did not follow the traditional Jesuitic tendency to exaggerate the original barbarianism of the future neophytes (he refused to believe that initially "Indians were not human beings like us, but were an animal species between man and monkey, that is, human-looking beasts"),[24] he did insist on the beneficial effects of evangelization on the heathen. In fact, until the end of the eighteenth century the belief persisted that Americans were ruled by a dangerous wildness that only

---

a long time. It is true one usually finds food, feeding one time on wild fruit, another time on turtle, other times on other animals. Still, there are many places where one finds nothing to eat! . . . This type of wandering life seems to me at first quite noble, God helping the Wayfarer, as it offers incredible sweetness. Although this journeying might seem thoughtful and melancholy, the contrary is true. . . . I must naively confess that I drew inexplicable pleasure from these difficult travels in Orinoco country" (3:91-92). Bougainville, in *A Voyage Round the World Performed by Order of His Most Christian Majesty In the Years 1766, 1767, 1768, and 1769 by Lewis de Bougainville*, 2 vols., trans. John Reinhold Forster, F.A.S. (London: printed for J. Nourse, etc., 1772), also recalls the holy apostolate of the Jesuits in Paraguay: "The Jesuits entered upon this carrier with the courage of martyrs, and the patience of angels. Both these qualifications were requisite to attract, retain, and bend to obedience and labour, a race of savage, inconstant men, who were attached to their indolence and independence. The obstacles were infinite, the difficulties increased at each step; but zeal got the better of every thing, and the kindness of the missionaries at last brought these wild, diffident inhabitants of the woods, to their feet" (1:98). On the other hand, Voltaire's interpretation of the Jesuits in *Candide* is ironic: in it, the protagonist, kidnapped by the Oreillon cannibals of South America, is considered a delicacy because he is believed to be a Jesuit.

22. Ibid., 2:72.
23. Ibid., 2:146.
24. Ibid., 1:9.

the Gospel's message could miraculously transform into meekness. As Gilij also indicates:

> Let it therefore be said that Indians (I am speaking especially of the savages and exclude the ancient Mexicans and Peruvians) are an uncultured people. Their features are not displeasing; they have unusual rites and customs. They are a strange and very often cruel people, with an intellect which is not bad, but unsteady in doing good; they are however easily trainable both in the Christian religion as well as in the customs of civilized life. In conclusion, they are a people who, unlike us, have not made great progress in the sciences and the arts, but who are capable of doing so once they conquer their laziness.[25]

Through both the violence of its conquistadors and the peaceful message of its preachers, Todorov writes, Europe "has tried to assimilate the other, to do away with an exterior alterity, and has in great part succeeded. As Columbus wished, the colonized people have adopted our customs and have put on clothes."[26] Already Rousseau had declared that the process of civilization of the savage world was leading only to illusory results:

> It is something extremely remarkable that, for all the years that the Europeans have tormented themselves in order to acclimate the savages of various countries to their lifestyle, they still have not been able to win over a single one of them, not even by means of Christianity; for our missionaries sometimes turn them into Christians, but never into civilized men.[27]

For Rousseau, as had been the case for Montaigne, "to civilize" did not mean "to convert"; in turn, to convert did not mean to come to know these new populations:

> To preach the Gospel in a useful manner, zeal alone is needed, and God gives the rest. But to study men, talents are needed which God

---
25. Filippo Salvatore Gilij, *Saggio di storia americana*, 2:xi.
26. Tzvetan Todorov, *The Conquest of America*, 247-48.
27. Jean-Jacques Rousseau, *Discourse on the Origin of Inequality*, in *Basic Political Writings*, trans. and ed. Donald A. Cress, intro. Peter Gay (Indianapolis: Hackett, 1987), 106 n. 16.

is not required to give anyone, and which are not always the portion of saints.[28]

According to Rousseau, the entire earth is covered with nations of which we know only the names and none of the four categories into which travelers are divided—navigators, soldiers, merchants, and missionaries—was able, thus far, to know the peoples of the Earth. This merit clearly belonged to the professional travelers and explorers.

1. Travelers and Explorers Between Two Centuries

Throughout the seventeenth century, the exploration of new lands made possible a widening of Europe's horizons and therefore a partial emancipation of the New World from a background steeped in fable and legend. The exciting era of discoveries was followed by an era of exploration, of verification, of travels understood as a search for curiosities and as an experience of "difference." At the turn of the century, alongside the missionaries and the explorers who continued to plough the ocean, the former driven by an evangelical spirit, the latter by a spirit of discovery, new stereotypes of travelers began to emerge, such as the collector, the aristocrat, and the merchant.[29]

The travel diary of the Franciscan Louis Hennepin (1640-1701?), *A Description of Louisiana*,[30] printed for the first time in Paris in 1683 and translated into Italian three years later, must be situated within this new perspective of geographical and anthropological notions. In 1678, along with La Salle, the author had made his way to the source of the Mississippi, and the account of his exploit represents the first description to appear in Italy of the Great Lakes area and of the American populations of the central and northern areas. A careful examination of Indian customs, and the observation of an evident similarity between their customs and Jewish

---

28. Ibid., 99.
29. On the new types of travelers who emerge during the seventeenth century, see Daria Perocco, *Viaggiatori barocchi in America*, in *Le Americhe: Storie di viaggiatori italiani* (Milan: Electa, 1987), 106.
30. Louis Hennepin, *A Description of Louisiana*, trans. John Shea (New York: J. G. Shea, 1880).

Fig. 2. Geographical map of North America, from Louis Hennepin's *Description of Louisiana*.

customs, led Hennepin to believe in a common genesis of Hebrews and Americans:

> One might even question whether the Indians are not of Jewish origin because of their similarity to the Jews in several respects. They, like Jews, make tent-shaped lodges. They anoint themselves with oil. They are superstitiously influenced by dreams. . . . It seems also that God's curse has fallen on them as on the Jews, for they are brutal and extremely stubborn. They are without fixed and settled abode.[31]

This was not an isolated observation, since the theory of the genesis of Americans from Hebrews was already widespread in the sixteenth century and was used by its supporters to interpret a European expansion in the New World as a continuation of the *Reconquista*.[32]

In *A Description of Louisiana* Hennepin emphasized that Indians were obstinate barbarians and that attempts to recall them to civilization

31. Ibid., 143.
32. See Giuliano Gliozzi, *Adamo e il Nuovo Mondo*, 69.

through religion often failed. They seemed meekly to receive the preaching of the Gospel, but the next day they would retain no trace of it; they forgot the admonishments of the patient missionaries, and reverted to their barbaric state. As Muratori would specify, Americans are, in fact, "of a fickle and voluble mind, because one day they seem fervently converted Christians, and the following day they all escape back to their Gentile rites."[33] Even Benjamin Franklin wrote:

> The Missionaries who have attempted to convert them to Christianity, all complain of this as one of the great Difficulties of their Mission. The Indians hear with Patience the Truths of the Gospel explained to them, and give their usual Tokens of Assent and Approbation: you would think they were convinced. No such Matter. It is mere Civility.[34]

With the exception of the Hurons and the Iroquois of Canada, who stood out on account of their higher degree of civilization, the natives from Louisiana still lived immersed in a state of wildness and were extraordinarily successful in facing ferocious beasts, natural calamities, and inclement weather. According to Hennepin, the physical strength of the Illinois tribe's children was truly amazing:

> Indian children are so hardened to cold that in midwinter they run naked through the snow and wallow in it like little pigs without ill effect. In summer when the air is full of mosquitoes, they also go naked and play without noticing the pricks of these little insects.[35]

Hennepin found the same degree of savagery among all the natives of Louisiana:

> They never wash their plates, which are of wood or bark, or their bowls and spoons.... They almost never wash their hands or faces.... They often eat off the plate from which their dogs have eaten without cleaning it.... Those who have ... shirts almost

33. Ludovico Antonio Muratori, *Il Cristianesimo felice*, 1:23.
34. Benjamin Franklin, *Remarks Concerning the Savages of North America*, 971.
35. *A Description of Louisiana*, 144.

never wash them but let them rot on their backs. They rarely cut their nails.[36]

As early as the last ten years of the century, *A Description of Louisiana*, which would become a leading text in the libraries of the "Americanists" of the eighteenth century, met with notable success. In 1691 Valerio Zani (anagram of Aurelio degli Anzi) from Milan included some pages from Hennepin's work in an anthology of travel stories he edited.[37] As Ramusio[38] and Moltalboddo[39] had already done, Zani collected four volumes of several accounts of Italian and foreign travelers, often accompanied by comments. Sometimes these were accomplished reviews of contemporary texts, such as the *Histoire générale des Antilles, habitées par les François*[40] by the Dominican Father Du Tertre:

> He divides his book into two parts. The first part contains an account of events up to the present, as [an island in the Antilles] was already inhabited by Caribs. These people were so barbaric and crude that they neither knew how to read nor write stories; and their traditions are so absurd that none can be taken seriously. . . . The second part contains a wealth of information about the island's natural life; as its climate is quite different from ours, there exist plants and animals so different from ours that some may not even seem believable.[41]

The anthology selections, however, indicated a singular taste for the unusual and the mysterious, which led the editor to choose stories where the subject matter was natural prodigies or monstrous human beings.[42]

---

36. Ibid., 159.
37. *Il genio vagante: Biblioteca curiosa di cento e più relazioni di viaggi stranieri de' nostri tempi* (Parma: Giuseppe dall'Oglio e Ippolito Rosati, 1691-93).
38. Giovanni Battista Ramusio (1485-1557) had published three volumes of various witness accounts by explorers and travelers. The third volume is devoted to America: *Terzo volume delle navigationi et viaggi nel quale si contengono le navigationi al Mondo Nuovo* (Venice: Stamperia De Giunti, 1556).
39. Fracanzano da Montalboddo had published in 1507 several reports of voyages around the world; among these, the first three voyages by Columbus: *Paesi novamente retrovati* (Vicenza: Henrico Vicentino, 1507).
40. (Paris: Jolly, 1667-71).
41. *Il genio vagante*, 3:72-73.
42. See *Lettera di M. Cristien scritta dall'isola Martinica a un licenziato della Sorbona intorno ad un Uomo Marino vedutosi nelle coste di quell'isola il 23 maggio 1671*, in ibid., 3:102-3.

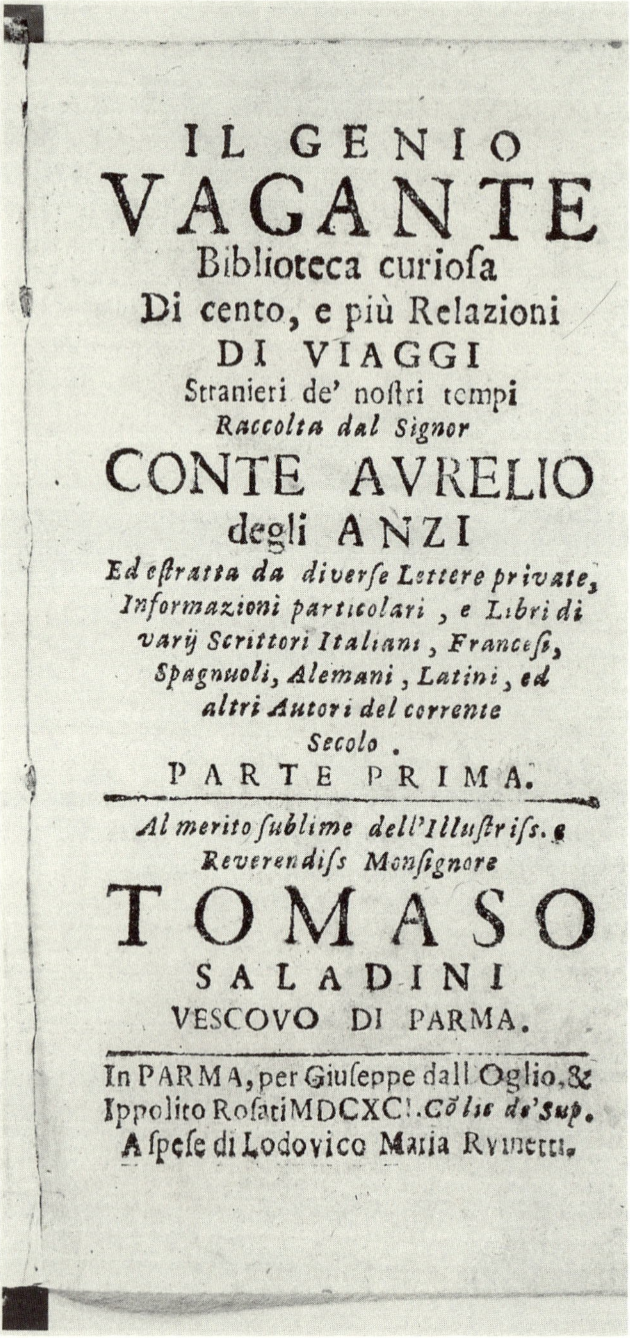

IL GENIO
VAGANTE
Biblioteca curioſa
Di cento, e più Relazioni
DI VIAGGI
Stranieri de' noſtri tempi
Raccolta dal Signor
CONTE AVRELIO
degli ANZI
Ed eſtratta da diverſe Lettere private, Informazioni particolari, e Libri di varij Scrittori Italiani, Franceſi, Spagnuoli, Alemani, Latini, ed altri Autori del corrente Secolo.
PARTE PRIMA.

Al merito ſublime dell'Illuſtriſs. e Reverendiſs Monſignore
TOMASO
SALADINI
VESCOVO DI PARMA.

In PARMA, per Giuſeppe dall'Oglio, & Ippolito RoſatiMDCXC!.*Cō lic de' Sup.*
A ſpeſe di Lodovico Maria Rvmetti.

Fig. 3. Title page of *Il genio vagante*.

The following passage from Gomberville on the Indians of the Amazon River is worth reading:

> Among several nations which dwell in the proximity of this river are populations which are sixteen palms high, others which are no taller than children, others which have their feet turned backwards yet whose members run so fast that it is impossible to overtake them. Others consider themselves beautiful because their head is flat like a hand, and to reach said shape they constrict the head of newborn babies inside a small press and allow it to extend only from one ear to the other.[43]

During this time Enrico Tonti (1650–1704), a Frenchman of Italian origin, had summarized his experiences as an explorer in North America in his *Account of Monsieur De La Salle's Last Expedition and Discoveries in North America*.[44] In his work, Tonti offered a precise analysis of the Iroquois nation, pointing out their respective virtues and excesses:

> Those inhabitants have nothing of man but the shape and the name; they live without any laws, religion, superiority or subordination. . . . Their life is always wandering, having no settled possessions; they take several wives, if they please. . . . However, notwithstanding that brutish temper, they have as good a sense as the rest of mankind to know their true interests, and therefore are capable of negotiations, commerce, and counsel.[45]

It must be pointed out, however, that the passages in Tonti's diary that are dedicated to the Indians amount to only brief, fleeting reflections. Although he came into contact with the Indian world, the author had no intention of exploring it in depth in order to arrive at a definition. Unlike the majority of travelers between the two centuries, who advanced reckless or bizarre hypotheses on America's geological structure or on America's fauna, Tonti limited himself in his work to a faithful recording of the routine work of exploration.

43. Ibid., 3:420–21.
44. In *Collections of the New York Historical Society, for the Year 1814*, vol. 2 (New York: Van Winkle and Wiley, 1814). About Tonti's explorations in America, see Giovanni Schiavo, *The Italians before the Civil War* (New York: Vigo, 1934), 111.
45. Ibid., 222–23.

At the close of the 1690s, the famous traveler Giovanni Francesco Gemelli Careri (1651-1725), mentioned by Parini in his "Sciolti per un'accademia di geografia,"[46] published in Naples an account of his journeys around the globe, *Giro del mondo*.[47] Gemelli Careri was Calabrese, held a law degree, and was governor of several cities in the kingdom of Naples. He began his trip around the world in 1693 by traveling to Egypt. After stays in Palestine, India, and China he sailed for the Philippines and from there to Mexico where he arrived in 1697 and where he sojourned for over a year.

Lively observations and faith in progress constitute the leitmotif of *Giro del mondo*, which given a certain methodological coherence, can be considered an eighteenth-century journal. The author, in fact, was fully conscious of the autonomous nature and the educational dignity of travel literature that made it possible to "secure dignity in the Republic of Letters by publishing for the benefit of all, what was seen and observed."[48] The merit, however, went to a chosen few, since "many travel, but few can do it well, and even fewer can give an educational account of their travels to the public."[49] The educational aim of Gemelli Careri's short accounts resulted in a list of necessary commandments for the model traveler: write one's observations every night in a "journal" since "memory is deceptive"; keep two copies of the "journal" since, "if one should get lost in a suitcase, the other copy will be in the hands of a trusted friend";[50] take into consideration the country's physical geography, its distances, customs, habits, arts, and the people's illnesses; obtain information from experts about the places to see and "become friends with a worthy man of letters, if that country should have any, or with the wisest among the elders." Finally,

---

46. "Per un'accademia di geografia," in *Opere di Giuseppe Parini*, ed. Ettore Bonora (Milan: Editoriale Vita, 1976), 374, lines 30-40.

47. For a profile of Gemelli Careri, see *Viaggiatori del Seicento*, ed. Marziano Guglielminetti (Turin: Utet, 1967), 683-84.

48. *Giro del mondo* (Venice: Sebastiano Coletti, 1719), 6:287. [Translator's note: A first English translation (*A Voyage Round the World*) was published in London in 1704, in A. & J. Churchill's *A Collection of Voyages and Travels*; however, it contained only an account of Gemelli Careri's voyage to the Spanish and Portuguese possessions in the Far East. Volume 4 of the third edition of A. and J. Churchill's *A Collection of Voyages and Travels* (6 vols.), published in London in 1745, includes in its Parts V and VI, Gemelli Careri's account of his voyage to the New Spain territories in the Americas.]

49. *Giro del mondo*, 6:287.

50. Ibid., 6:292.

one must be able to draw "so as to sketch beautiful statues, buildings, and ancient objects."[51]

The aim of the *Giro del mondo*—a faithful description of the countries visited—was emphasized by Giosef-Antonio Guerrieri in his preface. While pointing out the difference between the account of a journey and "an imaginary journey," Guerrieri praised Gemelli Careri for the reliability of his experiences, and criticized those who were prone to fantasize over geographic maps:

> He knows full well that some people who never left their nest, just because they pored over a few geographic maps or read a few accounts, believe they have acquired a perfect knowledge of foreign countries. Thus it happens that when other accounts do not agree with the ones they already studied, they call these new accounts "the dreams of a sick man, or novelistic fairy tales." As if tracing some imaginary lines could in a few pages express the life of the voyages, the strangeness of the climates and the wonders of Nature and of Art, as new mysteries are bye and bye revealed to us; or as if true knowledge could be found only in books, and only in those which they have read, and any other opinion could be only the invention of the writer.[52]

For many years scholars and experts did not consider Gemelli Careri's adventurous journey authentic. With time, however, its truthfulness was proved, and it was also ascertained that he collected important historical documents in order to know those exotic realities in greater detail. Indeed, the sixth volume of *Giro del mondo*, which covers only Mexico, contains information gathered from codices that existed prior to the Conquest; it also contains several illustrations of Aztec warriors gathered from these codices. In New Spain, Gemelli Careri had the opportunity to study the

---

51. Ibid., 6:289.
52. *A chi legge*, in *Giro del mondo* (Venice: Sebastiano Coletti, 1719), 2-3. The distinction between a travel record and a "novel" recurs often during the eighteenth century. Muratori, in *Il Cristianesimo felice*, writes: "Whenever my tired spirit needs rest, no reading touches me more deeply than the accounts of the travelers who journeyed to the least known corners of our globe. I speak of the travel reports of knowing, prudent, and truthful men. I do not speak of novels, although we have seen the genius of fiction penetrate this realm also and with false wonders entice and amuse those who are content with the surface of things and the shadow of truth" (2:iii).

pyramids carefully (their affinity to the Egyptian pyramids led him to believe that the ancient Egyptians and the Amerindians both descended from the inhabitants of Atlantis),[53] the Aztec hieroglyphics and the customs of its present inhabitants. Concerning the natives he wrote:

> The *Indians* are naturally very fearful; but excessively cruel. The vices the Spaniards generally charge them with are, first, the want of a sense of honour (for they make nothing of robbing one another of it, besides the incests they commit with their mothers and sisters); being beastly in eating, lying on the bare ground, and dying without any concern. They are very great thieves, cheats and impostors.[54]

Sloth and lack of self-discipline were seen as the distinguishing traits of the Mexican Indian and, as it will be possible to verify for the coming century, these were the presuppositions upon which the thesis of the congenital inferiority of the Americans would be founded (see Chapter 3). The theme of a slothful life reappears in a description of the Otomite Indians:

> Thus it appears that the first inhabitants of *New Spain* were a sort of wild people, since they lived amid the uncouth mountains, without tilling the land, without religion, without any form of government and without clothes, lived in a disorderly manner like beasts, feeding upon what they killed . . . [as] though they were wild creatures; and when these were lacking, on roots; and lying in dens, and under thick bushes.[55]

In addition to reflections about the populations and culture of New Spain (which the traveler continued to call "India"), Gemelli Careri carefully observed the country's physical geography and natural resources. He

---

53. John Francis Gemelli Careri, *A Voyage Round the World*, in A. and J. Churchill, *A Collection of Voyages and Travels* 3d ed., 6 vols. (London: H. Lintot and J. Osborn, 1745): "The building of these pyramids is attributed to the *Ulmecos*, the second planters of *New Spain*, who came from that island *Atlantis*, Plato speaks of in this *Timaeus*. This conjecture is made because all the *Indian* histories unanimously agree, that these *Ulmecos* came by sea from the east; and on the other side, according to *Plato*, the inhabitants of the island *Atlantis* derived their original from the *Egyptians* who had the custom of raising pyramids" (4:pt. 5:514).
54. Ibid., 4:pt. 5:492.
55. Ibid., 4:pt. 5:482.

dwelled upon exotic plants such as vanilla and cocoa, on silver mines and on the abundance of pearl oysters in California's waters. ("There are good pearl fisheries, and salt made. . . . They eat raw fish, and exchange pearls, in which all their coast abounds.")[56]

Before Parini, who in his *Vespro* would evoke the mythical image of an "extreme California, rich in many pearls" (lines 3-4), several sources had confirmed the extraordinary wealth of California's seas: the entry "California" in Moreri ("The Sea-Fish there are good, and plentifully furnished; but the Pearl-fishing is that which makes the Coast particularly famous"),[57] world histories,[58] and the accounts of the missionaries.[59]

56. Ibid., 4:pt. 5:471.
57. Louis Moreri, *The Great Historical, Geographical, Genealogical and Poetical Dictionary* 2d ed., 2 vols. (London: Jer. Collier, for Henry Rhodes, 1701), vol. 1, s.v. "California," and appendix to the *Three English Volumes in Folio of Morery's Great Historical, Geographical, Genealogical and Poetical Dictionary* (London: Jer. Collier, 1721), s.v. "California." See *The American Gazetteer* (London: A. Millar and J & R Tonson, 1762): "The abundance of pearls of exceeding lustre has rendered California famous all over the world, and now extensive pearl fisheries are carried on along its coasts, from which those concerned raise large fortunes in a short time" (s.v. "California"). Pearls exerted their exotic charm on the Jesuit Giambattista Roberti who in those years published a short poem, *Le perle* (Bologna: Lelio della Volpe, 1763).
58. William Robertson, *The History of America* (1777; published in Italy as *Storia d'America* [Venice: Gatti, 1778]), recalled that the minister of the West Indies, visiting California, found "the pearl-fishery on its coasts to be valuable, and he discovered mines of gold of a very promising appearance." Robertson, *The History of America*, 4 vols. (London: Sharpe and Sons, 1820), 3:359. Francesco Saverio Clavigero (*The History of [Lower] California*, trans. and ed. Sara E. Lake and A. A. Gray [Stanford: Stanford University Press, 1937]), pointed to the pearl trade of the Spanish captain Giovanni Iturbi who "when he returned to Mexico . . . brought very many pearls, partly fished for on his own account and partly acquired from the Californians in exchange for some things of small value. . . . Among the pearls was one which was valued at 4,500 *scudi*. . . . The Indians of California, on account of this trade, had to suffer a thousand vexations from those greedy fishermen; but sometimes they knew how to revenge themselves" (134).
59. Oyster fishing was considered one major cause of Spanish expansion, as documented in a letter of the Milanese Jesuit Salvaterra, included in Muratori's *Il Cristianesimo felice*: "Some say that if I were to make a gift of Pearls to the Lord Viceroy he would immediately open the Royal Treasury. But this is neither proper before God, nor before men. We did not come here to lose our reputation and I would sooner die than be a Pearl Trafficker. It is on account of this greed for pearls that we have been unable to secure the Holy Cross in this Kingdom. We must first conquer this land. This accomplished and made secure, the King will then be free to reap whatever fruits he may wish to. All will be lost if we let the tyranny of Pearls dominate these endeavors. . . . Truly, they [the Spaniards] yearned only for Pearls, this gift bestowed by the Maker of Nature on the beaches of California. When on the contrary, far from being interested, not only was he not seeking Pearls, but he also did not allow them as Church ornaments" (2:170).

On geographic maps, California was represented as an island, until the beginning of the eighteenth century.[60] After several expeditions, the Jesuit, Eusebio Francisco Kino (1645-1711), from the city of Trento, superintendent of missions in Baja California, finally determined that it was a peninsula.[61] Forty years later this exploit would be remembered by Muratori:

> Up to now there has been great debate between travelers and writers: the former asserted that California was an island, the latter that it was a Peninsula. The argument was finally resolved when Father Eusebio Kino of the Company of Jesus, who made several trips to those parts between 1698 and 1701, wrote that the sea channel separating California from Sinaloa and Sonora, which are maritime Mexican provinces, ends at the Continent, that is, where the unknown lands of New Mexico are joined to California. Thus it was discovered that California is not an island but a peninsula.[62]

Muratori's testimony therefore documents the exposure of the early eighteenth century's intellectuals to the accounts of the explorers and missionaries, especially the Jesuits,[63] who furnished the most reliable information on the Americas.

---

60. In the early decades of the century, with the advance in explorations and the widening of horizons, a need was generally felt for precision and revision. This led cartographers to engage in careful reconstructions of the Americas as a valid alternative to a roughly approximate and mythical geography. This work of revision included atlases, maps annexed to the missionaries' accounts and Venetian geography manuals. It was taken for granted that Venice would take the initiative since, as Piero Del Negro noted, "the city of St. Mark played, along with some Venetian inland centers, a major role in the processing and circulation of the literature of discovery" (*Il mito americano*, 13).

61. *Passage par terre à la Californie découvert par le Rev. Père Eusèbe-François Kino Jésuite depuis 1698 jusqu'à 1701* (Paris: Nicolas Le Clerc, 1705). Giovanni Schiavo's pages on Kino are enlightening: *The Italians in America before the Civil War*, 88-93. For a history of California, see Robert Ernest Cowan, *A Bibliography of the Historical and Pacific West (1501-1906)* (San Francisco: J. H. Nash, 1914) and *California from Legendary Island to Statehood: An Exhibition at the Huntington Library* (San Marino, Calif., 1933).

62. Ludovico Antonio Muratori, *Il Cristianesimo felice*, 164-65. Muratori placed this unusual discovery within an evangelical context: "The more closely they approached those coasts, the more clearly they saw that the sea narrowed, so that in the year 1690 they could clearly see the lands of California. Thus they began to hope they could soon glimpse the end of that sea channel, and California joined to the Continent of New Spain. This they fervently sought, so as to be able to comfortably pass to that land to preach the Gospel" (2:147).

63. For further information on Jesuit and Franciscan missionary activity in the New World, see Francis Parkman, *Jesuits in North America* (Boston: Little, Brown, 1867); Zephyrin Engelhardt, *The Franciscans in California* (Harbor Springs, Mich.: Holy Child-

Christian America and "Savage" America 23

Fig. 4. Geographical map of California from Francisco Eusebio Kino's *Passaggio per terra alla California*.

---

hood Indian School, 1897) and *Missions and Missionaries in California* (San Francisco: James H. Barry, 1912); Maynard J. Geiger, "Franciscan Missionaries in Hispanic California" (1769-1848), in *Bibliographical Dictionary* (San Marino, Calif.: Huntington Library, 1969); Herbert Ingram Prietley, *Franciscan Explorations in California*, ed. Lillian Estelle Fisher (Glender: Arthur H. Clarks, 1946).

2. The Comparative Approach: Lafitau, Vico, and Boturini Benaduci

In 1724 the French Jesuit Joseph-François Lafitau after five years as a missionary in New France, systematically summarized and studied the usages and customs of the Canadian nations.[64] Lafitau was a careful observer of the Indian and he overthrew the traditional prejudice, according to which he continued to be defined as "a species of naked man, covered with hair, living like an animal in the forest without social organization, having only the imperfect appearance of man."[65] In his work, one of the most significant eighteenth-century studies of the American Indian world, Lafitau accomplished an accurate examination of the Canadians' character. They have:

> good minds, quick perceptions, admirable memories. They all have at least traces of an ancient and hereditary religion and a form of government. They think justly about their affairs, better than the masses of the people do among us. They reach their goals by sure paths. They act with cold common sense and a self-control which would wear out our patience. As a matter of honour and through greatness of soul, they never loose their tempers, seem to be always masters of themselves and never angry. They have lofty and proud hearts, courage when put to the test, intrepid valour, heroic constancy under torture, and an evenness of disposition which hindrances and ill success do not alter.[66]

Although valuing other characteristics of the Indians, such as respect for the aged and hospitality, Lafitau added that "these good qualities are undoubtedly combined with a number of faults, for they are light-minded and changeable, inexpressibly lazy, excessively ungrateful, suspicious, vindicative."[67]

---

64. *Moeurs des sauvages amériquains comparés aux moeurs des premiers temps* (Paris: Saugrain l'aîné, 1724). Lafitau is also author of *Histoire des découvertes et conquêtes des Portugais dans le Nouveau Monde* (Paris: Saugrain Père, 1733).
65. *Customs of the American Indians Compared with the Customs of Primitive Times*, ed. and trans. by William N. Fenton and Elizabeth Moore, 2 vols. (Toronto: the Champlain Society, 1974), 1:88.
66. Ibid., 2:90.
67. Ibid.

MŒURS
DES SAUVAGES
AMERIQUAINS,
COMPAREES AUX MŒURS
DES PREMIERS TEMPS.

Par le P. LAFITAU, *de la Compagnie de Jesus.*

Ouvrage enrichi de Figures en taille-douce.

TOME PREMIER.

A PARIS,

Chez {
SAUGRAIN l'aîné, Quay des Augustins, près la ruë Pavée, à la Fleur de Lys.
CHARLES ESTIENNE HOCHEREAU, à l'entrée du Quay des Augustins, à la descente du Pont S. Michel, au Phœnix.
}

MDCCXXIV.

AVEC APPROBATION ET PRIVILEGE DU ROY.

Fig 5. Title page of Joseph François Lafitau's *Moeurs des sauvages amériquains comparées aux moeurs des premiers temps.*

Fig 6. Iroquois dances in Lafitau's *Moeurs des sauvages amériquains comparées aux moeurs des premiers temps*.

7. Canadian Indians in Lafitau's *Moeurs des sauvages amériquains comparées aux moeurs des premiers temps.*

As Duchet correctly noted, the Jesuit "catalogues a great deal of information in accordance with a synthetic, not an analytic, method: in comparing, term by term, the beliefs and customs of populations that are separated by centuries, by time, or by insuperable spatial obstacles, he lays the foundation for a universal science of man; he replaces a historical and geographical perspective with an anthropological perspective."[68] Lafitau's originality consisted in the fact that he used a "comparative" methodology, as the very title of his work suggests, which led him to draw recurrent parallels between the Americans' customs and those of the ancients. Putting forward the hypothesis of the transmigration of peoples to the Americas through the Pacific Ocean, Lafitau identified in the Canadian natives the vestiges of the most remote antiquity and in their myths, a key for interpreting the classical myths. "I have made a comparison of these customs with each other. I confess that, if the ancient authors have given me the information on which to base happy conjectures about the Indians, the customs of the Indians have given me information on the basis of which I can understand more easily and explain more readily many things in the ancient authors."[69] For example, the legend according to which the Iroquois originated from a woman who fell from heaven is compared to the legend of Ate recounted by Homer,[70] and several affinities are noted between classical and American mythology. One must, however, recall that matching America's aborigines to the prehistory of Europeans, was already a common occurrence at the end of the sixteenth and beginning of the seventeenth century; however, it merely resulted in idealizations or in erudite references. For Lafitau, on the other hand, comparing Americans to the ancients was a criterion of interpretation that bore a clear affinity to Giambattista Vico's approach.

Vico was acquainted with Lafitau's work; this is confirmed by a note in which he pointed out the inadequacies of *Moeurs des sauvages amériquains comparées aux moeurs des premiers temps*:

> We have been told, because we have not ourselves seen it, that Father Lafitau, a Jesuit missionary in America, has written an erudite work, *Moeurs des sauvages amériquains*, where he observes that these

---

68. Michèle Duchet, *Anthropologie et histoire*, 15.
69. Joseph-François Lafitau, *Moeurs des sauvages amériquains*, 1:27.
70. Ibid., 1:83. Lafitau broadened the comparison to the linguistic field, identifying the common roots of several Indian and Greek terms.

people are extremely similar to the very ancient people of Asia: whence he wants to prove that men and women were transported from Asia to America. But it is too difficult to prove such a point. Possibly, he might have been able to work closer to the truth, had he been assisted by this *Science*. Wherefore, the reader should verify his work with our principles, trusting he will accordingly find these principles happily verified.[71]

Vico proposed an anthropological and polygenetic interpretation of the comparison, rather than the "migratory" interpretation proposed by the French Jesuit. The analogy between the current state of the American populations and the state of infancy of the Europeans was therefore not justified by a migration hypothesis, but rather by the parallel course of "nations": Americans were survivors of previous stages of civilizations. As Landucci pointed out, integrating Americans into a historical and therefore diachronic perspective allowed the philosopher to escape addressing them as "living fossils" against which to measure humanity's progress; Indians acquired a time and a history that was their own; "they are not fossils because they represent humanity's 'infancy,' not only conceptually but also *chronologically*."[72] Compared to the four thousand years of the Asians, the Indians had been a "nation" for only fifteen hundred years.[73] The natives of the New World continued to err with respect to the nations of the ancient continents and were still immersed in the first age when "every new or great thing they saw, they believed to be Gods," and they used an enigmatic or sacred language, the sign of a symbolic theology. Lafitau had analyzed this last aspect in the final chapter of his *Moeurs des sauvages amériquains* where he discussed the linguistic system of the savages. Thus it is clear that in Vico's vision, the traditional *American/Savage* pair is split insofar as they "know something about reckoning and reasoning," although their "customs [are] so excessive for our refined nature."[74] For Vico, who was not knowledgeable on the most

---

71. *Del ricorso delle cose umane nel risurgere che fanno le nazioni*, in *Tutte le opere di Giambattista Vico*, ed. Francesco Flora (Milan: Mondadori, 1957), 694. This observation was removed from the final version of the *New Science*.

72. See Sergio Landucci, *I filosofi e i selvaggi, 1580-1780* (Bari: Laterza, 1972), 314.

73. See *Principi di una scienza nuova, d'intorno alla comune natura delle nazioni* (1744), in *Tutte le opere*: "The American [nation must have originated only] one thousand and five hundred years ago, as at the time of its discovery it was ruled by dreadful religions and was still at the stage of families" (689).

74. Ibid. (1725), 785.

recent debates on the New World, due, in part, to his scant knowledge of foreign languages,[75] the people of the New World appeared to him in a global vision, as one sole "nation." The opinion that the American Indians were an indistinct mass survived, in any case, until the second half of the eighteenth century, as documented by the entry "Indians" in the *American Gazetteer*:

> Indians, the name by which the aborigines of America are generally called. These people are scattered through the extent of the two prodigious continents, and divided into an infinite number of nations and tribes; differ very little from each other in their manners and customs, and all form a very striking picture of the most distant antiquity.[76]

Within this American "totality," Vico distinguished only the *Patacones*, "men of vast bodies and unshapen strength." These giants who "even to this day have retained much of their most ancient origin, in their customs as well as their language,"[77] were evidence of a more archaic evolutionary stage than other American natives, because they retained physical and mental characteristics that were closer to those of the men who reverted to a wild state after the Deluge. Vico continued with a description of their characteristics:

> Because of their recent gigantic origins, the heroes were gross and wild to the highest degree, such as we have found the Patagonians described, very limited in understanding but endowed with the vastest imaginations and the most violent passions. Hence they must have been boorish, crude, harsh, wild, proud, difficult, and obstinate in their resolve, and at the same time easily diverted when confronted with new and contrary objects.[78]

---

75. Vico's readings on the New World for the most part went back to the sixteenth and seventeenth century. The philosopher was definitely acquainted with José de Acosta (*De natura novi orbis libri duo et de promulgatione Evangelii apud barbaros, sive de procuranda indorum saluti libri sex*, 1589; *Historia natural y Moral de las Indias*, 1590), and Joannes de Laet (*Descriptio Indiae occidentalis*, 1640).

76. *The American Gazetteer*, s.v. "Indians."

77. *Principj di una scienza nuova* (1725), 689.

78. Thomas G. Bergin and Max H. Fisch, *The New Science of Giambattista Vico*, rev. trans., 3d ed. (1744), 2 vols. (Ithaca: Cornell University Press, 1968), 2:267, para. 708. [Translator's note: the 1725 edition of the *Scienza nuova* was not translated into English.

Christian America and "Savage" America 31

The anthropological dilemma of the dwarfs of Madagascar or the giants of Patagonia continue to arouse the curiosity of other members of Neapolitan cultural circles in the eighteenth century, such as Antonio Genovesi who, in his *Lettere accademiche*, contrasting the values of civilization to the feral state, wrote:

> We ferry through the Atlantic Ocean. Here are the Patagonians from Magellan's lands. The sky is harsh and the earth frozen for ten months. What do you want me to say? . . . It is everyone's ever-present feeling that their favorite food is human flesh. They think nothing of eating their dead: when there is no other food, they slaughter each other.[79]

Convinced of the man-eating customs of this American tribe, Genovesi went on to report an unusual event experienced by the English explorer Anson, who, after taking a Patagonian woman and her children prisoners:

> gave them cooked food to eat: they did not like it. He brought the mother a raw penguin, a kind of young goose from that country, with very long legs and very short wings. The wild woman tore it to pieces at once with her claws: she removed the heart, liver and intestines and gave them to the lads who gobbled them up raw. Blood flowed like dribble from their jaws, much like it is said of Homer's Cyclops when he tore Ulysses' companions to pieces and devoured them while they still throbbed with life. She then bit into the penguin, bones, feathers and all, as if it had been a butter-pear or angelica root. What a gentle Patagonian lady![80]

Except for the citation in this endnote, it was not possible to locate citations from the 1744 edition in the Bergin-Fisch English translation of same, given the fragmentary nature of the text itself.] In 1721 Roggeween discovered the monumental Easter Island statues and therefore another proof of the existence of giant populations; however the news did not arouse the curiosity of contemporaries (see Michèle Duchet, *Anthropologie et histoire*, 64) and it is unlikely that Vico knew about this.

79. Antonio Genovesi, *Lettere accademiche*, in *Autobiografia, lettere ed altri scritti*, ed. Gennaro Savarese (Milan: Feltrinelli, 1962), 400. On the Patagonian legend, see Antonello Gerbi, *The Dispute of the New World*, 139ff.

80. Ibid., 401. The legend of the Patagonians continued to influence eighteenth-century travelers and intellectuals such as Louis Antoine de Bougainville: "They have a fine shape; among those whom we saw, none was below five feet five or six inches, and none above five feet nine or ten inches; the crew of the Etoile had even seen several in the preceding voyage,

Also the Milanese aristocrat Lorenzo Boturini Benaduci (1698-1755), in his *Idea de una nueva historia general de l'America septentrional*,[81] recalled the American giants scattered, not over Patagonia, but throughout Mexico, after Babel's confusion:

> The giants of the lineage of Cham were routed to Phoenicia, Egypt, and Africa, and some of them to America, and were the first inhabitants of the back country of New Spain, as they came directly without staying long in any of the places along their pilgrimage. The Indians have an illustrious memory of these ancestors, and say that they were called *Quinamètin, Hueytlacàme*, which means, *Big and deformed men*.[82]

Boturini Benaduci, a honorable adventurer of the eighteenth century, traveled to New Spain in 1736, having been appointed to manage the property of the countess of Saintibañez, a descendant of the emperor Montezuma, with the goal of retracing the origins of the cult of Our Lady of Guadalupe. Between 1736 and 1743 he gathered a precious collection of Indian manuscripts, after having lived among the natives for seven years and having studied their customs, usages, and beliefs. While the Church regarded every residual local superstition as having been in some way vanquished by Christianity, Boturini was able to prove that certain autochthonous cults were still alive in various parts of Mexico. It was a dangerous discovery, which led the Inquisition to confiscate his collection of Indian documents and deport him to Spain. In 1746, although deprived

---

six feet . . . high. What makes them appear gigantic, are their prodigious broad shoulders, the size of their head, and the thickness of all their limbs. They are robust and well fed: their nerves are braced, and their muscles are strong and sufficiently hard; they are men left entirely to nature, and supplied with food abounding in nutritive juices, by which means they achieve the full growth they are capable of: their figure is not coarse or disagreeable; on the contrary, many of them are handsome: their face is round and somewhat flattish; their eyes very fiery; their teeth vastly white, and would be only somewhat outsized in Paris" (*Voyage*, 1:142). Pernety also devoted a section of the account of his journey in Magellan's lands to the Patagonian enigma. See *Histoire d'un voyage aux îles Malouines, avec des observations sur le détroit de Magellan et sur les Patagons* (Paris: Saillant et Nyon, 1770).

81. (Madrid: Juan de Zuñiga, 1746). A recent edition was published in Mexico, edited by Miguel Leon-Portilla (Mexico: Editorial Porroa, 1974). John B. Glass's studies on Boturini Benaduci should be consulted, especially *The Boturini Collection: The Legal Proceedings and the Basic Inventories, 1742-45* (Lincoln Center, Mass.: Conemex Associates, 1981).

82. Benaduci, *Idea de una nueva historia*, 133-34.

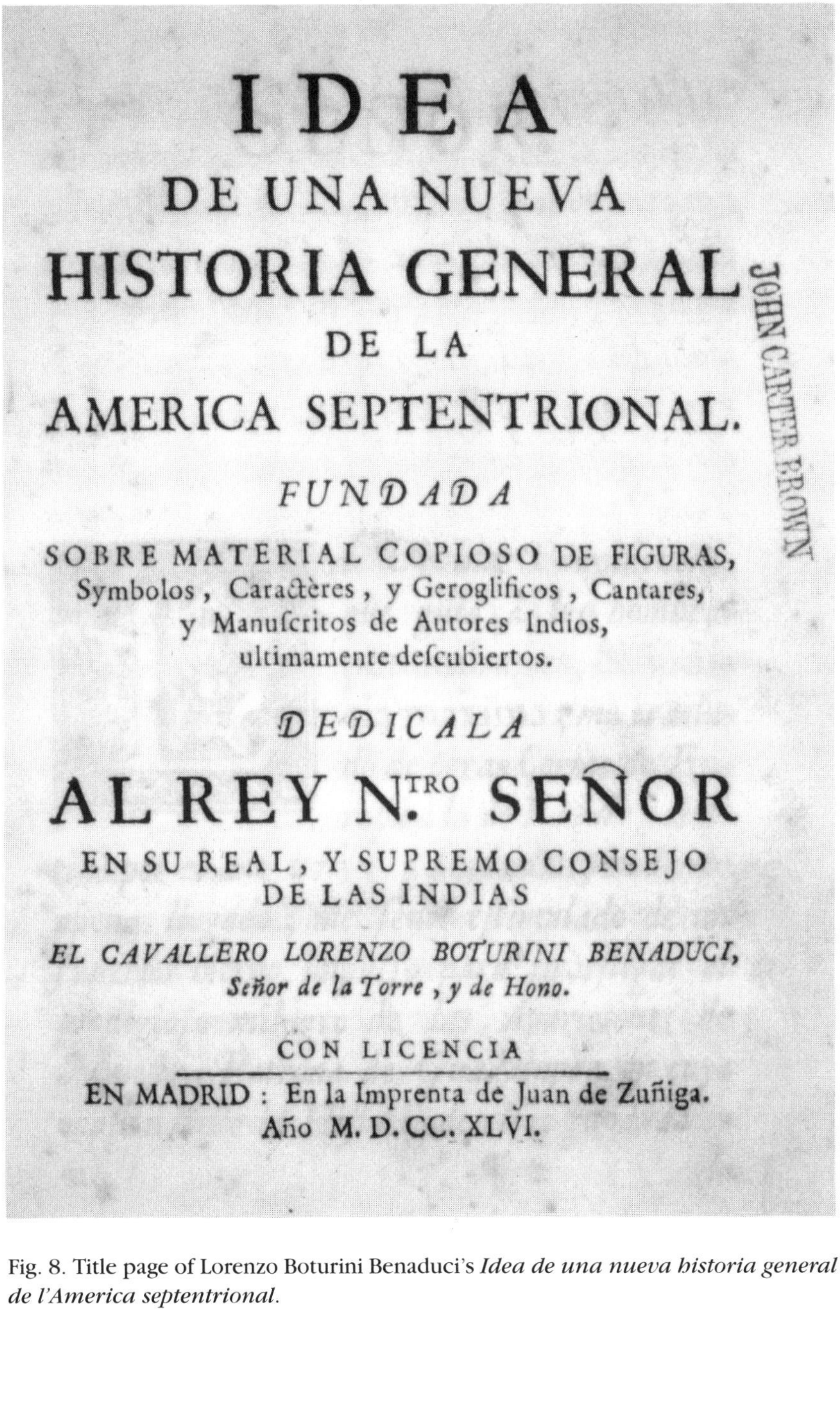

IDEA
DE UNA NUEVA
HISTORIA GENERAL
DE LA
AMERICA SEPTENTRIONAL.

FUNDADA

SOBRE MATERIAL COPIOSO DE FIGURAS,
Symbolos, Caractères, y Geroglificos, Cantares,
y Manufcritos de Autores Indios,
ultimamente defcubiertos.

DEDICALA

AL REY N.ᵀᴿᴼ SEÑOR
EN SU REAL, Y SUPREMO CONSEJO
DE LAS INDIAS

EL CAVALLERO LORENZO BOTURINI BENADUCI,
Señor de la Torre, y de Hono.

CON LICENCIA

EN MADRID : En la Imprenta de Juan de Zuñiga.
Año M.D.CC.XLVI.

Fig. 8. Title page of Lorenzo Boturini Benaduci's *Idea de una nueva historia general de l'America septentrional.*

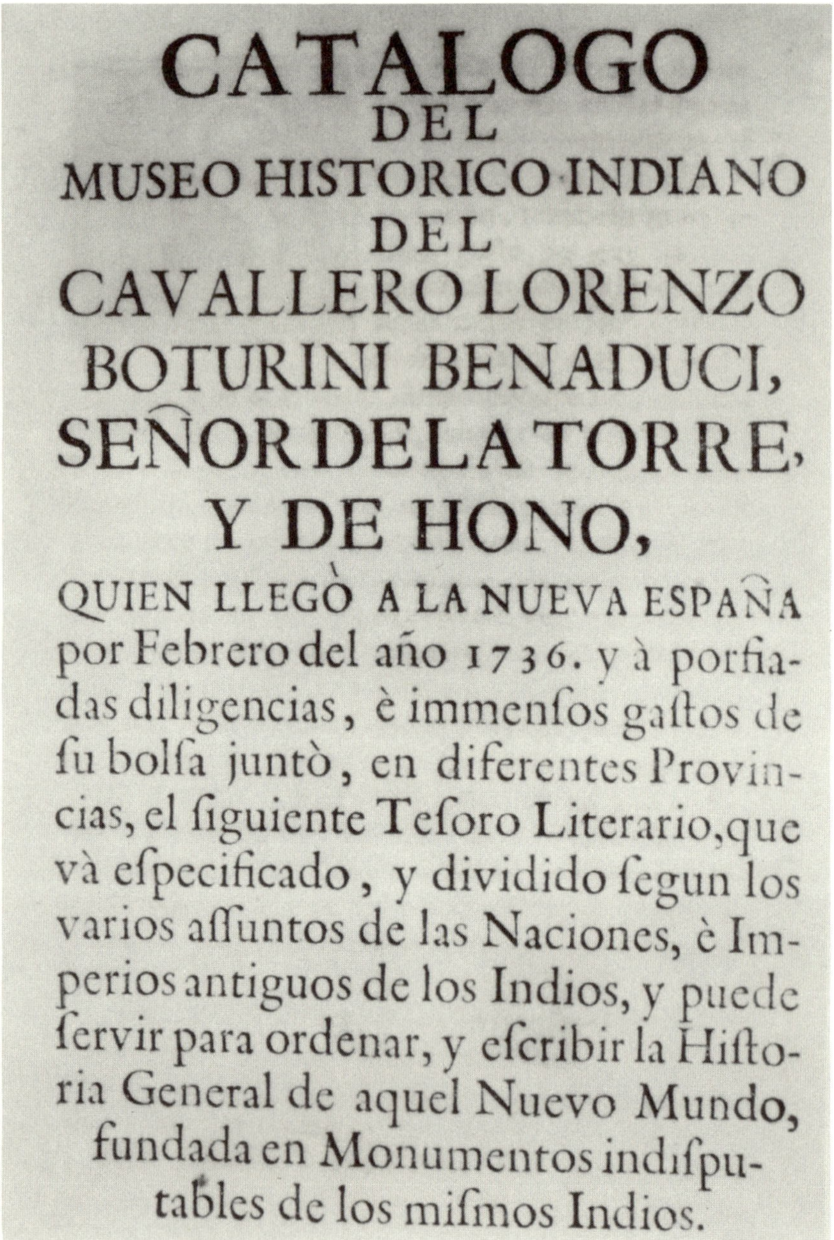

CATALOGO
DEL
MUSEO HISTORICO INDIANO
DEL
CAVALLERO LORENZO BOTURINI BENADUCI,
SEÑOR DE LA TORRE, Y DE HONO,

QUIEN LLEGÒ A LA NUEVA ESPAÑA por Febrero del año 1736. y à porfiadas diligencias, è immenſos gaſtos de ſu bolſa juntò, en diferentes Provincias, el ſiguiente Teſoro Literario, que và eſpecificado, y dividido ſegun los varios aſſuntos de las Naciones, è Imperios antiguos de los Indios, y puede ſervir para ordenar, y eſcribir la Hiſtoria General de aquel Nuevo Mundo, fundada en Monumentos indiſputables de los miſmos Indios.

Fig. 9. Title page of the *Museo Historico Indiano* catalogue in Benaduci's *Idea de una nueva historia general de l'America septentrional*.

PROTESTA PRELIMINAR.

AUnque con ocafion de efcribir
efta Idèa Hiftorica, me ha fido
forzofo meditar en los Arcanos, y
Planos Cientificos de los Indios, y
ufar, efpecialmente en la primera, y
fegunda Edad, de fus mifmos con-
ceptos para explicarla ; no obftante
tan lexos eftoy de apartarme en lo
mas minimo de la pureza de la Religion Catholica, en que nacì, que an-
tes me hallo prompto à morir por
ella, y todo lo que digo aqui lo fo-
meto con la mas humilde obediencia
à la cenfura, y correccion de nueftra
Santa Madre Iglefia Catholica Apof-
tolica Romana.

PRO-

Fig 10. Portrait of Lorenzo Boturini Benaduci in *Idea de una nueva historia general de l'America septentrional.*

of his Indian manuscripts and under constant censorship control, he published in Madrid the *Nueva historia*. This work illustrates a system for reading the Indian codices and contains a variety of information on the culture and religions of New Spain. It opened with two sonnets (dedicated to the author "on the occasion of the new, beautiful and erudite history of the Indies, which is being published to the advantage and praise of the Republic of Letters") and ends with a detailed catalogue of his scattered "museum."[83]

The general approach of the *Historia* follows Vico's example, as it distinguishes three evolutionary ages of the Indians: "Following the idea of the famous division of time taught by the Egyptians, I divided Indian history into three ages: the first, that of the Gods; the second, that of

---

83. Among the collectors of exotic objects, we recall Ludovico Moscardo, a nobleman from Verona, and Mario Saverio Bottoni, from Messina. The former listed several Mexican trophies in the catalogue of his "museum" (*Note ovvero memorie del Museo di Ludovico Moscardo nobile veronese* [Padua: Paolo Frambotto, 1656]); the latter, in the first half of the eighteenth century, collected precious oriental and American objects.

the Heroes; and the third, that of Men."[84] In chapter 28 of his *New Science* (1744) Vico had said that "from Egyptian antiquity two important ruins have reached us. One is that the Egyptians reduced all times past to three ages: the age of the gods, the age of the heroes, and the age of men."[85]

The first age of the Indians corresponds to the age of the gods, when men enslaved by idolatry and divination used a sacred or enigmatic language. The second age is the age of heroes, a "fabled time" in which "the origin of Heroes, whom our Indians believed had been divine" is celebrated.[86] The third age is that of men,

> an age when the masses mastered languages, which previously had been in the control of only the fathers and the heroes of the nation, shrouded in the obscurity of divine hieroglyphics and heroic symbols. And since the masses desired to be justly governed, monarchy was the chosen form of government desired by most, and the

---

84. *Idea de una nueva historia*, 7. "And with the passing of time our Indians, who descend from them, imagined Gods of different natures, composed of bodies of a strength superior to human strength, which gods they worshiped submissively with sacrifices. During the sacrificial rites they carefully searched for any visible signs of divine acceptance, and in this manner there developed at the same time among them idolatry and divination. The Romans likewise derived the word *divinity* from *divination*, which means to search for the visible signs of future events which are known only to the gods, and they thought it was a mute form of speech of the very Divinity" (ibid., 8-9). In this chapter Boturini Benaduci goes on to analyze the major Mexican deities and their corresponding symbols and hieroglyphics, and inevitably recalls a page from Vico's 1744 *Science (Principj di una scienza nuova)*: "In the West Indies it was found that Mexicans wrote in hieroglyphics, and in describing the New Indies, Joannes de Laet wrote that their hieroglyphics consisted of several heads of animals, plants, flowers and fruits by which they distinguished their families; just as we do with our coats of arms" (307). In 1758 Father Joseph Gumilla also postulated, in his *Histoire naturelle, civile et géographique de l'Orénoque* (Avignon: La Veuve de F. Girard, 1758), 1:99-100, a correspondence between the three ages of the inhabitants of Orinoco and the populations of the ancient continents: "I compare the first state of these populations to the darkness in which the human species was plunged before Abraham's vocation; the second state to the times when the Medes, the Persians, the Egyptians, the Greeks and the Romans forced with the help of their weapons the barbarian nations of our continent to embrace a more civilized kind of life; and finally the third state, which is the one in which we found the New World, the first time that it was discovered, to the kingdom of Tiber who extended his domination over the most beautiful provinces of our continent."

85. *Principj di una scienza nuova* (1744), 180.

86. *Idea de una nueva historia*, 35-36. Like Vico, Boturini Benaduci also acknowledged that the first individuals who recounted the histories of their nations were the poets of heroic verse. Thus heroic verse precedes all other forms of poetry in New Spain, as documented by the Indian *cantari* that celebrate the heroes and their illustrious exploits.

promulgation of laws that would be intelligible and truly human, not constructed with a hero's hammer and out of proportion, but tempered by a natural equity.[87]

There is an analogy with Vico's reflections on the three languages of humanity: "The third was human language, as agreed among each people, over which the people have total mastery, and is typical of popular republics and monarchies."[88]

Boturini Benaduci was deeply impressed by the religiosity in New Spain and delineated a parallel between the Aztec cults and the Catholic cults. This led him to believe that Indians were "unconsciously" Christian before the arrival of Cortés or that one of Christ's disciples must have reached Mexico and preached the Gospel there.[89] Several coincidences between the Christian and the Mexican worlds, already noted during the pilgrimage to the sanctuary of Our Lady of Guadalupe, which was already worshiped under the native dynasties, appeared to him to be a confirmation of the ideas of the *New Science* and therefore of the parallel course of nations.

It is certainly amazing that the author, who became a follower of Vico, never mentioned the Neapolitan philosopher in his *Historia*. This was probably not the result of an "anxiety of influence."[90] But the cultural environment in which Boturini Benaduci came to the idea of writing his history did influence his silence, as confirmed by Venturi:

> Why didn't Boturini ever mention Vico's name in these pages, which all echo Vico's line of thought? Manuel Bellesteros y Gambrois says it is because of caution, and that probably was the reason. Caution, one could say, especially toward his friends and protectors who were very willing to encourage and support him in his plan to write the great history of Mexico on condition, however, that he set forth facts rather than ideas, research rather than hypotheses, archeological data rather than debates with preceding historians.[91]

---

87. Ibid., 161.
88. *Principj di una scienza nuova* (1744), 113.
89. See Franco Venturi, "Un vichiano tra Messico e Spagna: Lorenzo Boturini Benaduci," in *Rivista storica italiana* 87 (1975), 777. As Gerbi points out in *Il mito del Perù* (Milan: Angeli, 1988), 306-97, before Boturini Benaduci, Oviedo, Acosta, and Lipsio had ascertained the presence of traces of Christianity in South America.
90. The expression is taken from Harold Bloom's theory in his *Anxiety of Influence: A Theory of Poetry* (London: Oxford University Press, 1975).
91. Venturi, *Un vichiano tra Messico e Spagna*, 773.

Unfortunately, once deprived of the precious objects of his Indian "museum," this unhappy writer could not achieve the great history of Mexico he had planned. He thus resigned himself to composing a lesser history—which, however, represents one of the first systematic treatises on American archeology in eighteenth-century Italy.

2

The Alibis of Exoticism: Myth, Parody, Utopia

1. The Italian Enlightenment and the Denunciation of the Return "To All Fours"

After reading the *Discourse on the Origins of Inequality*, Voltaire in a letter of June 30, 1755, wrote to Rousseau:

> A desire seizes us to walk on four paws when we read your work. Nevertheless, as it is more than sixty years since I lost the habit, I feel, unfortunately, that it is impossible for me to resume it, and I leave that natural mode of walking to those who are more worthy of it than you and I. Nor can I embark to go among the savages of Canada: first, because the maladies with which I am afflicted retain me near the greatest physician in Europe, and I should not find the same succors among the Missouris; secondly, because war has broken out in that country, and the example of our nations has rendered the savages

almost as wicked as we are. I limit myself to be a peaceful savage in the solitude which I have chosen in your country, where you ought to be.[1]

Rousseau's *Discourse,* in which he longed for an idyllic and primitive lifestyle that found a real correspondence in the harmonious existence with nature of the African and New World natives, proved to be heretical and provocative with respect to the canons of the Enlightenment. According to Rousseau, the state of nature represented the ideal condition of humanity and an antidote to civilization:

> The more one reflects on it, the more one finds that this state was the least subject to upheavals and the best for man, and that he must have left it only by virtue of some fatal chance happening that, for the common good, ought never have happened. The example of savages, almost all of whom have been found in this state, seems to confirm that the human race had been made to remain in it always; that this state is the veritable youth of the world; and that all the subsequent progress has been in appearance so many steps toward the perfection of the individual, and in fact toward the decay of the species.[2]

Among Italian intellectuals, this polemical conviction raised certain reservations about the primitivistic mirage and about the *noble savage:* a nostalgic return "to all fours" coincided with a regression of the spirit and a consequent collapse of the achievements of the Enlightenment. The traditional suspicion about Rousseau's return to origins was expressed

---

1. Voltaire, *Works.* 22 vols. Critique and Biography by the Rt. Hon. John Morley, Notes by Tobias Smollett, Revised and modernized new translation by William H. Fleming. Intro. Oliver H. G. Leigh (Akron: St. Hubert Guild, 1901-3) 21:223. Rousseau replied to Voltaire (letter of September 7, 1755, ibid., 227): "You see that I do not aspire to make men return to the condition of beasts, although I regret much, for my part, the little I have lost of that condition. With regard to you, monsieur, such a return would be a miracle, at once so great and so injurious that it would belong to God alone to perform it and to the devil alone to desire it. Do not try, then, to fall upon four paws; no one in the world would less succeed in the attempt than you. You set us up too well upon our two feet for you to cease to stand upon yours." In a letter to his brother Pietro, Alessandro Verri denounced Voltaire's unscrupulousness toward Rousseau; *Carteggio di Pietro ed Alessandro Verri,* ed. Francesco Novati and Emanuele Greppi (Milan: Cogliati, 1910), 2:24-25.

2. *Discourse on the Origin of Inequality,* 65.

in a series of writings critical of the state of nature. While Vincenzio Martinelli, in his *Lettere familiari e critiche* (1758), defended Europe's intellectual superiority by refuting the myth of the noble savage, Antonio Genovesi, who had assimilated the lessons of Vico and Voltaire,[3] rejected the unconscious isolation of the savage in the state of nature: "Those politicians who said there exist many nations in a pure, natural state, ignore history. All savages, unless they are a herd of scattered families, have theocracies."[4] He also rejected as illusory any return to origins, as favored by "ignoramuses [in] our times." In his *Lezioni di commercio o sia d'economia civile*, and even more strongly in his *Lettere accademiche*, the Neapolitan economist entered into a polemic with the "many Rousseaus found here among us"[5] who looked upon the primitive world as a perfect model. Genovesi went on to reassert the unquestionable advantage of "civilized living," which could be practiced only where arts and letters were present. He made the following point:

> But where are the arts ignored? Where there is no knowledge of civilized living. Can there be civilized living without letters? Come on: let us do away with letters: let us banish the wisdom of civilization. The arts will have fled. The cities will have been removed. We are savages, friend; to me—with Mr. Rousseau's permission—*savage* and *unhappy* are synonymous terms.[6]

Without the civilizing function of culture Europe would still be steeped in the barbarianism of its origins and "we would still be living in caves and huts, clothed with tree bark or rough wild animal skins, and eating wild nuts or the raw flesh of animals, like the savages of America."[7] The accounts of travelers and explorers such as Hennepin's *A Description of Louisiana* and the reports of the Jesuits led Genovesi to identify

---

3. Although he agreed with Rousseau about the Americans' docility, Voltaire ranked the human races in hierarchies according to their physical qualities and intellectual abilities. The Europeans' rank as rulers, first in the classification, was justified not by their degree of civilization, but by their "different nature."
4. Antonio Genovesi, *Lezioni di commercio ed economia civile*, in *Economisti italiani classici* (Milan: De Stefani, 1803), 7:70.
5. Letter to Orsola Garappa of March 19, 1768, in *Autobiografia, lettere e altri scritti*, 214.
6. *Lettere accademiche*, 405.
7. *Discorso sopra il vero fine delle lettere e delle scienze*, ibid., 257.

Rousseau's savages with the giants of Patagonia and the "Chirochesi" [translator's note: Iroquois] of Canada, whose unusual cannibal habits were evidence of an irreversible barbarity.[8]

According to the Neapolitan intellectual, savages were not naturally good, and they above all did not have a pleasing aspect: "Even the ones from Chile frighten me. Their face resembles that of wild boars: forehead, cheeks, they are all bristles. They run hither and thither naked through the woods: they throw themselves upon each other: they devour each other like fish."[9]

In any case, the novelty of Genovesi's arguments, as noted by Gerbi,[10] lay in having pointed out that savages are not just wretches from Africa or America, since some are present in Europe also, including the kingdom of Naples. Not far from one of the four most civilized cities of Europe lived not just the Hottentots[11] and the Patagonians, but also "Lapps" and "Kalcas":

> I have seen nearby in Vico's mountains some real Lapps and Carchas; after they have swallowed a piece of stale bread and drunk a glass of sabbath wine, that even the Jews wouldn't drink, you can go around with gold dobla coins, it won't be possible to make them even take one step. They despise any type of comfort: but with the same pride of savages, they consider work vile.[12]

Christianity was still unknown to the inhabitants of Southern Italy; for Genovesi, this lack of religiosity was a corroboration of a certain affinity

---

8. Ibid., 401-2: "Let us move to the northern part of America. What courteous people are the Issati, the Scotilandi [Translator's note: Scots], the Chirochesi [Translator's note: Iroquois]! Do delight in reading for a while F. Hennepin and the French Jesuits who were in Canada. Wolves, foxes, bears live better and more happily. There is no farming, no animal breeding, no crafts of any sort. . . . They steal from each other, they set each other on fire and butcher each other with no trace of compassion. To the Chirochesi their enemies' blood is as delicate as Rhine wine. Their best roasts are of human ribs. They make nice stews with human liver and heart. Do not ask whether they are happier than cultivated people: it's very clear. An ignorant people is always more carefree than a wise one."

9. *Lettere accademiche*, 401.

10. See Antonello Gerbi, *Il mito del Perù*, 324; and Franco Venturi, *La Napoli di Antonio Genovesi*, in *Settecento riformatore: Da Muratori a Beccaria* (Turin: Einaudi, 1969), 4:606.

11. See Letter to Romualdo Sterlich of October 27, 1753, in *Autobiografia*: "They [the inhabitants of the Sorrento peninsula] are so lazy and careless that I think I am seeing Hottentots in the proximity of this city, which is one of the four most cultivated in Europe for its gentility, aristocracy and greatness" (75).

12. *Lettere accademiche*, 492.

between the primitive world and the current condition of the lower classes of the Neapolitan province. The objective of this comparison, then, was to call attention to the "savages" of the *Mezzogiorno*, and to invite historians, scholars, and naturalists not to stray into shaky and bizarre hypotheses about exotic populations.

Francescantonio Grimaldi, from Apulia, also attacked Rousseau. In his *Riflessioni sopra l'ineguaglianza tra gli uomini* (1779-80) he stated that the isolation of the savage was deceptive and he pointed to comparison and to "dependency" as solutions to the primitive state of lack of comparisons:

> When we observe the course of the moral development of humankind, we find that the lonely and wandering savage is completely independent of his fellow creatures; later he is grouped in a family but is in some way independent of wife and children. Later, we find among savage populations that although they enjoy no government and no law, their members do cherish a certain independence one from the other. Later we find, in their proper order, the barbarian nations, where the dependence of individuals is more visible, yet where individuals maintain a part of their original independence and trust their safety to physical strength. Finally, among civilized nations we no longer notice any independence of individuals one from the other. This is the last link in the chain of the development of social order.[13]

13. *Discorso sull'ineguaglianza tra gli uomini*, in *Illuministi italiani*, ed. Franco Venturi (Milan: Ricciardi, 1962), 5:558. On this point Robertson wrote (*History of America*, 2:223): "As the condition of man in the savage state is unfavourable to the progress of the understanding, it has a tendency likewise, in some respects, to check the exercise of affection, and to render the heart contracted. The strongest feeling in the mind of a savage is a sense of his own independence." In his *Vita di Diogene cinico* (1777), Grimaldi uses the savage as a term of comparison to define the cynical philosopher (*Illuministi italiani*): "The difference between the savage and the cynical philosopher is that the former has few needs, few passions, and proportionally little reason. The latter is in a situation where he feels the stimuli of all passions, therefore his reason can expand to the fullest. But insofar as he lives in society detached from social relations, he avoids those passions which might make him unhappy: in sum, he enjoys the savage's happiness and peace of mind and at the same time the reason enjoyed by social man, which he contrasts to the savage's. This comparison makes him happy, for where there is no comparison, happiness cannot be perceived. For which reason the savage does not know his happiness because he is unable to make comparisons" (553).

Sociality guarantees the progress of civilization and the development of history. Grimaldi's thesis was summarized and praised in an issue of the *Giornale enciclopedico*:

> Have you ever noticed that when we have no comparisons in our mind, the faculty of reasoning is also lacking? . . . Should you like to read an author who does not take a step without the escort of experience, I would invite you to read the following work by Grimaldi, a Neapolitan, who, in examining the condition of solitary man, shows us that such an individual, because of a lack of comparisons, cannot reason.[14]

Thus, reflections on the state of barbarianism, on civilization, on freedom and progress could not be resolved within the egalitarian utopia of the state of nature. A return to origins, as yearned for by Rousseau, was in the end an image of pure possibility, and therefore a dangerous vision that did not coincide with the expectations of a generation of intellectuals who placed their trust in "civilized life." Beyond any primitivistic idealization, only a faith in progress could guarantee the advent of the golden age, as solemnly prophesied by Genovesi:

> I firmly believe that we shall be able to see among us the rebirth not of the fabled, but of the true golden century, where everyone emulates every one else to assure the triumph of justice, faith, honesty, work, beautiful and useful information, arts and crafts as well as general wealth and happiness, over vice, ignorance, hypocrisy and poverty.[15]

During these years, while Genovesi believed in a cultural and social palingenesis based on his faith in the progress of humanity, Gasparo Gozzi saw fragments of the golden age in certain aspects of the simple, natural life enjoyed by the common people:

> Although some believe that the golden age never existed, it did in fact exist, and is still present in certain places. Wherever there is

---

14. *Giornali veneziani del Settecento*, ed. Marino Berengo (Milan: Feltrinelli, 1962), 466.

15. Antonio Genovesi, *Opuscoli economici*, in *Lezioni di commercio ed economia civile*, 8:253. Franco Venturi sheds light on the relationship between Genovesi and Rousseau; see his *Settecento riformatore*, 4:605-6.

simplicity of customs, a rustic life, huts instead of houses, cornmeal cooked in water, milk, and fruit instead of other foods, there is the golden age. Images of such an age were found in almost all the countries penetrated by the Portuguese and Spanish discoverers. It still survives for the most part among the Hottentots. Some may criticize me if I say that in Venice I also see a resemblance to those times in certain customs. When small children swim naked in the summer, isn't that the golden age? Wherever people dance at the sound of a tambourine and rattles and sing certain songs which just come out of one's throat, I see a ray from those times. Here I find people who eat watermelon in the street; there someone, who with a tiny pick, removes the meat from the shell of small sea snails and enjoys eating it. In some districts you find poor little women who do this the whole day: they live carelessly, their slippers hit their heels, their hair is unkempt and they are only half-dressed: if you talk to them, they will easily give you a straight or crooked answer: here is a picture of the golden age.[16]

The "lost paradise" of the Americans, then, was not an absolute symbol of the golden centuries, since in the "paradise of the poor"[17] fragments of authentic happiness also survived.

When the golden age lost its quality of being beyond reach and was brought back inside familiar and possible horizons, it was no longer a mirage or a hypothesis. In discussing the relationship between Gozzi and Rousseau, Fido writes:

> Gasparo's axioms are similar to Rousseau's: and like Jean-Jacques' paradise, that of Gasparo also is a lost paradise. But unlike the author of *Emile*, he feels separated from it not by centuries of injustice and oppression, but rather by a thin and transparent social screen, a sort of shatterproof glass, through which the aristocratic Venetian author can admire the carefree, gay life of the masses, while enjoying the opposite and complementary pleasures of a fine education and a delicate melancholy.[18]

16. *La gazzetta veneta* (May 14, 1760), ed. Antonio Zardo (Florence: Sansoni, 1905), 134.
17. See Franco Fido, *Il paradiso dei poveri: immagini veneziane della vita felice*, in *Il paradiso dei buoni compagni* (Padua: Antenore, 1988), 18.
18. Ibid., 20.

According to Gozzi, the masses were still able to enjoy a state of happy unconsciousness because they were separated from any cultural adulteration, but not because they were still primitive or pre-civilized, as Rousseau thought.

The mirage of primitive lifestyle would continue to enjoy scarce success among Italian intellectuals even when it was reproposed in the *Account of the European Settlements in America* by the Burkes (London, 1757; Venice, 1763) and by the myth of Tahiti[19] in the 1770s. Inspired by the Burkes' *Account* and by the discovery of the Pacific islands, the revival of a savage world that still enjoyed primitive communism, and simple traditions, would not lead eighteenth-century Italians to regret an original innocence.

2. The American Indian in Eighteenth-Century Social Debates

In the satirical novel *L'ingénu* (1767),[20] the vicissitudes of a Huron who was brought to France were used by Voltaire to build a polemic against the traditions and conformity of contemporary society. Although he was aware of the advantages of civilization, Voltaire identified its inadequacies, and he employed the exotic element—because it lay outside of the social context—to unmask the limitations of civilization. The objective of the novel was therefore not an inquiry into the American native, but a denunciation of contemporary contradictions through the "popular myth" of the noble savage. These premises, however, did not prevent the author from singling out certain distinctive traits that contemporary naturalists were busy classifying in order to form an *identikit* of the American Indian.

The silence and good manners that the Americans displayed in conversation were certainly some of the qualities most appreciated by eighteenth-century intellectuals:

19. On the myth held in Europe about the islands of the Pacific ocean, see Michel Devèze, "La question du continent austral: Bougainville, Cook et leurs émules," in *L'Europe et le monde à la fin du XVIII*ᵉ *siècle* (Paris: Albin Michel, 1970), 228–72.
20. *L'ingénu, histoire véritable tirée des manuscrits du Père Quesnel*, in *Zadig. L'ingénu*, trans. and with intro. John Butt (Baltimore: Penguin, 1964), 107.

The news that there was a Huron at the priory spread quickly. All the best society of the district made haste to have supper there. The Abbé de St. Yves came with his pretty sister, a fine Low Breton girl who had been very well brought up. The Magistrate and the tax collector and their wives were there too. The stranger was given a seat between Mademoiselle de Kerkabon and Mademoiselle de St. Yves. He was the centre of admiration and the target for a continual barrage of questions and conversation; yet nothing disturbed the Huron, for his motto seemed to be that of Lord Bolingbroke, *Nihil admirari.*

But in the end the noise was so great that he was tired out, and said to them politely but with a touch of firmness: "Gentlemen, in my country we speak one at a time; how can I answer you when you prevent me from hearing what you say?"

Reason always brings people to their senses for a short time. Silence fell.

As documented in the *History of America* by Robertson, the taciturn savage was isolated in mental seclusion:

A savage, frequently, placed in situations of danger and distress, depending on himself alone, and wrapt up in his own thoughts and schemes, is a serious melancholy animal. His attention to others is small. The range of his own ideas is narrow. Hence that taciturnity which is so disgusting to men accustomed to the open intercourse of social conversation.[21]

Also, the Burkes continued to sketch the Indian's distinctive features:

The character of the Indians is striking. They are grave even to sadness in their deportment upon any serious occasion, observant of those in company; respectful to the old; of a temper cool and deliberate by which they are never in haste to speak before they have thought well upon the matter, and are sure the person who spoke before them has finished all he had to say. They have therefore the

---

21. William Robertson, *History of America*, 2:228. Hennepin also mentioned the Iroquois discretion in conversation (*A Description of Louisiana*): "These Iroquois, almost all of them large men, wore only robes of beaver, wolf, or in a few instances black squirrel, and were puffing often at calumets. Yet never did Venetian senators bear themselves more gravely or speak with more poise than the old men of the Iroquois in their assembly" (25).

greatest contempt for the vivacity of the Europeans, who interrupt each other, and frequently speak all together.[22]

Pietro Chiari also listed among the "privileges of ignorance" the wise silence of the Americans who were free from the snares of European eloquence. Either because of "scarcity of ideas" or because of "scarcity of language . . . they did not say any thing more than the need called for at their congresses."[23] The pseudo-author of *I privilegi dell'ignoranza* noted:

> Usually Americans are not great speakers; nor are there among us women as loquacious as the thousands I have heard elsewhere. Maybe then our language is one of the scarcest when it comes to words; for so few are our needs, what would we need different expressions for? This privilege bestowed on us by our ignorance is not small. Sometimes there are twenty or thirty of us who do not utter a syllable for most of the day.[24]

Voltaire's silent Huron brings to mind a short story by Alessandro Verri which appeared in *Il Caffè*[25] several years before *Ingénu*. In the story,

---

22. William and Edmund Burke, *An Account of the European Settlements in America*, 2d ed. with improvements, 2 vols. (London: R. and J. Dosley, 1758). (New York: Research Reprints, 1970, 2 vols.), 1:170.

23. Pietro Chiari, *I privilegi dell'ignoranza: lettere di un'Americana ad un letterato d'Europa* (Venice: Bassaglia, 1784), 2:letter 2, p. 95. Concerning native assemblies, Franklin, in *Remarks Concerning the Savages*, wrote: "He that would speak, rises. The rest observe a profound Silence. When he has finished and sits down, they leave him five or six Minutes to recollect, that if he has omitted any thing he intended to say, or has any thing to add, he may rise again and deliver it. To interrupt another, even in common Conversation, is reckoned highly indecent. How different this is from the Conduct of a polite British House of Commons, where scarce a Day passes without some Confusion that makes the Speaker hoarse in calling to *order*; and how different from the mode of Conversation in many polite Companies of Europe, where if you do not deliver your Sentence with great Rapidity, you are cut off in the middle of it by the impatient Loquacity of those you converse with, & never suffer to finish it" (970-71).

24. Ibid., 2:letter 2, p. 65. In another passage from the same work Chiari returns to the same topic (ibid., 2:letter 8, p. 66): "Blessed be these American women! Who, insofar as they need facts more than words, do not drive others crazy with long and loud gossip which says nothing, or says merely that they are head-over-heels in love with you; and that this or that other friend of theirs received sumptuous presents from her sweetheart. Should you, my friend, be forced to come and live with us—which I do not wish for you—you would be able to philosophize, and even write in the middle of the square, without the danger of being distracted or benumbed by savage speakers."

25. *Lo spirito di società*, in *Il Caffè ossia brevi e vari discorsi distribuiti in fogli periodici (dal giugno 1764 a tutto maggio 1765)*, ed. Sergio Romagnoli (Milan: Feltrinelli, 1960).

a Canadian Indian arrives in Peking and, having been led to a "meeting," voices his surprise:

> A confused and incessant murmuring of grave, middle and acute voices began to stop him, surprised, at the door: "What is this noise?" he said. "This is the noise the sea in my country makes when the winds start troubling it!" "Ah, not at all," answered the Peking man, "these people have so many things to tell each other, that they will never finish their business unless they all talk at once."[26]

The wonder, however, is reciprocal, and the entrance of the American Indian in the sparkling assembly hall provokes a resounding chorus of inquisitive queries and scornful complaints:

> Who is that character? Who is that figure? Who is that ugly animal? You heard no other comments but these throughout the assembly. . . . "If you please, from what country are you Sir? "Canada" he said. "Oh this is a good one, your excellency is Canada!" exclaimed a witty character. "Oh," said another; "what a figure!" "Hey, Mr. Confucius," said another, "listen, this gentleman is Canada! Oh, Canada, damn it!" And so, little by little everyone exclaimed "A Canada! A Canada!"[27]

Information about the American savages arrives during these years through several sources, including, also, *La Gazzetta di Milano* of February 11, 1769 (edited by Arnaldo Bruni [Milan: Ricciardi, 1981], 1:88), which described a savage from Labrador who landed at Cadiz: "From Cadiz it is reported that a young savage man from the land of Labrador, in North America, recently taken by the English, arrived here on an English war frigate. This young man who seems to be no older than fourteen years, disembarked yesterday in the same boat with which he had been taken prison in America. Said boat is constructed of a thick hide, seemingly of seal skin, tied together with whalebones; it is about twenty feet long, and no wider than twenty two inches. There is space for only one person, and this person sits inside a hole in the center of the boat. The savage maneuvers it with just one oar. He is also dressed in what appears to be seal skin, in the fashion of his country. A large number of curious people came to the inn where he is staying, and where the boat was exposed to the public." Later, the account continues: "Two young Delawari men, the sons of a tribal chief, having learned English, are now studying Medicine and practical surgery with an excellent professor, and specializing in smallpox inoculation, a disease which plays havoc among Indians" (1:291).
26. Ibid., 280.
27. Ibid., 281. The Canadian Indian continues to wonder at the odd reception given him by the Chinese: " 'You are odd, you Pekingese', said the American, of course: 'if one of you came to my country, no one would wonder at your appearance, as you are of mine. . . .' 'Eh, this is a good one' said a witty character from the group, 'Mr. Savage, are you comparing yourself to us?' " (181-82).

Poor "Sir Canada," insulted by the members of this strange assembly, finally runs across a "Pekingese" lady who scolds him because he did not treat her with due respect, having failed to enumerate all her appellations, and identifies him as one who belongs to that "dog-like race which inhabits North America."

It should not be surprising that Verri and Voltaire chose a Canadian Indian, since the eighteenth century continued to recognize in Hurons and Iroquois qualities and virtues that were unknown to other New World natives. "In North America," writes Francesco Algarotti in his *Saggio sopra l'imperio degl'Incas*, "the Iroquois republic stands out among the other populations: and it well deserves this special place on account of its accomplishments, its passionate love of freedom, its inextinguishable thirst for glory, and a deeply rooted conviction of being the most excellent of all nations."[28]

Through "Sir Canada's" naive reflections, Verri denounced abstract values such as friendship and brotherhood, which in sophisticated eighteenth-century society had lost all freshness and authenticity. However, the overall meaning of the fable should not be seen as a vague aspiration to escape to the primitive world, but rather as a search for equilibrium. "In my opinion there are two extremes," he concluded, "that spoil human intercourse: wildness and frivolity. The former produces rough customs and fierceness; the latter makes men indifferent, scarcely capable of true friendship and of enjoying its delights. . . . This finally is the true spirit of society, neither American nor Pekingese."[29]

Verri's observations were not subversive and did not propose a pre-civilized alternative to eighteenth-century society. On the contrary, he wished for an ideal condition that would fall between the extremes of the sophisticated "Pekingese" and the primitive "Americans."

Social satire hides behind the alibi of exoticism. The picture, almost completely invented, of a foreign universe, allows an ironic liberation

---

28. Francesco Algarotti, "Saggio sopra l'imperio degl'Incas," in *Saggi*, ed. Giovanni da Pozzo (Bari: Laterza, 1969), 320-21. Algarotti's panegyric is to be interpreted in the light of certain exemplary texts such as the Jesuits' reports from New France, Lafitau's investigation and especially Cadwallader Colden's *History of Five Nations of Canada* (London: Locker Davis, 1755). For a bibliographical survey of travels made in Canada from the seventeenth through the eighteenth century, Gemelli Careri furnishes exhaustive documentation (*Voyage Round the World*, vol. 10). Prévost also recognized that the Iroquois are "the Canadian nation which seemed to occupy first place in the last two centuries"; *Histoire générale des voyages* (Paris: Didot, 1746), 4:15.

29. *Lo spirito di società*, 282.

that, as pinpointed by Starobinski, "enable[s] the mind to move back into the unreal, either to be intoxicated by it or to find in it the point of view from which reality may be described as a comedy."[30]

The New World native, rather than representing a romantic symbol of savagery, was a projection of the ethical expectations and aspirations of eighteenth-century intellectual society.

3. Carlo Goldoni's "American" Tragicomedies

The Italian eighteenth century tended to lead the myth of the noble savage back within bourgeois horizons and therefore within a realistic and familiar context. The theater confirmed this orientation, which developed along two tracks: on the one hand, the realistic representation of the American Indian as reflected in bourgeois ideals, and on the other hand, the parody of the primitive man, a recurrent theme in comedies, farces, and librettos.

Two of Goldoni's "American" tragicomedies belong to the first trend: *La Peruviana* (1754-55) and *La bella selvaggia* (1757-58). The playwright showed, especially in the second play, that he was acquainted with the more common American traits, both from a character point of view (indolence, stubbornness, individualism) and from an ethical standpoint (frankness, equality, freedom). The typical aspects of the savage world, already known to the eighteenth century, are presented in *La bella selvaggia* and summarized in the reply of Papadir the savage to the Portuguese Don Alonso, who is curious to know the "tasks" the Americans practice in the Guyana forest:

> We follow the law of bountiful nature
> The larger our herd, the greater the esteem enjoyed.
> Hunting animals in these forests
> With bow and arrow is our preferred amusement.
> The hairy hide which we skin from animals
> We use for clothing in harsh winter.
> The happy hunter devours the still bloody

---

30. Jean Starobinski, *The Invention of Liberty, 1700-1789*, trans. Bernard C. Swift, 1st paperback ed. (New York: Rizzoli, 1987), 56.

Flesh of the animals he hunted.
Herbs, fruits and plants are in abundance.
Our soil in every season fertilizes its seeds;
And crystal clear waters from the mountain
Spring, to extinguish our thirst.[31]

In *La bella selvaggia* two sources are clearly identifiable: the chapters on Guyana from the *Histoire générale des voyages* by Prévost, from which Goldoni claimed he had gathered the topic for his work,[32] and Voltaire's *Alzire*, which had been staged at the San Samuele theater in 1738. Against the backdrop of a Peru threatened by the Spanish conquistadors, in the tale of the heroine Alzire—contested by the evil "civilizer" Gusmane and the proud Peruvian prince Zamore—Voltaire staged one of the favorite themes of the Enlightenment: the conflict between barbarism and civilization. Goldoni's Delmira is modeled after Voltaire's heroine (just as Zadir is reflected in Zamore and Don Alonso in Gusmane). Instead of taking place in the Inca kingdom, the action is located in the "hitherto unknown lands of Guyana," and more precisely in a new island discovered by the Spaniards, *La Trinité,* according to the description by Prévost.[33] As the

31.   Di provvida natura noi seguitiam la legge
      Quel più tra noi si stima, che più fecondo ha il gregge.
      Un arco, una faretra, ci dà fra queste selve
      Il nobile diletto di abbattere le belve.
      L'ispida pelle irsuta che agli animai si toglie,
      Suole nel crudo verno formar le nostre spoglie.
      E delle membra loro insanguinate ancora
      Dal cacciator contento la carne si divora.
      L'erbe, i frutti le piante son comuni fra noi.
      La terra in ogni tempo feconda i semi suoi;
      E a spegner della sete i consueti ardori,
      Scaturiscon dal monte i cristallini umori.
La bella selvaggia (act 1, scene 4), in *Tutte le opere di Carlo Goldoni*, ed. Giuseppe Ortolani (Milan: Mondadori, 1959), 9:829-30.

32. See *Mémoires*, 1:387.

33. See Antoine François Prévost, *Histoire générale des voyages*, 15:335. The island was certainly a favorite exotic space, as confirmed by Goldoni, Chiari, and Metastasio. In the theater piece *L'isola disabitata*, Metastasio fantasizes that "the young Gernando, his young bride Costanza and her little sister Silvia, then still a baby," travel by ship "to reach his father in the West Indies, where the latter was governor of one of those lands"; *L'isola disabitata*, in *Tutte le opere di Pietro Metastasio*, ed. Bruno Brunelli (Milan: Mondadori, 1965), 2:325. After a violent storm the travelers land in a deserted island where Gernando is kidnapped by the pirates. The adventure, however, ends happily when, thirteen years later, the protagonists find each other in the same place.

Portuguese replace the Spanish rulers, Zadir's plan to kill Don Alonso fails and the solution is reversed: the rebel savage is condemned to death, but after being pardoned by Alonso, he generously gives up Delmira. The abandonment of tragedy and the need to "find comic material," even on the Amazon river,[34] led Goldoni to graft humoristic devices onto the "shaved wild man" Schichirat, who thirsts after European wines, the sole positive effect of the conquest:

> Blessed be the moment when you arrived here,
> You, happy possessors of delicate wines.
> And would Zadir want I, with my hands,
> To cut their captains veins and so betray them?
> Were I to sit on the throne of such sweet liquor,
> I would give them in exchange all of America's gold.
> Europeans' sight is restored when they see gold.
> I indulge my throat's pleasure with wine.
> My pleasure consists in drinking whenever I can.
> The more I drink, the more I want to drink
> (*He drinks*).
> Steady yourself, what is this? It's as if the ground were dancing.
> No, I am the one who is dancing full of mirth.
> It seems I have lost my sight. Well, I need no sight.
> A bottle in my hands I can empty in the dark
> (*He drinks*).[35]

---

34. See *Mémoires*, 388.
35.   Benedetto il momento che qui siete arrivati,
              Felici possessori di vini delicati.
              E vorrebbe Zadir che il loro capitano
              Potessi a tradimento svenar colla mia mano?
              Per sì dolce bevanda s'io possedessi il trono,
              Tutto l'oro d'America vorrei dar loro in dono.
              La vista agli Europei coll'oro si consola.
              Io pascolo col vino il gusto della gola.
              Nel bere quando posso stan tutti i gusti miei.
              E quanto più bevo, più ancor ne beverei
              (*beve.*)
              Saldi, saldi, ch'è questo? par che balli il terreno.
              No, son io che ballo coll'allegrezza in seno.
              Pare che non ci veda. Eh, di veder non curo.
              Se ho la bottiglia in mano, posso vuotarla al scuro
              (*beve*).
La bella selvaggia, act 4, scene 5, p. 864.

Prévost mentioned that in Guyana a fairly good wine was produced and that natives were in the habit of abusing a liquor made with "American powder and the juice of several herbs."[36] Drunkenness was one of the excesses of American Indians. The cause was to be found, if not in "delicate wines," then in various alcoholic beverages. This was confirmed by several eighteenth-century sources. Muratori, for example, describing the habits of the "Paraguayesi" before the coming of the Jesuits, remembered that "drunkenness [is] a common vice among them. They are sure to exceed when they have *Chica* at discretion, and particularly when they are presented by Europeans with some bottles of wines and spirits."[37] Their feasts and dances "hold out usually two or three days and nights, of which the greatest part is spent in drinking; and frequently the fumes of *Chica* getting into their heads, disputes, quarrels, and murders suceed to their diversions and pleasures."[38] Like Muratori, the missionary Jesuits in Paraguay found this vice of the natives to be an obstacle to conversion. Father Fernandez recalled that after a sermon, the Indians would "return to their dances and to *Chicha*, which is their drink, and soon, their minds overheated from excessive drinking of this liquor, the feast turns into fights, leaving several of them wounded or dead."[39]

To activate the comic mechanism Goldoni blended certain distinctive American traits into the character of the Indian Schichirat: drunkenness, sloth, inactivity ("Up to now, I ate quite well. / Herbs, fruits and plants are my delight; / I care not to eat your nasty food")[40] and, in the final analysis, the question of the beards. Naturalists and historians of the New World

36. Antoine François Prévost, *Histoire générale des voyages*, 15:383.
37. *A Relation of the Missions of Paraguay*, 29.
38. Ibid.
39. *Lettres édifiantes et curieuses*, 25:134-35. The Burkes also wrote, in *An Account of the European Settlements in America*, about the dissoluteness of Americans in this respect: "Before we discovered them they wanted spiritous liquors; but now, the acquirement of these is what gives a spur to their industry, and enjoyment to their repose. This is the principal end they pursue in their treaties with us; and from this they suffer inexpressible calamities; for, having once begun to drink they can preserve no measure, but continue a succession of drunkenness as long as their means of procuring liquor lasts. In this condition they lie exposed on the earth to all the inclemency of the seasons, which wastes them by a train of the most fatal disorders; they perish in rivers and marshes; they tumble into the fire" (1:169). Bougainville (*Voyage*, 1:25) and Gilij (*Saggio di storia americana*, 2:114) also describe the tragic consequences alcohol had on the Indians.
40. "Finor senza far nulla, benissimo ho mangiato. / L'erbe i frutti, le piante son le delizie mie; / Mangiar io non mi curo le vostre porcherie." *La bella selvaggia*, act 2, scene 1, p. 35. In America, as Pietro Chiari wrote, "the land sprouted by itself, without waiting for the plough" (*I privilegi dell'ignoranza*, 1:letter I, p. 3).

had more or less come to the shared conclusion that Americans were "beardless"; this issue, turned upside down and used to comic effect, is reflected in the Indian who is proud of his beard, as in the dialogue between Schichirat and Rosina:

Schi. Were I to fall in love, I would look for a pretty one.
Ros. But not with such a beard.
Schi. And why not?
Ros. Because we care not to look at faces
Swaddled in such beards.
Schi. Oh well, I do say and have so decided:
I was born with a beard, and bearded I will die.
Ros. And if a pretty girl, one much prettier than me,
Should ask you as gift this cute beard of yours?
Schi. Her charms notwithstanding, I would answer her
That in higher esteem I hold my beard.
Ros. But you would be kind of handsome without that beard!
Schi. I would not barter it for a jug of wine.
Ros. What! Do your people appreciate wine more than women?
Schi. Yes Ma'am, I esteem it much more than beauty.
. . . .
Ros. Come, I will make sure you get your fill of wine,
But you must please me and cut off that beard.
Schi. My poor beard! How has it hurt you?
Why should I appear deformed and in disguise?
Ros. What do you say, should I cut it?
Schi. If you are furious,
Cut off my life, but not my beard.[41]

41. *Schi.* Se avrò da innamorarmi, cercherò una vezzosa.
 Ros. Ma non con questa barba.
 Schi. No? Perché?
 Ros. Perché i volti
  noi non vogliam vedere da queste barbe involti.
 Schi. Oh in quanto a questo poi, lo dico ed ho fissato:
  Son nato con la barba e vo' morir barbato.
 Ros. E se donna vezzosa, più assai di quel ch'io sono,
  Questa bella barbetta vi domandasse in dono?
 Schi. Con tutti i vezzi suoi, io le risponderei
  Che questa mia barbetta la stimo più di lei.
 Ros. Senza di quella barba sareste pur bellino!

Once shaved by Rosina, that "damned witch," Schichirat fears the other savages' derision: "Should I show up without beard on my chin? / What will our Americans say to this? / Pert insolent women will make fun of me."[42] Ortolani felt the artistic limitations of *La bella selvaggia* and found the reason for its failure in the play's "comic vulgarity." In addition, the critic submitted his reservations about Rousseau's influence on this tragicomedy, based on the following observations: "We cannot accept that Goldoni, writing in '57, knew of the doctrines of Jean-Jacques Rousseau, as Rabany seems to state: it was only later that Chamfort's *La Jeune Indienne* (1784) was staged, and that Marmontel's novel about the *Incas* (1778) came out. Attilio Momigliano is therefore not correct when he mentions *La bella selvaggia* and affirms that it is purposely Rousseauian throughout."[43] The *Discourse on the Origins of Inequality* came out only two years before

---

        Schi. Non la darei nemmeno per un boccal di vino,
        Ros. Come! più bella donna il vin da voi si apprezza?
        Schi. Sì signora, lo stimo più assai della bellezza.
        . . . .
        Ros. Via, posso far io stessa che di vin vi saziate,
             Ma vo' che per mercede la barba vi tagliate.
        Schi. Povera la mia barba! cosa di mal vi ha fatto?
             Perché ho da comparire deforme e contrafatto?
        Ros. Che sì, la taglio?
        Schi.   Se siete inviperita,
             piuttosto della barba toglietemi la vita.
Ibid., act 2, scene 1, p. 838.

    42. "Dovrò farmi vedere senza la barba al mento? / I nostri Americani di ciò cosa diranno? / Le donne insolentissime di me si burleranno." act 5, scene 1, p. 876. A page from Hennepin (*A Description of Louisiana*) sheds some light on the Indians' aversion to beards: "These uncouth people, who until then had been without faith and without law, ridiculed everything I said. 'How can it be', they asked, 'that these two men with you have wives? Ours would not live with them because they have hair all over the face, while we have none either there or anywhere else.' In fact, they were never better pleased with me than when I was shaved. I humored them, since it involved no sin, and shaved every week" (110). In *Il costume antico e moderno di tutti i popoli*, it is stressed that "although the Indians' heads are quite thick with hair, they have no other hair on their bodies. Only elderly men have a very sparse beard, much like that of very old European women" (1:280).

    43. Giuseppe Ortolani, *Nota storica*, in *Opere complete di Carlo Goldoni*, ed. the Municipality of Venice in the second centennial of his birth (Venice, 1927), 24:585. Felice Del Beccaro ("L'esperienza 'esotica' del Goldoni" in *Studi goldoniani* [1979], 62) is in agreement on Rousseau's influence on *La bella selvaggia*. Krzysztof Zaboklicki's analysis ("Le commedie 'esotiche' di Carlo Goldoni: rassegna della critica novecentesca," in *L'interpretazione goldoniana, critica e messinscena* [Rome: Officina, 1982], 158-73) is also enlightening.

La bella selvaggia, and although we have no proof that Goldoni read it, it is surprising that he intended "in imitation of the best writers, to let nature speak with its plain language, without the aid of acquired notions."[44] Certainly among the "best writers," Goldoni must have included Prévost and Voltaire, but an allusion to Rousseau as well cannot be confirmed. Here we must acknowledge with Sestan that the claim to trace any reference to the primitive back to the context of Rousseau's *Discourse* is not always justified, as "deep universal upheavals in feelings have, of course, neither one sole healing sorcerer nor one specific birthday."[45] Even before the diffusion of the *Discourse on the origin of inequality, La Peruviana* (1754) conforming to the taste for exoticism, had already shown an inclination for those egalitarian ideals that Goldoni would boldly associate with the state of nature in his next tragicomedy. *La bella selvaggia* was certainly "the strong piece in Goldoni's natural primitivism,"[46] although his noble savage stereotype ultimately projected a temperate bourgeois ethic, as Delmira's speech to Don Alonso confirms:

> What wicked concept of our savages do you have?
> That they do not appreciate virtue? Sir, you are mistaken.
> Foreign lands have other laws, other rites
> But reason reigns in all human hearts;
> And perhaps we savages better obey
> The time hallowed truths of honest living.
> Among us, no desire spurs animals to plunder,
> Nor do we wreck havoc and ruin.
> Content and satisfied with our state,
> We do not attempt to benefit a good by harming others.
> We are taught to succour those in need.
> For us, a promise given is an eternal pledge.
> And if an honest life be called virtue,
> Then savages possess it in their hearts.
> Such is their virtue.[47]

44. *L'Autore a chi legge,* in *Tutte le opere,* 588.
45. Ernesto Sestan, "Il mito del buon selvaggio americano e l'Italia del Settecento," in *Europa settecentesca e altri saggi* (Milan: Ricciardi, 1951), 136.
46. Manlio Dazzi, *Carlo Goldoni e la sua poetica sociale* (Turin: Einaudi, 1957), 145.
47.   Qual dei nostri selvaggi rio concetto formate?
        Non apprezzan virtude? Signor voi v'ingannate.

The necessity of "spreading the seeds of good philosophy," as stated in the dedication to Dolfin Tiepolo, led Goldoni to create a heroine that, as in the earlier case of Zilia in *La Peruviana*, "supporting herself on the mere principles of nature, loves honesty and prefers virtue to any type of riches."[48] This observation continued to persuade Momigliano[49] that there is a Rousseauian influence on Delmira, but convinced Ortolani of the opposite opinion: *La bella selvaggia* meant to celebrate only "the beautiful simple virtues of nature dreamed in the eighteenth century and dear to the Abbé Prévost in his novels, before Chiari."[50] And we must agree with Ortolani: in bringing the Americans to the stage, Goldoni did not mean to idealize the primitive world, but rather to offer the eighteenth-century public an exotic escape, within the limits and platitudes of bourgeois theater tradition.

4. The Parody of the "State of Nature": Francesco Cerlone and Ferdinando Degli Obizzi

In the second half of the century, Francesco Cerlone (1722-79), a prolific playwright from Naples, combined contemporary exotic stereotypes with elements of the Arcadic tradition in works such as *Gl'Inglesi in America, o sia il Selvaggio* (1764). Author of fifty-six comedies and several opera librettos, including *Il Colombo nell'Indie* and *Li Napoletani in America*,

---

          Altre leggi, altri riti hanno i paesi estrani
          Ma la ragion per tutto regna nei cori umani:
          E di onesto costume le massime onorate
          Forse da noi selvaggi saran meglio osservate.
          Quivi desio non sprona gli animai alle rapine
          A seminar non vassi le stragi e le rovine;
          Ciascun del proprio stato si appaga e si contenta,
          Suo ben coll'altrui danno di procacciar non tenta.
          Ai miseri soccorso porgere a noi s'insegna.
          Fra noi la data fede perpetuamente impegna.
          E se virtù si chiama vivere vita onesta,
          L'hanno i selvaggi in petto. La lor virtude è questa.
La bella selvaggia, act 1, scene 5, p. 833.
    48. Ibid., 818.
    49. Cf. Attilio Momigliano, *Saggi goldoniani*, ed. Vittore Branca (Venice: Istituto per la Collaborazione Culturale, 1959), 163.
    50. Giuseppe Ortolani, *Nota storica*, 582.

Cerlone took as his model the theater of Gozzi and especially of Goldoni, having translated some of Goldoni's comedies into Neapolitan. The exotic theme, especially in *Il Colombo nell'Indie,* underwent a grotesque deformation, which disappointed the public as well as the critics, as reported in an article that appeared in *Nuovo giornale letterario d'Italia:*

> In Naples Cerlone, not unlike Gozzi, used the most trivial ridicule and the most indecent tricks to amuse the rabble, which comes running whenever it sees Harlequin and Punchinello. These kinds of authors reveal what the national taste is and prove how much the people need to be educated.[51]

In *Gl'Inglesi in America, o sia il Selvaggio,* staged for the first time at the San Carlino theater in Naples in 1764 by the Compagnia della Cantina, Cerlone conformed to the exotic fashion of the time and situated the Americans in a pastoral setting. Urania, daughter of noble Europeans and entrusted to Aminta, whom she believes to be her father, lives among the savages of Canada. Sought after by both the American Arensbergh ("a black prince, Lord of Savages and Cannibals"), and Milord Arespingh ("a rich English nobleman"), the young girl in the end succumbs to the latter's flattery and leaves behind "her unhappy life, in horrid desert lands, separated from the world," following him to England. Thus Cerlone, like Goldoni's and Chiari's American heroines,[52] adopted the theme of the European man who falls in love with the young American girl, smitten by her innocence and her natural beauty.

Milord Arespingh confesses to his confidant Beautif his passion for Urania:

---

51. "Lo stato presente della letteratura italiana," in *Giornali veneziani,* 646.
52. We must also recall the protagonist of a short story by Francesco Soave, *L'ingratitudine.* Jariko, a young American girl, saves and looks after the Englishman Inkle, shipwrecked on her island. The young man persuades her to follow him to England after having talked to her of "lovely and magnificent houses where she would live much better that in rough caves or under an open sky; of splendid garments, which, instead of being naked, would protect her from the seasons' blows and would add taste and decorum to her beauty; and of the exquisite foods and precious liquors she would taste, much more valuable than the water she drank or the forest fruit she ate" (*Novelle morali* [Naples: Marotta, 1777], 2:84-85). But the "barbarian Inkle . . . attracted by his own avarice, and forgetting everything" sells the unlucky Jariko at a slave market; she dies shortly thereafter. When Inkle returns to the American island to bring gold and silver back to Europe, he will be killed in fatal revenge by the natives.

Mil. I burn, I am with love inflamed; my heart was smitten by two lovely eyes.
Be. What do I hear! You love! Who inflamed you? Can America produce a beauty such as to make an English nobleman fall in love?
Mil. Ah Beautif! my sweet friend! have pity on me, for I am lost. A thousand European beauties I despised, only to be in turn conquered and scorned by a rustic beauty.
Be. Black?
Mil. No, whiter than snow and more vermilion than a European rose. . . . The day before yesterday I heard her sing in the shadow of those cypress trees; slowly I approached and was at her side before she knew it. At the sound of footsteps she turns, sees me and sets out to flee and all the while I notice that she shyly looks at me, curious and surprised. Her soul fearless, she takes two steps backward, fixes her eyes on my face and then starts to examine me from head to toe. I greet her and speak to her; shyly she replies, then no longer fearful she asks me a hundred things about Europe. I please her, and finally dare talk to her of love, and sighing, with languid eyes, try to tell her of the fire burning in my heart.[53]

Milord Arespingh ignores the European origins of Urania who, through the resolutory device of sudden recognition, rediscovers her father Ernesto. The latter, called "the Savage," is an Irish prince who for years has been living "in a reverted state of wildness in an American desert" and who makes his appearance "clothed with several animal skins, with long hair flowing about his shoulders."[54] Unlike Urania, who unwillingly finds herself among American "blacks and cannibals," Ernesto is a European, now become "naturalized American," who consciously opted for a primitive life:

Ur. Were you not born here?
Er. No: I am European.
Ur. Who brought you here? why do you flee all living souls? why do you live like a beast?

53. *Gl'Inglesi in America, o sia il Selvaggio*, act 1, scene 1 (Naples: Ruffo, 1770), 5.
54. Ibid., act 1, scene 2, p. 14.

Er. Because to this life I am sentenced.[55]

Although Ernesto's vicissitudes, as one who was converted to walk "on four feet," lets one guess this is a conscious comical version of the Rousseauian idealization of the primitive, the central theme of the comedy is not however a polemical stance with reference to Rousseau, but rather a celebration of the ancient values of honesty, moderation, and simplicity. Exoticism is modeled after virtuous bourgeois ideals as Urania's scolding words to Milord Arespingh show:

> And I want to convince you that love of one's father is at the same time sacred, it is law and duty; all other loves are uncertain, deceptive, merely a choice; this nature teaches us, without your science.[56]
>
> You are the unjust and cruel barbarian who acts against the laws of nature and heaven.[57]

These observations bring Urania closer to Goldoni's Delmira and to Chiari's American heroines, whose novels, according to Croce,[58] constitute the main sources for Cerlone.

Thus, if in *Gl'Inglesi in America,* the objective was not a parody of Rousseau's theory, the case of two comedies of Ferdinando degli Obizzi, a nobleman from Padua was quite different: *Il bel Selvaggio,* which takes place at the Cape of Good Hope, and *Il filosofo e il pazzo.* The latter, especially, made explicit reference to the *Discourse on the Origin of Inequality,* insofar as the protagonist, Roberto, having read Rousseau's "damned book" decides to join the American natives and return to the state of nature. His intention to "want to live among men today with ancient customs" creates havoc with his family and worries his mother Clarice, his sister Eleonora and his servant Cecco:

> *Cla.* Oh wretched me, oh disgrace on my family! My only family support, my dear son Roberto, gone mad; poor me, who would have believed it?

---

55. Ibid.
56. Ibid., act 1, scene 1, p. 11.
57. Ibid., act 2, scene 3, p. 35.
58. See Benedetto Croce, *I teatri di Napoli* (Bari: Laterza, 1926), 170.

> *Cecc.* I would have believed it; and why not? Don't you think he should go mad, seeing how he pores over all those books of his, in this horrible dog-day heat? Moreover, when he takes in his hands one of those books that talk about, so he says, inequality among men, nothing can stop him; all he can say is: Oh lovely state of nature, oh wretched human society full of discomfort! Then he undresses down to the light covering you made for him when he was born, which never goes out of fashion.[59]

Roberto's bizarre behavior and his reasoning which is restricted to Rousseauian maxims, lead to the need for medical assistance from a physician who tries to dissuade him from his mad intent. But Roberto persists in his mulishness, setting up a contrast between the genuine condition of the savage world and the corruption of modern society:

> Poverty is a word which is unknown in the state of nature, given that nature provides equally for everyone's needs. The inequality in shares causes some to be lacking in need, and others to have a surfeit.[60]

> According to my Author, in the state of nature all man has to do is eat, sleep and look for a woman.[61]

> I did in fact learn that man was born to live in the woods and that it was fear and suspicion that induced him to live with other men in cities; that it was greed and ambition that kept him there; and that even if one were to find virtue, it has been so sophisticated by constant human practice that it has been reduced to excess and degenerated into fanaticism.[62]

All attempts to lead Roberto back to normality fail; Roberto continues to think and to dress according the "savage fashion." He does not come back to his senses and at the end, although he decides to marry the young servant Bice, he will remain insensitive to the revelation that her origins are noble, and will confess to her: "Bice, since you have been noble and

---

59. *Il filosofo e il pazzo: Commedia per la villa*, act 1, scene 1 (Padua: Conzatti, 1766), 5.
60. Ibid., act 1, scene 5, p. 13.
61. Ibid., act 1, scene 6, p. 15.
62. Ibid., act 3, scene 2, p. 35.

rich, you have seemed to me less beautiful."[63] This convinced Rousseauian unwillingly gives up the American paradise and stays in a society that has lost all sense of authenticity.

5. Pietro Chiari's Primitivism

Pietro Chiari, the "incurable scribbler," could not resist the charm of the New World, as seen in his three novels with an American theme: *La donna che non si trova* (1762), *L'Americana raminga* (1763) and *La corsara francese della guerra presente* (1780-81). The protagonists are American heroines who, following Prévost's and Defoe's models, relate their adventurous and involved vicissitudes in the first person. Among Chiari's American cultural sources, as Fido has noted,[64] there are Lafitau's works, and Burke's *Account of the European Settlements in America*, whose Italian translation was published in Venice in 1763 by the publisher Zatta. These readings, and probably others as well, gave this prolific writer the idea to develop a comparison between the two worlds, and to stress the inadequacies of contemporary life while assessing the qualities of primitive life.[65] In any case, even before the "American" novel cycle, in *L'uomo d'un altro mondo*,[66] Chiari had earlier compared the primitive protagonist to civilization, and denounced the excesses and limitations of the old continents. The solitary hero, after abandoning a desert island where he had always lived, goes to Asia and Europe. Disappointed by the pretenses and deceits of civilization, he finally decides to return with a servant and some friends to his island in order to found an ideal republic.[67]

---

63. Ibid., act 5, scene 9, p. 77.

64. See Franco Fido, "I romanzi: temi, ideologia, scrittura," in *Pietro Chiari e il teatro europeo del Settecento* (Proceedings of the Conference "Un rivale di Carlo Goldoni. Pietro Chiari e il teatro europeo del Settecento," Venice, March 1-3, 1985), ed. Carmelo Alberti (Vicenza: Neri Pozza, 1986), 286.

65. See William Boelhower, "New World Topology and Types in the Novels of Abbot Pietro Chiari," *Early American Literature* 19 (1984): 153-72.

66. *L'uomo d'un altro mondo, o sia memorie d'un solitario senza nome, scritte da lui medesimo in due linguaggi, chinese e russiano, e pubblicate nella nostra lingua dall'abate Pietro Chiari* (Parma: Carmignani, 1760).

67. Marchesi, in *Studi e ricerche intorno ai nostri romanzieri e romanzi del Settecento* (Bergamo: Istituto Italiano di Arti Grafiche, 1903), 99, identified the sources of Chiari's novel in Swift's *Gulliver's Travels*, Defoe's *Robinson Crusoe*, and Marivaux's *Effets surprenants de la sympathie*.

Two years later, *La donna che non si trova,* the only American novel truly influenced by primitivistic themes, revived the topic of the state of nature and celebrated simplicity over the corruption of civilization. Quivira and Delingh's adventures in the forest of Canada allowed Chiari to dwell upon the character of the North American Indians, free of any religion, law, and moral or educational conditioning. "The soul of a nation is its liberty" and natives were endowed with an "unquenchable spirit of independence, sustained by nature and regulated by the light of natural reason."[68] As already noted by the Burkes, the Indian's propensity for freedom was his distinguishing trait: "Liberty in its fullest extent is the darling passion of the Americans. This is what makes a life of uncertainty and want, supportable to them; and their education is directed in such a manner as to cherish this disposition to the utmost."[69] The affront committed by the "civilized" populations to this spirit of independence with the imposition of European conventions, raised Chiari's indignation against past conquistadors and present settlers: but his protest cannot fit neatly within a Rousseauian context. A deviation from Rousseau's principles occurred when, although applauding the perfection of the state of nature, he was convinced that reason would allow the savages to integrate themselves into an enlightened society and into a process of acculturation ("the enlightened, industrious European," Delingh, directs the Canadian natives to civilization; Quivira wins a decorous position in London and Paris, and another savage, Criqué, becomes captain of a British regiment). But the fundamental contradiction of this conception was revealed in Chiari's certainty that Americans, although in the midst of a process of maturation based on Enlightenment premises, could remain faithful to

68. *La donna che non si trova o sia le avventure di Madama Delingh scritte da lei medesima e pubblicate dall'abate Pietro Chiari* (Venice: Pasinelli, 1768), 167.
69. William and Edmund Burke, *An Account of the European Settlements,* 1:175. On this point, Robertson observed: "Men, thus satisfied with their condition, are far from any inclination to relinquish their own habits, or to adopt that of civilized life. The transition is too violent to be suddenly made. Even where endeavours have been used to wean a savage from his own customs, and to render the accommodations of polished society familiar to him; even where he has been allowed to taste of those pleasures, and has been honoured with those distinctions, which are the chief objects of our desire, he droops and languishes . . . [and] seizes the first opportunity of breaking loose from them, and returns with transport to the forest or the wild, where he can enjoy a careless and uncontrolled freedom." One thus comes to believe that savages are fatally destined to solitude and to a life much like "that of beasts, than [to a life] of men born to live in society and to reason." William Robertson, *History of America,* 2:235-36.

their natural ethics. The survival of a primitive spontaneity in a civilized context was undoubtedly the most utopian aspect of Chiari's thought.

The savages' ascent toward civilization did not alarm a cosmopolitan and tolerant Illuminist, who was convinced that "whether in Asia, Africa or America or even in Europe, we are all men and by virtue of our minds, we are capable of everything."[70] The exotic theme thus became an ideological pretext and projected reformist ethics that saw enlightened ideas as the means to refine the natives.

The "naturalist" perspective of Pietro Chiari, as recently shown by Del Negro, was evolutionary, and must be related to the events that occurred on the other side of the ocean. According to Del Negro, Chiari's discourse on America proceeded from two incompatible and opposing points: "on the one side, that between the noble savage and the European who is a victim of a cultivated and 'artificial' society, on the other side that between the rough savage and the enlightened European."[71] Before independence, the first dichotomy prevailed, as documented in the *Lettere d'un solitario a sua figlia per formarle il cuore e lo spirito nella scuola del mondo* (1777). Here Chiari confessed that, circumstances permitting, he would have chosen "a solitary life among the savages of America."[72] With the birth of the United States and the dissolution of a homogenous America, Chiari insisted on the second alternative. He modified the *identikit* of the noble savage and made a distinction between the enlightened American of the North and the still primitive American of the central and southern part of the continent. The originality of this new perspective by Chiari lay, in any case, in his opinion of the insurgents as "a mixture . . . of Americans and Europeans of every fatherland, every sect, every language and every custom," ready to seize "arms together and free themselves of their ancient first mother, as soon as they were able to sustain by themselves such a war and no longer needed her."[73] The singular perception of a fusion of settlers and Indians in the struggle for independence, involved a conversion of the American that would seem to legitimize Chiari's total conversion to a "philosophical" and "enlightened" native as opposed to Rousseau's noble savage. But this expectation failed, in that Chiari's last

---

70. Pietro Chiari, *Il secolo corrente: Dialoghi d'una dama col suo cavaliere scritti da lei medesima* (Venice, 1783), 172-73.
71. Piero Del Negro, *Il mito americano*, 250.
72. *Lettere di un solitario a sua figlia per formarle il cuore e lo spirito nella scuola del mondo* (Venice, 1777), 136.
73. *Il secolo corrente*, 249.

work with an American theme, *I privilegi dell'ignoranza* (1784), was, within the eighteenth-century Italian literary panorama, one of the few texts completely inspired by Rousseau's ethics and by an apology for the state of nature. This was, therefore, a new perspective that coincided, not with a return to Rousseau, but with an arrival, since Chiari had never admitted to be a follower of Rousseau. Even in his first "American" novels, an exaltation of primitive life appeared side by side with faith in the conversion of the savage to the civilization of the Enlightenment.

The praise of "ignorance" and of a utopian state of nature represented a radical turn that took the disappointed intellectual to a conclusive assessment of the victories of the Enlightenment. This ideological change, as noted by Marchesi, coincided with "a moment of weakness and discouragement" that led Chiari to consider "happy only he who knows nothing, rejecting almost completely his past of free thinker."[74] "Ignorance" was synonymous with "frankness, . . . that is, with an American-style simplicity,"[75] and it was a privilege that was destined to vanish with the conversion to civilization:

> Blessed ignorance! kindly let me tell you how the most sophisticated human minds only yielded similarly most unhappy consequences! My Americans recall none of these, although they orally preserve the glorious memories of their ancestors. America possibly had no nations more educated than Mexico and Peru. For this reason they were the first to surrender to the greed and might of the European discoverers and conquerors. Another such people of note among us are, perhaps, the Canadians; although presently their number has been greatly reduced, they are still about half savage.[76]

Thus the most cultivated nations were the first to undergo a fatal decline and to pay the price of their advanced degree of civilization. A similar conclusion had been reached twenty years before Rousseau, by Joubert de la Rue, in his *Lettres d'un sauvage depaysé* (1738), where it was emphasized how the loss of "savage reason" on the part of the Peruvians and of the Mexicans was an indication of folly:

74. Giambattista Marchesi, *Studi e ricerche*, 70.
75. *I privilegi dell'ignoranza* 1:letter 7, p. 58.
76. Ibid., 1:letter 3, pp. 23-24.

The Alibis of Exoticism 67

Do not quote to me as example the senseless Populations of Peru and of Mexico, or other similar American Nations. They are a thousand times more senseless than all the other Nations of the Earth because while they rejected the Maxims of Savage Reason, they failed to imitate those of Civilized Nations, not unlike Monkeys which imitate the actions of Men.[77]

Americans, who lived in accordance with "savage reason" and were steeped in the "darkness of common ignorance" were satisfied with their condition and "would not know how to make it better, nor [did] they want to, precisely because they [knew] no other state, and have always lived in the same miserable condition."[78] As Rousseau had already pointed out, the savage did not desire more than what he owned: "Whence it follows that since savage man desires only the things he knows and knows only those things whose possession is in his power or easily acquired, nothing should be so tranquil as his soul and nothing so limited as his mind."[79]

The absence of any comparison and the consequent lack of desire beyond one's needs was one of the American privileges listed also by Robertson:

> Thus in every situation where a human being can be placed, even the most unfavourable, there are virtues that peculiarly belong to it; there are affections which it calls forth; there is a species of happiness which it yields. Nature, with most beneficent intention, conciliates and forms the mind to its condition, the ideas and wishes of man extend not beyond that state of society to which he is habituated.[80]

The revival of the noble savage proposed by Chiari in *I privilegi dell'ignoranza* went against the tide, as it developed within a cultural climate that was not favorable to idealizing the primitive; the Italian literati of the 1780s are still indifferent to any mythical facet of a return "to all fours."

77. Hector Joubert de la Rue, *Lettres d'un sauvage depaysé* (Amsterdam: Jean François Jolly, 1738), 50.
78. *I privilegi dell'ignoranza* 1:letter 7, p. 34. Genovesi also, in *Lettere accademiche*, noted: "The savages limit their needs to nature, and nature to their needs: nature does not require much, and the savages work little" (171–72).
79. Jean-Jacques Rousseau, *Discourse on the Origins of Inequality*, 101.
80. William Robertson, *History of America*, 2:232–33.

6. The Utopia of Peru

Such general reticence with respect to the savage world led eighteenth-century Italy to praise pre-Columbian civilization precisely because it evolved far beyond a primitive organization. Where the noble savage's antihistorical meaning could easily lead to heretical and subversive consequences, the Peruvian, backed up by a differently structured civilization, in a certain sense superior to the European, agreed more easily with Enlightenment orthodoxy. The very concept of "civilization" stimulated not just praise of advanced American societies, such as the Incas and Aztecs, but also a comparison between these and the ethical, political, and economic conditions of current Europe. As early as the sixteenth century,[81] the contrived "empire" of the Incas, known to the Europeans first as legend rather than history, had acquired the status of precious symbol.

In the 1750s the theme of Peru was consolidated in Italy with Goldoni's *La Peruviana* (1754). This tragicomedy represented Goldoni's "American debut" and signaled his new susceptibility to exotic French stereotypes. In fact, the topic was suggested to him by the epistolary novel, *Lettres d'une Péruvienne*, published by Madame de Graffigny in 1747. Goldoni's heroine is taken from the American forest to a French drawing room where, resisting the passion of the Frenchman Deterville, she continues to love the Peruvian prince Aza. Notwithstanding her passage from a state of nature to civilization, Zilia decides not to lose her "plain naive style":

> I accept the new laws; I confess the new God.
> Only I will keep in my soul this native custom
> Of speaking the truth with innocence to all,
> Not hiding behind my face the mystery of my thoughts.[82]

In Goldoni's tragicomedy, the contrast between two civilizations was slight. The protagonist differed from the French only in American frankness, and her adoption of European customs came about without the

---

81. See Antonello Gerbi, *Il mito del Perù*, 21-22: "A portrait of Peru cannot ignore the colored lenses through which this country was seen, nor the illusory mirrors in which it was reflected. . . . For centuries, Europeans spoke of Peru without knowing it. They repeated in verse and prose the hyperbolic expression 'it is worth a Peru' without truly knowing what the worth of Peru was."
82. Prendo le nuove leggi: confesso il vero Nume. / Serberò sol nell'alma questo natio costume / Di dir in faccia a tutti con innocenza il vero, / Di non celar col viso gli arcani del pensiero. *La Peruviana*, act 5, last scene, in *Tutte le opere*, 9:813.

traumas and polemics that characterized Graffigny's novel. Here, in her letters to Aza, Zilia often expresses her reservations about civilization:

> It is with regret, my dear Aza, that having admired the genius of the French people I have now come to despise the use they make of it. I once believed in good faith this was a charming nation; however I can no longer refuse to see its flaws.... The dominant French conceit is to appear opulent. Genius, art, possibly even science, all is related to luxury and contributes to the dissipation of fortunes.[83]

> Censure is the reigning taste of the French, as inconsistency is the characteristic of their nation. In their books you find the general criticism of human manners and in their conversation that of every particular person—provided he be absent . . .
> In a word, my dear Aza, their vices are artificial, as well as their virtues; and the insignificance of their character permits them to be but imperfectly what they are . . .
> Inconsistency is a consequence of the airy character of the French. . . . I cannot sufficiently wonder that they, with as much or more penetration than any other nation, seem unconscious of the shocking contradictions which foreigners remark in them.[84]

The French worshipped ephemera, while the Peruvians lived wisely, regulated by their own laws established by Manco Capac, founder of the Incas, and of an empire where the arts, sciences, and writing flourished.

Madame de Graffigny asserted that Zilia's letters, before being translated into French, were composed in *quipos*, "a great number of strips of different colours, which the Peruvians used instead of writing."[85] In these years also the Neapolitan prince Raimondo de Sangro di San Servero expressed fascination with the *Quipos*, and defended Graffigny's theory against its opponents, represented by an anonymous duchess. In 1750 this eclectic intellectual, who also dabbled in magic and medicine and was interested in the more heterodox aspects of the culture of his times,

---

83. Françoise de Graffigny (Mme de), *Lettres d'une Péruvienne* (Paris: Migneret, 1797), 341-43. The first Italian translation of the novel was published in Venice in 1754. [Translator's note: This particular passage could not be located in the English translation.]
84. Françoise de Graffigny (Mme de), *Letters of a Peruvian Princess, with the Sequel*, trans. Francis Ashworth, in *Novelist's Magazine*, vol. 9 (London: Harrison, 1782), 41, 44-45.
85. Ibid., 8n.

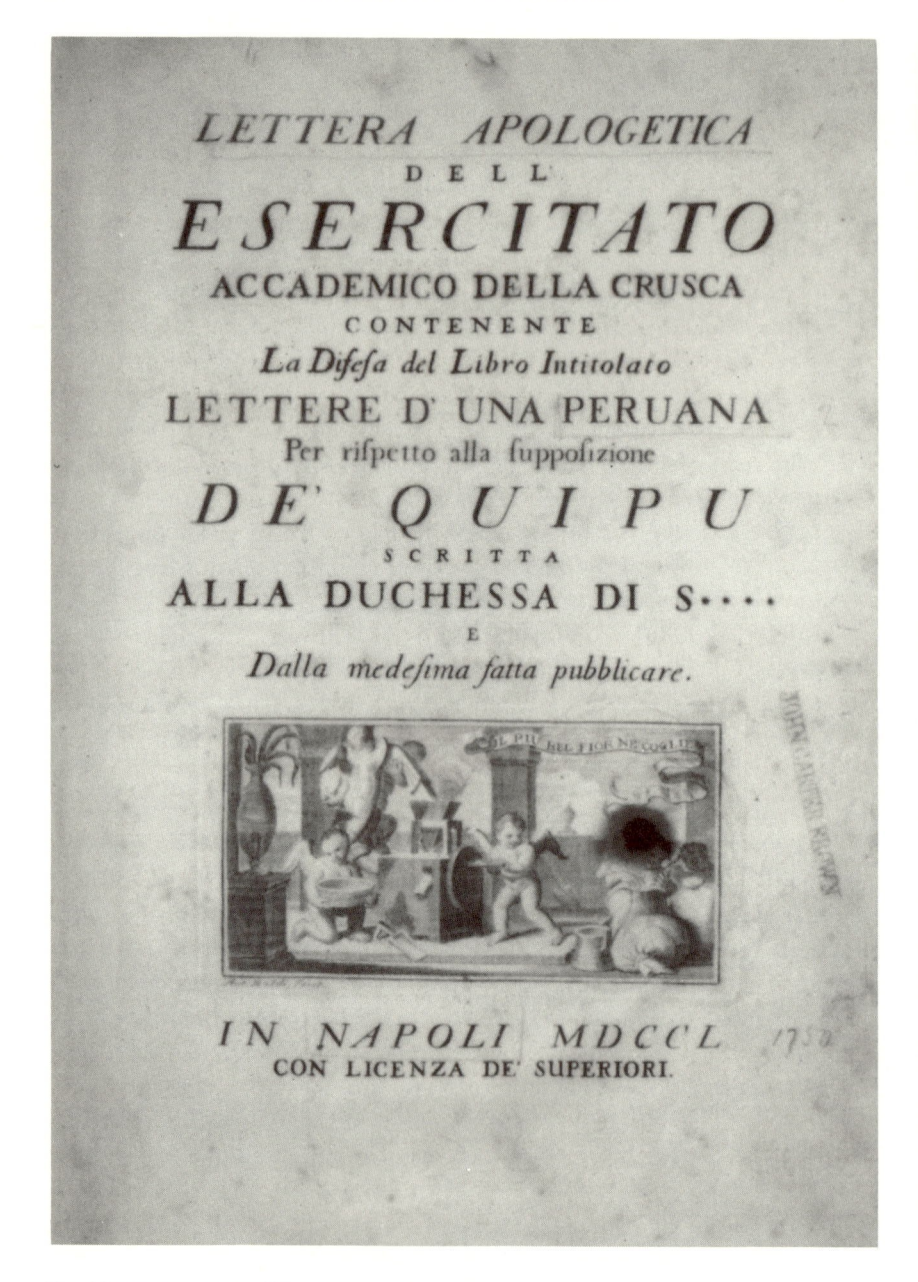

Fig. 11. Frontispiece of the Prince of San Severo's *Lettera apologetica*.

published a *Lettera apologetica dell'Esercitato Accademico della Crusca contenente la difesa del libro intitolato "Lettere d'una Peruana" per rispetto alla supposizione de' Quipu.*

With the pretext of sharing Graffigny's statement, the prince composed a treatise on the Incas' system of writing, probably the first to appear in the history of Italian culture. As Venturi correctly observed, he "thus reaches the core of an issue that was being debated at mid-century by various thinkers, from Warburton and Silhouette to Diderot, Condillac and Rousseau: the problem of the origin and meaning of any language."[86] Although he admitted that the author of the *Lettres d'une Péruvienne* used "some license," San Severo argued that it was totally "credible, for a young Peruvian girl to compose, by means of *Quipos,* those extremely elegant letters that the author had her write: but this skill is not as extraordinary and indiscreet as you might think; because . . . even if the Peruvians, a wise and industrious people, did not reach this high state of perfection, they could not be too far from it."[87]

The invention of this ingenious system of communication was derived from the cleverness of a nation that, far from being the "roughest and laziest people of this world," because of its "perfect morality" and "deep notions about natural law," deserved to be listed "among the best nations of the earth."[88] This conviction led San Severo to make frequent comparisons between the exploits of the Peruvians and those of the Greeks and Romans and to develop a comparison on the level of political and cultural excellence from which the Inca civilization emerged as an absolute model.[89] The comparison with the classics continued to constitute, as it had for Vico and Lafitau, a perspective from which the Americans could be known, although it often led to arbitrary associations and analogies.

Three years after San Severo's *Lettera apologetica,* Francesco Algarotti, in his *Saggio sopra l'imperio degl'Incas* (1753), suggested a similarity between the splendid Inca civilization and the legendary golden age:

---

86. Franco Venturi, *La Napoli di Antonio Genovesi*, in *Settecento riformatore*, 4:540.

87. Raimondo de Sangro di San Severo, *Lettera apologetica dell'Esercitato accademico della Crusca contenente la difesa del libro intitolato "Lettere d'una Peruana per rispetto alla supposizione de' Quipu"* (Naples, 1750), 183-84. A reprint of the eighteenth-century edition was recently edited by Domenico d'Alessando (Naples: Torre, 1984).

88. Ibid., 181.

89. Ibid., 183: "If we were just to compare the state of Ynca and the populations of Mexico to the Greeks and Romans, I am certain that the former would win, with respect to political government."

For over 200 years the golden age shone over Peru. Not an imaginary or poetic age, it was historical and real. That empire could not fail to prosper, given that the universal mind ruled like a prince over his people. In that empire, measures were taken against laziness that might weaken the state; excessive numbers of sects that might perturb it; the dangers of external wars that might subdue it. There, religion and law were guarded by military force; finally, the perfect obedience and full contentment of the people were achieved. This rule of politics was discovered only by the Incas of Peru and later by the Jesuits of the missions they founded in the nearby kingdom of Paraguay.[90]

The praise of Inca society within a perspective sympathetic to enlightened absolutism,[91] was inspired, not by a traditional admiration evoked by gold and silver and the magnificence of the cities and buildings, but by the ethical-political achievements of the Peruvians who "would equally enrich the science of legislation and morality."[92]

While Peru continued to be idealized, the following question was also asked: Why didn't the Peruvians, who were so evolved, adequately resist the Spaniards? This unsolved dilemma contrasted somewhat with the traditional myth, and led Inca "admirers" to justify this compliance in various ways. Algarotti wrote:

> How was it possible for such a small group of Spaniards to subjugate in such a short time such a vast empire ruled by so many good

---

90. Francesco Algarotti, *Saggio sopra l'imperio degl'Incas*, 338.
91. See Gustavo Costa, *La leggenda dei secoli d'oro nella letteratura italiana* (Bari: Laterza, 1972), 192.
92. Francesco Algarotti, *Saggi sopra l'imperio degl'Incas*, 239. Robertson, in *History of America*, inquiring about the weaknesses of Peruvians, came to the following conclusion "Though the traditional history of the Peruvians represents all the Incas as warlike princes, frequently at the head of armies, which they led to victory and conquest; few symptoms of such a martial spirit appear in any of their operations subsequent to the invasion of the Spaniards. The influence, perhaps, of those institutions which rendered their manners gentle, gave their minds this unmanly softness; perhaps, the constant serenity and mildness of the climate may have enervated the vigour of their frame; perhaps, some principle in their government, unknown to us, was the occasion of this political debility. Whatever may have been the cause, the fact is certain . . . [t]his character hath descended to their posterity. The Indians of Peru are now more tame and depressed than any people of America. Their feeble spirits, relaxed in lifeless inaction, seem hardly capable of any bold or manly exertions" (3:351).

laws? First of all, it was to be expected that a people to whom navigation was completely unknown, should be terrified at the sight of new people who came upon them as if flying over the sea. The shots from our firearms seemed to them thunderbolts, and horsemen centaurs.[93]

Genovesi was also surprised at the naïveté of the Peruvians:

Therefore a people, although very numerous, if composed of men who are either ignorant and rough or spineless and debauched, will always be a tiny, despicable and miserable people, not unlike a nation of boys and girls. . . . This is how the Peruvians and Mexicans were when we met them; and just like frightened children they were vanquished and subjected by a few hundred Europeans. Can one believe that someone is a man, who believes that vessels are people walking on waves, and cannons their thunderbolts? That a man on a horse is a centaur?[94]

In *Mattino* (lines 149-50) Parini referred to the Europeans as violators of "the boundaries for many ages inviolate" who, with the "thunder and lightning" of their firearms, spread terror among the American populations. Nevertheless, even before he composed *Il Giorno*, in a sonnet read

---

93. Ibid., 341. Twenty years later, in the preface to the Italian edition of *Colombiade* by Mme du Boccage, defending the New World inhabitants from the theory of American degeneration supported by De Pauw, the author noted that "neither is the very slight resistance that Pizarro and Cortés met in their conquest of Peru and Mexico an argument in favor of the imbecility of these two populations; just as imbecility cannot be directly inferred either from a terror of fire arms or swords, or from the general superiority that the people from cold climates have in warmer climates"; introduction to *La Colombiade, poema di Mme du Boccage* (Milan: Marelli, 1771), x. Leopardi also, in his *Dei Pigmei e dei Giganti*, in *Saggio sopra gli errori popolari degli antichi* (*Opere*, ed. Walter Binni [Florence: Sansoni, 1969], 1:854), wrote: "Many ancient scholars believed that the Thessalonians' skill in taming horses and their custom of horse combat gave rise to the legend of the centaurs. This was natural, and we know that similarly Americans mistook the Spanish horsemen for two-shaped monsters." Todorov, in *The Conquest of America*, wrote concerning Mexicans: "We cannot avoid wondering, when we read the history of Mexico: why did the Indians not offer more resistance? Didn't they realize Cortés' colonizing ambitions? The answer displaces the question: the Indians in the regions Cortés first passed through are not more impressed by his imperial intentions, because they have already been conquered and colonized—by the Aztecs" (58).

94. Antonio Genovesi, *Dello stato e delle naturali forze del regno di Napoli per rispetto all'arti e al commercio*, in *Autobiografia, lettere e altri scritti*, 576-77. On the question of America's gold, see Antonello Gerbi, *L'oro indiano corruttore*, in *Il mito del Perù*, 99.

to the *Trasformati* around 1760 (*Ecco la reggia, ecco de' prischi Incassi*), the poet had recalled the sad consequences of the Conquest and had imagined, on the prow of the enemy ship, the spirits of the Americans oppressed by the goldplundering Europeans ("But here your tyrant ship crosses / the sea with its spoils; and now I see your daemons from the sad prows / descend").[95] The "wicked gold" provokes conflict and disastrous consequences for Europe together with the diffusion of tobacco, rum, and diseases ("Quick were they to gather the unhappy gifts / that across the bright ocean / to them Americo brought; / with both hands they promptly caught").[96]

During those same years while Beccaria pointed out that American gold reduced "the Spaniards to greed and courage greater than love of life,"[97] Genovesi asserted that "nations where there is much gold are slaves, and the most miserable on the whole earth." Therefore "the Hottentots,

95. "Ma la vostra tiranna ecco attraversa / il mar con sue rapine; ed ecco io veggo i vostri demoni da la triste prore / discender seco" *Ecco la reggia, ecco de' prischi Incassi*, in *Opere di Giuseppe Parini* 455, lines 9-12. Concerning America's gold, Vico wrote in the 1730 *Scienza nuova*: "The first world had to be so rich in these mines, that when America was discovered, they were depleted as a result of human greed" (291).

96. "Ben fu presto a raccor gli infausti doni / che, attraversando l'oceano aprico, / lor condusse Amèrico; / ed ambe le man li trangugiaron pronte" (*L'innesto del vajolo*, 30, lines 117-21). Europe also imported "brown chocolate" from America. In *Mattino*, in the description of the breakfast of the "Giovin Signore," chocolate evokes the picturesque image of the "Guatemalan and the Carib, whose hair are with barbaric feathers adorned" ("[Il] guatimalese e il caribbèo, c'ha di barbare penne avvolto il crine.") Ludovico Savioli Fontana also referred to cocoa's "American foam" when describing the awakening of a young lady; see *Il mattino*, in *Lirici del Settecento*, ed. Bruno Maier (Milan: Ricciardi, 1959), 304. Gian Rinaldo Carli would write that "every morning [chocolate] gives us the occasion to remember poor America, so destroyed by the Europeans"; see *Delle lettere americane* (Florence: Cosmopoli, 1780), 1:letter 21, p. 209. The theme of American spices and chocolate recurred frequently. Lorenzo Bellini of Florence wrote a dithyramb, the *Bucchereide*, about the perfumed soil vases that came from Portugal or from the Americas; the Arcadian poet Marcello Malaspina dedicated to chocolate one of his poems, *Bacco in America*. A cheerful sonnet dedicated to "chocolate" opened a treatise by Giambattista Occhiolini, *Memorie storiche sopra l'uso della cioccolata in tempo di digiuno, esposte in una lettera a Monsig. Illustriss. Arcivescovo N.N.* (Venice: Occhi, 1748). Gemelli Careri emphasized its popularity in Mexico: "This drink is very ancient, and us'd by the *Indians* before the *Spaniards* conquer'd the country but the *Spaniards* improved it. In the *Indies* it is so common now that there is not a *Black* or a porter but drinks it every day, and the better sort four times a day" (*A Voyage Round the World*, 4: pt. 4, 517).

97. Quoted from *Carteggio di Pietro ed Alessandro Verri*, ed. Francesco Novati and Emanuele Greppi (Milan: Cogliati, 1910), 151. Concerning the *Prolusione*, where Beccaria mentioned American gold, Alessandro continued: "Even in his inaugural speech he says that Columbus brought back from America a disease which infects the source of life; I

who do not know this metal, are richer and happier than the people of Senegal or Guinea, and today the Californians, Appalachians, Canadians, and Caribs are happier than many Peruvians."[98] Gold, transitory and lethal, carried with it a curse that struck those who owned it by nature and those who acquired it by might.

In any case, not all the American gold disappeared because of the greed of Europeans. According to La Condamine, in his *Relation abrégée d'un voyage fait dans l'intérieur de l'Amérique méridionale*, certain tributaries of the Marañon "carry a sand mixed with specks and grains of gold" and "the Indians collect precisely the quantity they need to pay their tribute or poll tax."[99] Such statements, on the one hand convinced certain individuals of the discovery of El Dorado, but on the other hand led skeptics such as Voltaire to imagine the fabulous voyage of Candide and the Indian Cacambo amid the gold of the Orinoco:

> As they approached they noticed some children, covered with tattered gold brocade, playing at ninepins; and our two visitors from the other world stopped to watch them. Their skittles were large round objects of striking brilliance, some of them yellow, some red, and some green. The travellers had the curiosity to pick some up, and found that they were gold nuggets, emeralds, and rubies, the least of which would have been the grandest ornament in the Mogul

---

remember Voltaire said this, I don't remember where; and it says roughly that it infects life 'at its very source' " (Ibid.).

98. Antonio Genovesi, *Lezioni di commercio ed economia civile*, 9:18. Genovesi, in *Lettere accademiche*, returns to the topic of gold: "Gold, gold, gold. Next? Silver? Silver, silver, true? I haven't seen bigger or uglier beasts. It is very clear that gold and silver aren't worth more than what they represent, right? But what do they represent? Bread, cheese, wool, cloth, wood . . . what is needed in life; and furthermore these come to us from the soil, the sea, the crafts, from the labour of those who are envied just by clowns. There is no country which is more ragged and miserable: that is because one does not eat gold. In Chile not only the Indians, but many Spanish families who were attracted there by the mines, have these under their feet, and yet they step over them and laugh" (493).

99. Charles Marie de La Condamine, *Relation abrégée d'un voyage fait dans l'intérieur de l'Amérique méridionale* (Paris: La Veuve Pissot, 1745), 31. In the *Histoire des Pyramides de Quito* of 1751 La Condamine related the adventures of the expedition to the equator made by three members of the Royal Academy of Science. In the place crossed by the equator line, two pyramids were erected, and in commemoration of the undertaking an inscription was also going to be placed containing a sonnet of Scipione Maffei, translated into three languages (Latin, Spanish, and French). La Condamine's *Histoire*, known to Italian intellectuals such as Algarotti, had the merit of arousing interest in Peru's archaeology.

throne.... The travellers did not fail to pick up the gold, emeralds, and rubies.[100]

In a world that is collapsing only El Dorado saves itself, as there the Incas still ignore that precious stones and metals can have value and the wise Pangloss can still be right. But the best of all possible worlds, hidden in the Andes, is just a utopia.

7. Gian Rinaldo Carli's *Lettere americane* and the Apotheosis of Utopia

In the last two decades of the eighteenth century while Pietro Chiari proposed a hypothetical return to primordial "ignorance," Peru's utopia reached its apotheosis with the *Lettere americane*[101] (1780) by Gian Rinaldo Carli (1720-95), an eclectic personality that cannot easily be

---

100. Voltaire, *Candide; or, Optimism*, trans. John Butt (Harmondsworth: Penguin, 1947), 75. Already in his *Essais sur les moeurs*, Voltaire recalled that for a long time there was the belief that the Peruvians and Incas lived on a lake called *Parima* bordered by gold sand, in the proximity of a city called *El Dorado*. Voltaire had found the elements of this legend in Garcilaso de La Vega, *Histoire des Incas, rois du Péru; La relation des voyages pendant son séjour depuis 1666 jusques en 1697, avec une relation de Walter Raleigh*. At the end of the century, after several years of missionary work among the Orinoco people, Gilij also (see Chapter 3) wrote an account that was part history, part legend, *Saggio di storia americana*: "Under the name of *Dorado*, if we accept the meaning it has in those lands, goes an extremely rich city that was discovered in the new world. Unlike what travelers might think, neither the famous *Potosì*, nor *Cioccò* nor the mines of *Mexico*, nor many other places, can compare to this place, where precious treasures are excavated and there is no end in sight. If we listen to their accounts, in this happy land the rocks are gold; and the sands carried by impetuous waters are gold and silver. Furthermore, what should we say about the people who inhabit these lands? Like their city, as this metal is so lightly considered, these people are covered in gold. Gold are their vases, gold their ploughs and hoes, gold their implements of war; the height of wonder is that even their roofs are gold" (1:135). On the myth of *El Dorado*, see Antonello Gerbi, *El Dorado come riflesso del Perù*, in *Il mito del Perù*, 50-54.

101. The second edition of this work, *Le lettere americane: Nuova edizione corretta ed ampliata con l'aggiunta della parte III, ora per la prima volta impressa* (Cremona: Manini, 1781-83), revised and corrected, contained a third part, which examined "the hypotheses of Mr. Bailly about Plato's Atlantis, and that of the Count of Buffon concerning the subsequent cooling of the globe." For a recent edition of Carli's work, see *Delle lettere americane*, selections, with an introductory study and notes by Aldo Albonico (Rome: Bulzoni, 1988).

categorized in a precise segment of cultural history.[102] The great success of the *Lettere americane*, written between 1777 and 1779 and translated before the end of the century into French, English, and German, was due principally to two reasons: the cultural climate, which was favorable to the Peruvian myth (in these years Marmontel's novel *Les Incas ou la destruction de l'empire du Pérou* (1777) also met with success); and Carli's elegant and colloquial style, which allowed him to summarize with originality and aplomb actual debates on Peru and to address a public that was not necessarily expert in those issues. As a matter of fact, he made a point of stressing the dilettante character of his *Lettere:*

> I will talk about all these items, but piecemeal and without any real order; because I write what is presented to my eyes as it comes to me, and I write and reflect whenever I can, and my purpose in doing so is to amuse and divert myself. This is neither a treatise nor a history.[103]

Although he said that his *Lettere americane* did not aim to be a "history," it was with the contemporary "Americanists" and historians that Carli desired to enter into polemics and competition. "Ulloa and Algarotti," he noted, "are too limited to the general; Pauw writes with his pen poisoned by the black bile of a man-eater; Raynal is too succinct, and is too in awe of Pauw, and Marmontel according to his plan mixes in too much fiction."[104] Carli adopts a critical, revisionary perspective with respect to the theory of the "degeneration" of America, and particularly with

---

102. See *Colpo d'occhio sullo stato presente della letteratura italiana*, in *Giornali veneziani*: "For a long time we could not decide in what category to place this renowned literary figure, as he could be placed with distinction among economists, publicists, and erudite critics. He was a poet as well, and a tragic poet. But insofar as his main role was that of conducting careful examinations, with unbiased arguments and choice erudition on any topic, we thought we should list this personality, so distinguished by birth, work and talent, at the head of our literary critics. . . . He ended only recently his literary career with the famous *Lettere americane*" (699).

103. *Delle lettere americane*, 1:letter 7, p. 68. Isidore Bianchi, in the letter of dedication to Benjamin Franklin in the second edition of the *Lettere americane*, insisted on this point: "He [Carli] never claimed he was writing a history. I am the first to confess this to you candidly. Only, from the shapeless and complex mass of so much and such varied news, left us by the ancient and modern writers about your lands, he endeavoured to separate the false from the true, to conduct new examinations, new calculations, new conjectures, to bring physics to the aid of history, and to delineate a picture of America and of the world" (letter 1).

104. Ibid., 1:letter 12, p. 121.

respect to Cornelius de Pauw, author of the *Recherches philosophiques sur les Américains*[105] (1768). Convinced that there was a rigid causal relationship between the living and the natural realms, De Pauw believed the American native was fatally destined to regression because he had been subjected to a hostile and uncontrollable nature. "Monsieur Paw" was therefore for Carli the first enemy to rebut, also on account of his arbitrary and simplistic interpretation of the concept of civilization:

> It is truly strange that Paw while always arguing in support of the barbaric, wild state of the Americans has never defined what civilized society is and what are the boundaries of savage life, and of natural society. They had no coins, they did not use iron, he says. Are these, then, the characteristics of civilized society? I do not deem this a definition worthy of a philosopher.[106]

Such a convinced admirer of Inca civilization also found unacceptable the thoughts of Robertson who, in his *History of America*, affirmed that the American populations, Peruvians included, were definitely uncivilized:

> If the comparison be made with the people of the ancient continent, the inferiority of America in improvement will be conspicuous, and

---

105. Cornelius De Pauw borrowed from George Leclerc, count of Buffon (*Histoire naturelle, générale et particulière*; 1749), and exaggerated the thesis of the "degeneration" of America (see Chapter 3). The publisher Zatta, announcing his plan for an "American" series, on the occasion of the publication of Raynal's *Storia dell' America Settentrionale* (a series that was also to have included Carli's work), writes: "We flatter ourselves that our endeavors will meet the public's pleasure and that this will so encourage us as to lead us to publish, as we have planned, many other literary works that concern America, and which should certainly meet with the interest of the readers. Among these, we can announce to our erudite friends the *Lettere americane*, as yet unpublished work of a good author. It contains thirty-three philosophical and critical-historical letters divided in two parts. The main theme is a confutation of the untrue positions of the renowned Mr. Pauw, author of the *Ricerche filosofiche* on the Americans. It is a very erudite work, and reading it will be pleasurable" (Venice: Zatta, 1778), xi. In those same years when La Condamine was spreading archaeological news about Peru, in France and throughout the rest of Europe, with his *Histoire des Pyramides de Quito*, Pernety with his *Dissertation sur l'Amérique et les Américains contre les "Recherches philosophiques" de Mr. de Pauw* (Berlin: Decker, 1769) opposed the splendor of Peruvian civilization to De Pauw's thesis of the degeneration of America. On the success of De Pauw's *Recherches* in Italy, see Antonello Gerbi, *De Pauw: l'inferiorità dell'uomo americano* and *Le prime polemiche europee intorno a De Pauw*, in *La disputa del Nuovo Mondo*, 59-71.

106. *Delle lettere americane*, 1:letter 11, p. 106.

neither the Mexicans nor Peruvians will be entitled to rank with those nations which merit the name of civilized.[107]

In stressing the limitations of the Inca system such as limited commerce and absence of the use of metals, the Scottish historian concluded that "there is not an instance in history of any people so little advanced in refinement, so totally destitute of military talents and enterprize [as the Peruvians]."[108] It is easy to imagine the terms of Carli's reply to such a statement; it is not surprising that, at the conclusion of his work, he decided to "take up the pen again" to confute Robertson's thesis in the last letter of his work. "This research," he wrote, referring to his own studies, "should have been the object of Mr. Robertson's research. But we in fact did the work in the *Americane*. Therefore you will find in the above mentioned article [Robertson's *History of America*] nothing new, no solid reflection, nothing of import such as to convince the intellect of those who want at least to approach, or touch with their own hands, a historical truth."[109] Carli rejected Robertson's historical methodology because he was convinced, like Vico, of the parallel course of nations, and did not share a "paralyzing" criterion of interpretation that confined the New World to irreversible barbarianism.

The point must however be made, with Gerbi,[110] that the *Lettere americane* was not intended as an apology for all the populations of the Americas: in fact, for Carli "American" was the equivalent of "Peruvian" or "Mexican," and connoted no meaning of "wildness." Earlier, in *L'uomo libero* (1778), rejecting the notion of the noble savage, he had clarified his observations about Rousseau, whose formulas seemed to embody a "disease of the mind". He had, instead, praised the Peruvian governance, "the Patagonians of politics"; who, "having established a religious discipline, having maintained an opinion based on their religion, [they] were able to secure . . . the happiness and contentment of all their subjects."[111] According to Carli, Peru took on the function of representing an ethical and political model unknown in our "hemisphere," where lawmakers had said to men: "Let's build a happy and respectable society, and as a result

107. William Robertson, *History of America*, 3:268.
108. Ibid., 3:351.
109. *Delle lettere americane*, 2:letter 18, p. 286.
110. See Antonello Gerbi, *La disputa del Nuovo Mondo*, 256.
111. *L'uomo libero*, in *Illuministi italiani*, ed. Franco Venturi, 3:462.

Fig. 12. Frontispiece of Gian Rinaldo Carli's *Delle Lettere Americane*.

you will be happy." On the contrary, the Incas had said: "Let us make individual men happy, so that no one should desire what is best; and therefore we will have a strong and happy society."[112]

With respect to the image of an ideal society "which needs neither our laws, nor our crafts, nor our culture, nor ourselves," it was natural for Carli to resent the Spaniards' cruelty: "in the name of God the merciful they mercilessly massacred twelve million men."[113] This same crisis of conscience had caused Algarotti, Parini, and other intellectuals to admire and regret that vanished civilization.

Carli's unconditional admiration for Peru reflected his concerns as an enlightened reformer and his efforts to achieve a prosperous economy. One sees in it "the eighteenth-century philosophe who fully trusts in reason's mending virtues and fully believes in humanity's certain and happy destinies."[114] For Carli the well-structured Inca state became a projection of his reformist spirit and an embodiment of his ideals: "I am so full of the idea of the ancient government of Peru," he confessed, "that I feel as if I were a Peruvian, or at least I wish that in some other part of the globe a similar system would be planned so I could go there and live in full happiness the remainder of my life, away from mass riots, shielded by the storms of the tempestuous seas of politics, full of rocks and quicksand."[115] This statement was due to a partial lack of faith in eighteenth-century institutions and led to Carli's fantasizing a utopian model, as can be seen in his very first letter to Gravisi: "I am committed to developing with you my thoughts, or dreams, about the ancient peoples of the Americas, which I believe are for the most part descended from the most ancient inhabitants of Atlantis."[116] Carli proposed to conduct more precise research in the second edition of the *Lettere americane*, which contained a third part,

112. *Delle lettere americane*, 1:letter 20, pp. 193-94.
113. Ibid., letter 21, p. 208.
114. Ernesto Sestan, *Il mito del buon selvaggio americano e l'Italia del Settecento*, 4. On Carli's intellectual background, see E. Apih, *La formazione culturale di Gian Rinaldo Carli* (Trieste: Deputazione di Storia Patria, 1973).
115. *Delle lettere americane*, 1:letter 19, p. 182. Admirers of the Incas often used enthusiastic expressions. Concerning the ingenious *Quipo* system, the prince of San Severo notes, in *Lettera apologetica*: "In conclusion I can't see what else I could tell you about *Quipos*, as I have already said so much about them. I will only naively confess that the possibility you gave me to study this system has made it so familiar to me, that were it not for a scruple on behalf of the poor paper manufacturers and printers, I would be tempted to introduce the system here" (287).
116. Ibid., 1:letter 1, p. 7.

where he reviewed the *Lettres sur l'Atlantide de Platon*, published in Paris by Bailly. Like Plato, Carli was convinced that the dwellers of Atlantis "as has been ascertained, had, in part passed through Africa and Europe, where they brought their notions about astronomy and various usages and customs, and some of them even went to America."[117] Evidence of this sunken continent existed not only as islands (the Canaries and Azores),[118] but also in the form of linguistic analogies:

> Nothing was more common in America than the names *Atlas* and *Antaeus*. Next to the province of Meuchan was a city called Atlan. In that proximity were other cities with the same suffix, that is, Guatatlan, Cinatlan, Itz-atlan: all located between Mechuacan and Lelisco. The dwellers of these places were called Atlantids.[119]

An alteration in the earth's axis produced a huge flood, as a result of which "Atlantis may have sunk, as it was located in the middle of the Atlantic Ocean. From it sprang those populations that spread, in America as well as in Egypt and Europe, the first seeds of science, astronomy, the Atlantic writing—hieroglyphics—that was called sacred, customs and religion."[120] Citing ancient authors and modern naturalists, comparing, approving, and rejecting their hypotheses, Carli resolved the enigma of

---

117. Ibid., 2:letter 2, p. 20.

118. Carli believed that a flood sank lands that were inhabited on the Atlantic as well as the Pacific coasts: "If then, as shown, the Mediterranean is a new sea, and if the ancients preserved a constant, uninterrupted tradition handed down from generation to generation, of the Ocean breaking over that strait and flooding Atlantis; and if the physical observations of the seabed made by the modern geographic philosophers, and the discoveries effected over the whole ocean and the Pacific sea all combine and conspire to prove that on that side also there was such a phenomenon, I do not find it unreasonable to whisper in your ear that in ancient times, the globe was on this side for the most part dry, and that these spaces were cultivated and inhabited" (2:letter 16, p. 212).

119. Ibid., 2:letter 4, p. 62. Carli was aware that his thesis would be challenged (ibid., 2:letter 10, pp. 150-51): "I know well all the challenges you can bring. (1) Many writers considered Plato's account a fable. (2) One should have fathomed the ocean in order to be able to believe in the existence of such a land. . . . (3) If we were to imagine a lowering of the sea level that would have left such a large part of the globe dry, then the great Mediterranean basin, the Adriatic, and maybe even the Baltic and other seas would also have to have been dry. (4) As a consequence, great part of the face of the globe would have been different. . . . (5) Finally, one should be able to find a reason for such a great change and upheaval, independently from the Deluge, because this would postulate the survival of generations of men, on both sides of this new sea, where the memory and the knowledge of those prior times would have been preserved."

120. Ibid., 2d ed., 2:letter 12, p. 212.

Peru's high civilization: the common genesis of the Americans and of other populations from Atlantis[121] justified the surprising affinities between distant civilizations. But as Venturi suggested, "Carli's great weakness lay precisely in the eclectic wealth of his hypotheses and arguments which prevented him from tracing a directional line and limited him to a fanciful erudition."[122] Although he based his theories on reliable documents and witness accounts, the last letters undoubtedly show a tendency toward fantasy. This tendency must be seen as a lack of faith in the enlightened society at the turn of the century. While Chiari reacted with a primitivism that goes "against the tide," Carli "traveled with the mind" and in so doing, forgot his "physical location" and "unpleasant tasks." Enraptured by Atlantis's charm, he was overtaken by fantastic hypotheses that seem even riskier if one compares them to the analytic work of this economist and reformer. Even an enlightened minister was thus allowed license to escape:

> Sometimes the soul needs to be dazed, rather than yawning at large assemblies, where men unite without searching for each other, caress each other without love, and leave each other without desire. . . . I retire to my study and by stealing a few hours from my tasks I search for distraction in the pleasures of meditating, writing, reading, and being with you.[123]

Like Machiavelli, Carli put on "royal and curial robes" and took refuge in a cultural hermitage where he could embark on his utopian "journey."

---

121. Carli was firmly convinced that Atlantis had been located in the center of the Atlantic, between Africa and the Americas: "Therefore my Hypothesis, it seems to be, remains intact, notwithstanding the efforts of well-known authors, who are famous for moving Atlantis to Sweden or Spitzberg" (ibid.).
122. Franco Venturi, *Illuministi italiani*, 433.
123. *Delle lettere americane*, 1:letter XI, p. 104.

3

Tradition and Revision in Eighteenth-Century Histories of the New World

As early as the end of the 1770s a shift in European attention from Latin America to British settlements in North America implied a widening of geographic horizons and a partial revision of the traditional identification of "American" with "savage." In fact, as the image of a homogeneous New World faded and the United States emerged, the concept of America gradually lost its connotation of savagery and came to coincide with the young northern republic, taking on a different meaning. One must, however, acknowledge with Jantz that the change of perspective was not immediate, since this "radical change of location [was not accompanied by] a truly corresponding change of connotation. When the shift was made, the general image of America as it had been developed was transferred bodily to North America and then specifically to the new United States."[1] Although the geographical distinction between the Spanish and the English spheres of influence was by then well established, unconsciously the

1. Harold Jantz, *The Myths about America: Origins and Extensions*, 7.

general characteristics of the central and southern parts of the continent were applied en bloc to the New America.

The first text on America to promote an interest in the northern colonies was *An Account of the European Settlements in America* by the Burkes, whose Italian translation appeared in Venice in 1763. As mentioned in the introduction, it was "composed by the erudite English authors and published at a time when War was brewing between their country and the French nation";[2] the translator lets it be clearly understood that only at that time and with reference to international events does Europe "discover" America. Thus, the conflict between the English and the Franco-Spaniards had the merit of having awakened historians' attention to the overseas lands:

> The affairs of America have lately engaged a great deal of the public attention. Before the present war there were but a very few who made the history of that quarter of the world any part of their study.[3]

By devoting the first volume of the *Account* to the discovery of America and the destruction of pre-Columbian civilizations and the second volume to the European settlements in North America, the Burkes made a first attempt to clarify the geographical, historicopolitical, and anthropological features of the New World. The novelty of their work must nevertheless be grasped from two angles. By dedicating more than one-third of the second volume to the English colonies, they widened the American frame of reference; they also "revived" the myth of the noble savage[4] in a climate that, especially in Venice (with the exception of intellectuals such as Chiari), was not favorable to Rousseau or primitivism. The illustration that appeared next to the title page is interesting. It was

---

2. *Il traduttore a chi legge*, in *Storia degli stabilimenti europei in America* (Venice: Giambattista Novelli, 1763), 2:i.

3. Burke, *An Account of the European Settlements in America*, 2 vols. (New York: Research Reprints, 1970; repr. 2d ed., London, 1758), 1:A2. In his foreword to the Italian edition the translator, focusing on the British colonies, noted that "in those vast New World lands which had been discovered by an Italian, among all the European nations . . . Italians alone have no settlements, nor has any Italian group attempted to settle there. . . . Yet, I believe the generous prudence of the English would not have refused them a pocket of land" (*Storia degli stabilimenti europei in America*, 2:i). For the success of the Burkes *Account*, see Franco Venturi, *The End of the Old Regime in Europe, 1768-1776*, vol. 3, *The First Crisis*, trans. R. Burr Litchfield (Princeton: Princeton University Press, 1989), 405-9.

4. Cf. Piero Del Negro, *Il mito americano*, 59.

taken and sketched from a small picture which had been made to give . . . an idea of the Indians of North America, where a couple of natives are portrayed next to a couple from the province of Pennsylvania, whose capital, Philadelphia, gave birth to the ingenious and excellent young man who painted it in Leghorn last year.[5]

The artist, Benjamin West from Pennsylvania, continued to be inspired in his paintings by the Indian world which he knew well. His "exotic" style was certainly well known in Italy, especially in Rome where he had been twice and where he had spent a year, from 1760 to 1761.[6]

The chapter in the *Account* illustrating the anthropological characteristics of the savages was modeled after Lafitau's research and stemmed from a positive evaluation of the Indians, which was somewhat useful in investigating the prehistory of civilized populations:

Whoever considers the Americans of this day, not only studies the manners of a remote present nation, but he studies, in some measure, the antiquities of all nations; from which no mean lights may be thrown upon many parts of the ancient authors, both sacred and profane. The learned Lafitau has laboured this point with great success, in a work which deserves to be read amongst us much more than I find it is.[7]

The Burkes praised the findings of the *Moeurs des sauvages amériquains* as well as the comparative methodology employed by the author. Convinced of the parallel course of nations, the two English historians also believed that Americans represented Old World prehistory and that a thorough study of their customs could offer an important contribution to the study of ancient Europeans. In any case, although they praised the natives' qualities, in later chapters they insisted on the civilizing mission of the English settlers, so as

to do justice to the names of those men who by their greatness of mind, their wisdom and their goodness, have brought into the

---

5. *Storia degli stabilimenti europei in America*, 1:iii.
6. On West's popularity in Europe, see Michael Kraus, *Atlantic Civilization: Eighteenth-Century Origins* (New York: Russel & Russel, 1961), 12.
7. *An Account of the European Settlements in America*, 1:167–68.

STORIA
DEGLI STABILIMENTI EUROPEI
IN AMERICA
DIVISA IN SEI PARTI

Nelle quali oltre una breve Notizia della Scoperta e Conquiste fatte in quella parte di Mondo de' Costumi, e Maniere de' Popoli originarj, si dà un'esatta Descrizione delle colà stabilite Colonie dell'Estensione, Clima, Prodotti, e Commercio loro, Indole, e Disposizione degli Abitanti: si accennano gl'Interessi de'Potentati di Europa in riguardo à cotali Stabilimenti, e le Mire Politiche, e di Commercio degli uni rispetto agli altri.

TRADOTTA IN ITALIANO

DALLA SECONDA EDIZIONE INGLESE

VOLUME PRIMO

IN VENEZIA MDCCLXIII.
Presso Giambatista Novelli
Con Licenza de' Superiori, e Privilegio.

Fig. 13. Title page of the Burkes' *Storia degli stabilimenti europei in America*.

Fig. 14. Reproduction of Benjamin West's painting in the Burkes' *Storia degli stabilimenti Europei in America*.

pale of civility and religion these rude and uncultivated parts of the globe; who could discern the rudiments of a future people, wanting only time to be unfolded, in the seed; who could perceive amidst the losses and disappointments and expenses of a beginning colony, the great advantages to be derived to their country from such understanding; and who could pursue them in spite of the malignity and narrow wisdom of the world.[8]

This glowing tribute to the admirable results of English colonization was a forecast of the new continent's future glory:

> The ancient world had its Ossyris and Erichtonius, who taught them the use of grain; then Bacchus, who instructed them in the culture of the vine; and their Orpheus and Linus, who first built towns and formed civil societies. The people of America will not fail, when time has made things venerable and when an intermixture of fable has moulded useful truths into popular opinions, to mention with equal gratitude, and perhaps, similar heightening circumstances, her Columbus, her Castor, her Gasca, her De Poincy, her Delawar, her Baltimore, and her Pen.[9]

The Burkes came to this prophetic judgment after evaluating the prosperity of the English settlements. They presented an idyllic picture of the colonies of North America, especially Pennsylvania, which caused the translator to yearn to escape to "a good, glorious, free Fatherland."[10]

In 1763, the publisher Coltellini from Leghorn published an encyclopedic dictionary on America, *Il gazzettiere americano* (the Italian version of the *American Gazetteer of London*; 1762). In it, he wrote:

> The lack of books in the Italian language that deal with current American history or with recent and accurate accounts of current events, persuaded us to publish this translation of the *American Gazetteer*. . . . The primary subject of this book is neither the discovery of America nor its history before the conquest: for through it more than through anything else we have a view of the current

---

8. *An Account of the European Settlements in America*, 2:221-22.
9. Ibid., 2:222.
10. *Il traduttore a chi legge*, in *Storia degli stabilimenti europei in America*, 1:ii.

IL GAZZETTIERE AMERICANO
CONTENENTE
UN DISTINTO RAGGUAGLIO DI TUTTE LE PARTI
DEL
NUOVO MONDO
DELLA LORO
SITUAZIONE, CLIMA, TERRENO, PRODOTTI, STATO ANTICO E MODERNO, MERCI, MANIFATTURE, E COMMERCIO

Con una efatta defcrizione delle Città, Piazze, Porti, Baje, Fiumi, Laghi, Montagne, Paffi, e Fortificazioni

Il tutto deftinato ad efporre lo ftato prefente delle cofe in quella parte di Globo, e le mire, e intereffi delle diverfe Potenze, che hanno degli ftabilimenti
IN AMERICA

TRADOTTO DALL' INGLESE
e arricchito di Aggiunte, Note, Carte, e Rami.

VOLUME PRIMO.

IN LIVORNO PER MARCO COLTELLINI ALL' INSEGNA DELLA VERITA' MDCCLXIII.

CON LICENZA DE' SUPERIORI.

Fig. 15. Title page of *Il gazzettiere americano*.

state of affairs in our part of the world.... Our author interjected only brief information about the early discovery of the New World and only whenever he felt it was necessary to better understand the subject at hand. Therefore, those who are even minimally interested in the early discovery of the New World, might want to consult several other works that cover this matter and are available in their original language as well as in translation. Among these, especially, the *Account of the European Settlements in America* published, of course, in Venice. This work, as it covers different subjects from a different methodology, does not diminish the Priority of our work.[11]

Although the publisher recognized the chronological priority of the Burkes' work, he claimed the methodological originality of his *Gazzettiere*.

After the Burkes, it was Raynal, "the immortal author of *Philosophical and Political History of the Two Indies*,"[12] who furnished valid information on the New America. Undoubtedly, the work's popularity was favored by the war between the colonies and their fatherland. Also, "one should not underestimate that the Abbot's volumes provided the great majority of observers with the concepts which better enabled them to grasp the importance of the American revolutionary phenomenon."[13] Raynal's *History*, together with other best-sellers on America such as De Pauw's *Recherches philosophiques*, Robertson's *History of America*, Marmontel's novel *Les Incas* and Carli's *Lettere americane*, was one of the most widely read books in Italy at the end of the century. Still, the *History* has the merit of being a truly reliable source on North America. The same cannot be said for the *Recherches*, which were vitiated by the authors's belief in American "degeneration"; the *Lettere americane*, which culminated in a yearning for utopia; and the *History of America* in which Robertson focused on the Spanish settlements and ignored the northern colonies.

By 1773 Raynal's work was already known in Italy. Translated and published first in Siena in 1776, two years later another Italian version was also published in Venice by Zatta.

11. *L'Editore al Lettore*, in *Il gazzettiere americano*, 1:v. For an account of the success of the *Gazzettiere americano* in Venice, see Piero Del Negro, *Il mito americano*, 44.
12. *La gazzetta urbana veneta*, in *Giornali veneziani*, 586.
13. Piero Del Negro, *Il mito americano*, 84.

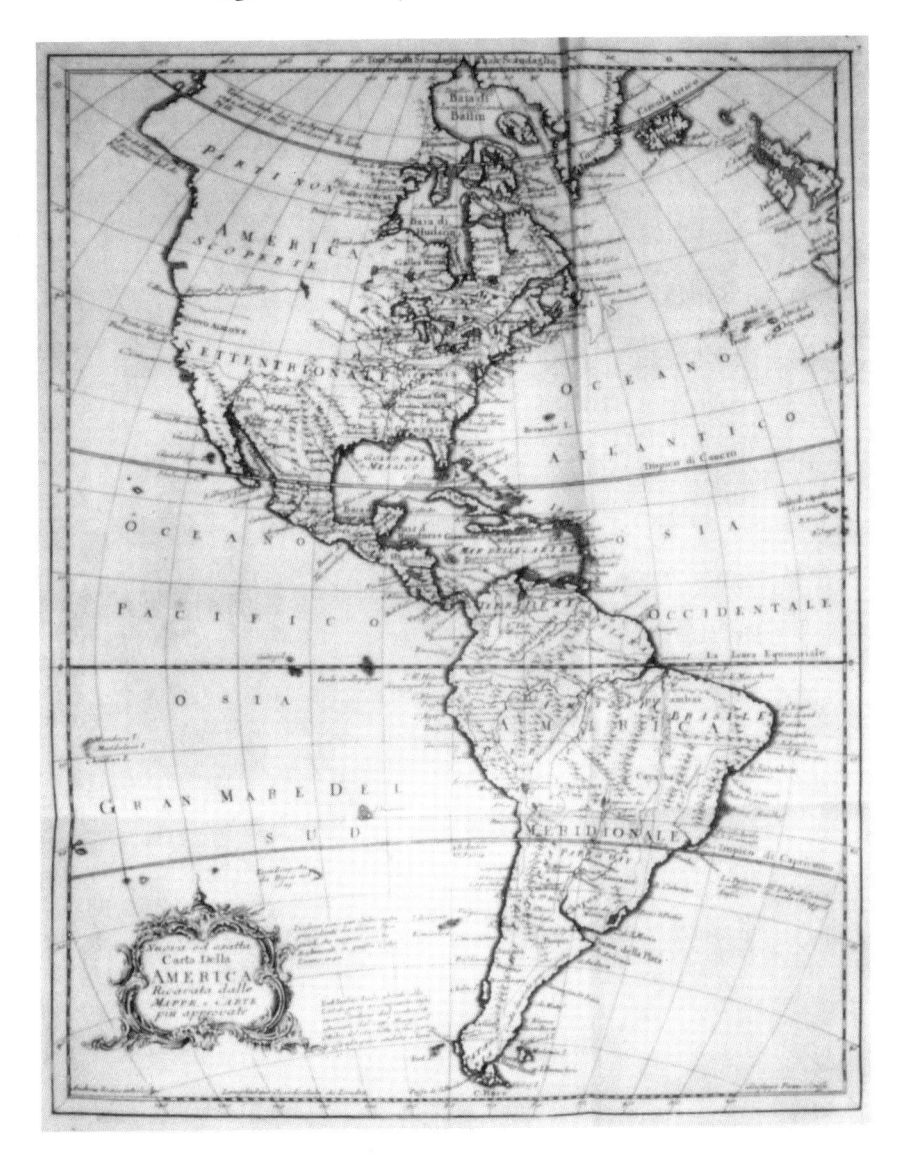

Fig. 16. Geographical map of the Americas in *Il gazzettiere americano*.

The *History*'s central design revolves around the belief that America is "prepubescent," "a child" that nature had neglected to nurture. The historian firmly asserted the inferiority of the new continent and its inhabitants with respect to antiquity. With respect to American animals he writes:

> None of them was useful to mankind. There is only one at present, which is the bee: but this is supposed to have been carried from the old to the new world. . . . The bee is not the only present which Europe has had in her power to make to America. She had enriched her also with a breed of domestic animals; for the savages had none.[14]

Lacking mastery over animals, the natives were settled in a stationary condition of indolence. Raynal wrote:

> The savages then gave themselves up to a total inaction, in the most profound security. This people, content with their lot, and satisfied with what nature afforded them, were unacquainted with that restlessness which arises from a sense of our own weakness, that loathing of ourselves and everything about us, that necessity of flying from solitude, and easing ourselves of the burden of life by throwing it upon others.[15]

Raynal participated in the debate on the nature of the Indian by supporting Voltaire's Eurocentric perspective as well as Buffon's and De Pauw's theories of "degeneration." However, as Gerbi noted, he contributed no new theoretical developments and his work was substantially "always a question of verbal or rather rhetorical emphasis."[16]

The French historian's belief that climate affects the human psyche led him to postulate that the Europeans who had settled in America would also be inevitably subjected to a process of degeneration. As confirmation of this thesis, he reported on the dissoluteness of the Canadian settlers:

> The manners of the French colonists settled in Canada were not always answerable to the climate they inhabited. Those that lived in the country spent their winter in idleness, gravely sitting by their fireside. When the return of spring called them out to the indispensable labours of the field, they ploughed the ground superficially without ever manuring it, sowed it carelessly, and then sank again into their former indolence till harvest-time. The people were too proud or

---

14. Raynal, *A Philosophical and Political History of the British Settlements and Trade in North America*, 2:144–45.
15. Ibid., 1:12–13.
16. Antonello Gerbi, *The Dispute of the New World*, 1:45.

Fig. 17. Engraving of Niagara Falls in *Il gazzettiere americano*.

too lazy to work for hire, so that every family was obliged to gather in their own crops; and nothing was to be seen of that sprightly joy, which on a fine summer's day enlivens the reapers, whilst they are gathering in their rich harvests. . . . This amazing negligence might be owing to several causes.[17]

After tracing the causes of the poor moral discipline of the inhabitants of the Cataraquí region to the rigors of the climate and their passion for weapons, Raynal went on to analyze the city dwellers' excesses:

The inhabitants of the cities, especially of the capital, lived, both in winter and summer, in a constant round of dissipation. They were alike insensible to the beauties of nature, and to the pleasures of the imagination; they had no taste for arts or sciences, for reading or instruction. Their only passion was amusement, and persons of all ages were fond of dancing at assemblies.[18]

In those same years the botanist Luigi Castiglioni, in his *Travels in the United States of North America*, wrote concerning the English soldiers who lived in Canada:

On the day of the 22nd of September I finally departed for Montreal in a boat with eight Canadians, gladly leaving a region where everything contributed to making me dejected and ill. Equally averse to satire and adulation, I would have liked to find that men were virtuous everywhere and to present them as an example for imitation, but inasmuch as I had set for myself the goal of pursuing only the truth, I cannot conceal the disorders of this new population. The officers of the British regiments reorganized at the end of the war, left with

---

17. *A Philosophical and Political History of the British Settlements and Trade in North America*, 2:88-89.
18. Ibid. After tracing a negative picture of the Canadians, Raynal concludes: "This way of life considerably increased the influence of the ladies; who were possessed of every attraction, except those soft emotions of the soul, which alone constitute the merit and the charm of beauty. Lively, gay, coquettes, and addicted to gallantry, they were more gratified with inspiring than feeling the tender passion. In both sexes might be observed a greater degree of devotion than virtue, more religion than probity, a higher sense of honour than of real honesty. Superstition took place of morality, as it does wherever men are taught to believe that ceremonies will compensate for good works, and that crimes are expiated by prayers" (ibid).

nothing to do in America and reduced to half pay, received a portion of land in the Bay of Kenty, and for the first few years they were furnished with the most essential supplies. However, since they were used to military life and completely ignorant of agriculture, they left to others the job of attending to their farms.[19]

Like Castiglioni, Raynal also, after harshly criticizing the flaws of the Canadians, praised Pennsylvania and William Penn who gave "an example of moderation and justice in America, never so much as thought of before by the Europeans."[20] The havenlike Pennsylvania was therefore not included in the process of decay to which the natives and the "naturalized" American Europeans were doomed. Here, then, Raynal deviated from the "degenerative" perspective, and this is especially clear at the end of his *General Reflections on the Anglo-American Provinces*, where he unexpectedly "predicted" America's glorious future:

Let us wait till a more ample burst of light has shone over the new hemisphere. Let us wait till education may have corrected the unsurmountable tendency of the climate towards the enervating pleasures of luxury and sensuality. Perhaps we shall then see that America is propitious to genius and the arts, that give birth to peace and society. A new Olympus, an Arcadia, an Athens, a new Greece, will produce, perhaps, on the continent, or in the Archipelago that surrounds it, another Homer, a Theocritus, and especially an Anacreon. Perhaps another Newton is to arise in New Britain. From British America, without doubt, will proceed the first rays of the sciences, if they are at length to break through a sky so long time clouded.[21]

---

19. Luigi Castiglioni, *Travels in the United States of North America*, 1:79-80. Castiglioni continued his description: "The inhabitants of Canada must be distinguished into Britishers, Frenchmen, Americans, and Indians. The first of these are merchants, or soldiers, or people employed in the government; and the second, coming from the French families that settled this country, are the true Canadians. The latter are divided into four classes, comprising the gentlemen, the clergy, the merchants, and the people" (1:81-82).
20. *A Philosophical and Political History of the British Settlements and Trade in North America*, 1:152-53.
21. Ibid., 2:164-65. Again, Raynal prognosticated: "In proportion as our people are weakened and resign themselves to each other's dominion, population and agriculture will flourish in America: the arts, transplanted by our means, will make a rapid progress; and that country, rising out of nothing, will be fired with the ambition of appearing with glory,

Thus, insofar as they were capable of acculturation, Americans would emancipate themselves from a causal, deterministic relation with the environment and overcome their inborn inferiority.

The publication of Robertson's *History of America* was contemporaneous with Raynal's work. In the foreword to volume 4 of Robertson's work, his publisher, Giovanni Gatti, wrote, to the detriment of the French Abbé's work:

> A few words must be said on the substantial difference between Mr. Robertson's work and the too well known work by the former Jesuit Raynal. Actually, the title alone suffices to indicate their different goals. . . . What is central to one author becomes peripheral to the other. The former sets as his goal a knowledge of America; the latter, America's influence over Europe. Robertson writes the history of the New World; Raynal weaves a kind of addendum to the history of the ancient world. . . . Robertson cautiously analyzes; Raynal boldly paints; the latter in 200 pages writes the history of the Spanish colonies, while the former accomplishes the same goal in no less than four volumes.[22]

The *History of America* (1777) by the Scottish historian Robertson, already known to eighteenth-century intellectuals in its French version, was translated in Florence in 1777 and published by Gatti in Venice a year later. A Voltaire-inspired text that popularized the naturalistic pessimism of Buffon and De Pauw in Europe, it forcefully resisted the theories of Rousseau and those who "seem to consider . . . the most perfect state of man [to be that] which is the least civilized," and "describe the manners of the rude Americans with such rapture, as if they proposed them for models to the rest of the species."[23]

The four volumes of Robertson's *History*, however, were limited to an analysis of just the Iberian possessions in the New World, in a perspective

---

in its turn, on the face of the globe and in the history of the world" (2:231). With reference to Raynal's changed perspective on the irreversible inferiority of Americans, Gerbi (*The Dispute of the New World*) noted: "Raynal [inquires] into who is happier, the savage or the civilized man, coming to an unexpected conclusion in favor of the savage, the very same savage to whom he had just denied the supreme pleasure of love" (49–50).

22. *Storia d'America*, 4:iv–v.
23. *History of America*, 2:57.

that often denounced Spain's conduct, as noted by the translator of the Italian edition:

> Readers will maybe think that Dr. Robertson is too severe [in his judgments] against the discoveries and conquests of an entire nation and portrays [that nation] as guided by an insatiable greed, so that, having seemingly forsaken all feelings of humanity, it oppresses her equals.[24]

The historian, however, was more severe toward the "Americans" than the conquistadors, since America was "gross and uncultivated"; based on this premise, Robertson easily sketched the physical and psychological traits of the natives. Although he differentiated the savages of the tropical regions from those of the moderate climes, and primitive tribes from "monarchies," he captured Americans in a global, generalized vision:

> But in the New World, the state of mankind was ruder, and the aspect of Nature extremely different. Throughout all its vast region, there were only two monarchies remarkable for extent of territory, or distinguished by any progress in improvement. The rest of this continent was possessed by small independent tribes, destitute of arts and industry, and neither capable to correct the defects, nor desirous to meliorate the condition of that part of the earth allotted to them for their habitation. Countries, occupied by such people, were almost in the same state as if they had been without inhabitants.[25]

---

24. *Il traduttore a chi legge*, in *Storia d'America* (Venice: Gatti, 1778) 1:xx. The translator further noted: "The two volumes which I am now publishing contain an account of the discovery of the New World and the progress which Spain's colonies and armies achieved there. This, the most splendid part of American history, is also detached from it so as to form a separate unit worthy of being examined on its own" (1:5). With reference to the relations between Spaniards and American Indians, Robertson wrote, in *History of America*: "Not only the incapacity, but the prejudices of the Spaniards, render their accounts of the people of America extremely defective. Soon after they planted colonies in their new conquests, a difference in opinion arose with respect to the treatment of the natives. One party, solicitous to render their servitude perpetual, represented them as a brutish, obstinate race, incapable either of acquiring religious knowledge, or of being trained to the functions of social life. The other, full of pious concern for their conversion, contended that, though rude and ignorant, they were gentle, affectionate, docile, and by proper instructions and regulations might be formed gradually into good Christians and useful citizens" (2:54-55).

25. *History of America*, 2:14-15. Robertson recalled the first impressions the Spaniards had at the sight of the American populations: "Their vacant countenance, their staring

Robertson built his theory of the inferiority of the American native populations on eight premises.[26] Finally, he speculated that the Indian's inborn apathy was a result of the climate's influence as well as the ease of survival. "In America, man appears under the rudest form in which we can conceive him to subsist" and Americans "apply [themselves] to work without ardor, carry it on with little activity, and, like children, are easily diverted from it. . . . Their work advances under their hand with such slowness, that an eye-witness compares it to the imperceptible progress of vegetation."[27]

Like Robertson, the Italian Jesuit Filippo Salvatore Gilij (1721–89), covered only Spanish America in his *Saggio di storia americana* (1780). His work was distinguishable from other histories of the turn of the century, however, in that it was an account of about twenty-five years of missionary work spent in South America prior to the Jesuits' expulsion in 1767. Gilij's contribution to the debate about the New World should be carefully assessed especially in view of his strong "Hispanophile" perspective, which differed from that of other Jesuits who, having been "expelled from America were very bitter toward Spain and quite ready to help England or any other power who might open the doors of their country to them again."[28] The originality of Gilij's position is to be found particularly in his "good sense," which made him wary of rigid schemes and eighteenth-century naturalist classifications. The purpose of the *Saggio* was to present his contemporaries with an objective view of Iberian America and, especially, of the Orinoco and Terranova:

> My objective (I know not if I shall succeed) is to present to my readers America as it truly is, or most certainly as it appears. In writing, I am

---

unexpressive eye, their listless inattention, and total ignorance of subjects which seem to be the first which should occupy the thoughts of rational beings, made such impression upon the Spaniards, when they first beheld those rude people that they considered them as animals of an inferior order, and could not believe that they belonged to the human species. It required the authority of a papal bull to counteract this opinion, and to convince them that the Americans were capable of the functions, and entitled to the privileges of humanity" (2:93).

26. "I. The bodily constitution. . . . II. The qualities of their minds. III. Their domestic state. IV. Their political state and institutions. V. Their system of war, and public security. VI. The arts with which they were acquainted. VII. Their religious ideas and institutions. VIII. Such singular detached customs as are not reducible to any of the former heads" (2:59).

27. Ibid., 2:50, 184.

28. Antonello Gerbi, *The Dispute of the New World*, 224.

spurred neither by a spirit of factionalism, nor by resentment toward anyone. I cared for religion; accordingly, should the occasion arise, my former profession of missionary will not leave me indifferent to religion but will spur me to its defense. With these intentions, I set out to write a history which I have entitled *American*.[29]

In order to portray America "as it truly appears," however, Gilij had to fight on several fronts: with those who idealized the noble savage, with the pioneers who espoused the theory of inferiority of the New World, and more generally, with the mystifying historians' tendency to "the strange and wonderful:"

> I noticed another feature about American writers, one which however is not totally harmful. Besides a nationalistic resentment, they have almost all inherited a tendency to exaggeration; from the very first writers who described that part of the world this tendency has spread almost fatally to everyone. The descriptions of Spanish America, only cursorily known to foreigners or reported by inexperienced individuals, are for the most part, if not invented, at least greatly exaggerated. America is known for its wonder. . . . [30]

The Burkes, reflecting, like Gilij, on the hyperbolic nature of New World accounts, observed that "it has been the fate of this country to create romantic ideas at all times"[31] and as such also aroused the imagination of historians.

Among the historians of the New World, Gilij acquitted only Oviedo and Gomara, whom he often quoted and praised:

> We had a better knowledge of America at the time of its discovery, than we do now. It is true. At that time, Italians received fresh news about America from the purest sources. They received the news from Oviedo, Gomara and similar Spaniards. A careful analysis leads us to believe that their writings have the appearance, nay the substance of truth. . . . But if we look at modern writers about America, my God! We find in them dark mazes which lead to most serious errors![32]

29. Filippo Salvatore Gilij, *Saggio di storia americana*, 1:xix.
30. Ibid., 1:xviii.
31. *An Account of European Settlements*, 2:36.
32. Filippo Salvatore Gilij, *Saggio di storia americana*, 1:xiv–xvi. Gilij again insisted on the scant reliability of information about the Americas: "People will read any book that

The Roman Jesuit countered the scant reliability of sources about the Americas with a well-pondered and meticulous portrayal of the natives, which his "missionary profession" led to evaluate as possible neophytes. Americans were uneducated, erratic and primitive, but if one "could defeat their slothfulness" they could be "easily trained" to religion and to civilized life. Thus the author's conception of the savage was framed by the traditional Jesuit perspective, which distinguished *before* and *after* conversion as two existential stages of the native's life:

> As I said elsewhere, at the very outset my poor *Orinochese* came before me, men and women, with their skin painted in different shapes, almost fully naked, and were not ashamed of their strange appearance. However, after much advice and preaching, they so much changed their customs that I was moved to tears.[33]

In analyzing the fervor of the neophytes, Gilij pointed to the extraordinary religious attitude of the blacks, thus introducing a new issue, that of slavery. This issue produced a lively debate in eighteenth-century Europe, especially in France, with the participation of the Abbot Grégoire;[34] however, it did not seem to take root in Italy. Gilij noted:

---

deals with America. No care is given to whether the author is knowledgeable or whether he is someone who either out of ignorance or on purpose, likes to spread fairy tales with ink. All books are good, as long as they amuse. But apart from the damage they often cause, these books do not lift the reader out of ignorance, although one should think this would be the reader's aim; on the contrary, they increase it and encourage it immensely" (1:xiii–xiv). Gilij based his reasoning on his conviction that South America exhibited a substantial "uniformity": "In any case, as the common saying goes, there is an egg to egg similarity among the various regions of America. Having seen one, one has the wherewithal to judge all. Like eggs however, although greatly similar one to the other, they differ in some accidental aspect" (3:v–vi).

33. Ibid., 4:250. In analyzing the various American cross-breeds, the Jesuit expressed his reservations with respect to the Zambi, "the children of an Indian woman and a black. Were that we had never met such a person in all America, there is no one worse. The Zambo is quiet, has an evil or cunning look and exhibits such a perverse temperament that he is easily led to evil. He sits beside you with lowered eyes and a thoughtful expression. He walks with you, acts in his own way as a friend; but very rarely does he speak and even more rarely does he laugh. Some will say: what evil have the *Zambi* done to you? None, nothing at all. I talk about them in this fashion because I do believe they deserve it. In one way or another, I like all the various kinds of Americans, except for these. My disposition does not agree with them" (4:320).

34. The Abbot Grégoire, a Jansenist, was not only a defender of the Jews, but a champion of the slave freedom movement in the French colonies of America. He died excommunicated after having been labeled a dissident and a heretic. Among his works, we mention: *Lettre aux philantropes, sur les malheurs, les droits et les réclamations des gens de*

Nor do these poor people, who rather than being idolatrous seem, like the Indians, superstitious, resist the Gospel. They listen to it with pleasure and embrace it with a good heart. They are also devout, frequently receive the Sacraments and are devoted to reciting the rosary and our other usual prayers. Having been accustomed to a life among the *Orinochese*, I could not tell whether these Indians are better Christians than the blacks. I do know that many favor the latter.[35]

In accordance with his "anthropological" perspective, the Jesuit's intent was to draw a psychological portrait of the South American slaves, pointing out the differences and analogies with the Indians. He continued:

The black is an excellent imitator of the actions of others, no less than the Indian. These two human races seem to have reason residing in their sight. Elsewhere I wrote about the Indians. Let us now observe a black. If he is slave to a Spaniard, you will see him copy his master so well, that he is totally like him in behavior and all the rest.[36]

Like the obedient African slaves, the "very barbaric" *Orinochese* were not hostile to the word of God and the charismatic virtues of the preachers who were forced to undergo uncomfortable "journeys" to carry out their evangelizing mission.[37] In the third part of his *Saggio* the Jesuit recalled several missionary treks into the forests of the Orinoco, vividly presenting a detailed description of the environment and circumstances experienced:

---

couleur de Saint Domingue, et des autres îles françoises de l'Amérique (Paris: Belin, 1790); *De la littérature des Nègres, ou recherches sur leurs facultés intellectuelles, leurs qualités morales et leur littérature* (Paris: Maradan, 1808); *De la traite de l'esclavage des Noirs et des Blancs; par un ami des hommes de toutes les couleurs* (Paris: Adrien Egron, 1815).

35. Filippo Salvatore Gilij, *Saggio di storia americana*, 4:305.
36. Ibid., 4:305-6.
37. Father Gilij wrote about a woman from the *Parechi* nation who asked for his rosary: "So that Jare also asked for my rosary, which I carried suspended from my belt and which, being made of glass beads, she saw as beautiful and shining. No, I said firmly, this I need to pray to the God of heaven. She was astonished in hearing this, and did not insist. But in her face I glimpsed a flash of vivid intelligence uncommon among the savages. And this thought was not unfounded. Later, as I was explaining doctrine to a group of Parechi and showing them sacred images, they asked surprising questions and I noticed in them a great frankness of mind" (3:121-22).

> When the guides tell us that we are getting close to Gentiles, we must abstain from making fires so as to avoid sending smoke into the air, which would indicate that foreigners are coming their way. Once in a while, a neophyte from the group climbs a tree and observes if any smoke is visible in any one direction. On the basis of his observation he advises his companions who march in the direction he gives them. They march very quietly; if they are traveling by boat, they row silently. They no longer do any cooking. Like a farmer who avoids disturbing a wasps' nest with smoke, they only eat food that needs no cooking, until they find the savages.[38]

Gilij took pleasure in narrating small anecdotes and in so doing vividly described the Jesuits' adventures. In recounting the arrival of *Parechi* ambassadors to the Jesuit settlement, he wrote:

> Lest anyone think that these *Orinochese* ambassadors had magnificent trains, four Indians arrived, naked like all Gentiles, covered only with a cotton loincloth held around the waist. The upper part of their body as well as their thighs and legs were all painted with *anòto*. I will not tell you the unusual surprise they expressed when they saw my house. They were so shocked at the sight of things they had never fancied before, that when they later came to converse in my sitting room, they did not understand or pretended not to understand, what I told them in the *Tamanachi* language. It should be noted that this language and *Parechi* differ from each other like Roman and Neapolitan, which is to say, they can be reciprocally understood.[39]

The issue of American languages drove Gilij to bizarre hypotheses. In a way, he fell prey to the same fanciful temptations he had strongly denounced. His refusal to follow the trend to the "strange and wonderful" and his intent of depicting the "true appearance" of the Spanish provinces, did not prevent him from noticing a similarity between the "Muscovite" and "Californese" languages.[40] He thus believed, although with some

---

38. Ibid., 3:97.
39. Ibid., 3:116-17.
40. On the basis of linguistic analogies, Gilij speculated that there had been contact between the populations of Siberia and those of California: "As far as I am concerned,

reservation,[41] in the satanic origin of certain Indian terms ("I would not however deny that some terms were introduced into the Indian languages by the devil")[42] and in some *Orinochese* legends, such as the ones about the mythical Dorado and the Savage, a woodland monster:

> In the vast bushes of the Orinoco there are, as everyone who lives there claims, certain beasts which apart from small details, resemble man. This beast that we would call a *Savage*, is called in *Tamanaco*, *Acci*. The *Savage*'s appearance is human, except for his feet whose ends are naturally pointed backwards, like the tracks left by the oxen which Caco stole and which he turned backwards by cunning artifice. It therefore looks as if the *Savage* is leaving, when in fact, he is approaching the travelers. Hairy from head to toe, he is extremely lecherous and when he has the chance, he abducts women.[43]

Although he claimed to be a champion of historical truth, as opposed to the "strange and wonderful," Gilij could not help slipping into brief flights of fancy. These are infrequent, however, and do not preclude the *Saggio di storia americana* from providing contemporary Italy with a wealth of geographical, anthropological, and environmental information on the New World. Together with Muratori's *Cristianesimo felice*, Gilij's work is eighteenth-century Italy's most valid and systematic documentation of the "Jesuit empire" of South America.

I am certain that prior to the famous navigator Bering, or possibly later, the Muscovites sailed from Kamczatka or another part of Siberia and reached the coast next to Spanish California. Many people have recounted this" (411).

41. A legend already circulating at the turn of the century recounted that the devil resided among idol-worshiping savages and that their languages, as they could not be traced back to a common source, must have originated in hell: "It is difficult to believe the many horrible deceptions incurred by some ancient writers about the Americas. They were shocked, so to say, by the vast number of different languages or dialects. And as they either could not or would not, for lack of time, determine their exact number or the true origin, they wrote that the number of American tongues was infinite, and that along with the natives, their author was the devil" (3:276).

42. Ibid., 3:278.

43. Ibid., 1:247.

4

Italy and the New America

1. The Quakers and the Myth of Pennsylvania

The 1760s saw a decline in hispanocentrism. Europeans turned their attention from Iberian possessions to the English settlements in North America. The Burkes' *Account* attests to this shift in direction in the many pages devoted to William Penn and the Pennsylvania Quakers. Although they stated that "William Penn in his capacity of a divine, and of a moral writer, is certainly not of the first rank," the two English historians granted that "in his capacity of a legislator, and the founder of so flourishing a commonwealth, he deserves great honour amongst all mankind."[1]

Voltaire's letters on the Quakers were clearly the source of the Pennsylvania myth and the legend of the "good Quaker." Voltaire praised Quaker

---
1. William and Edmund Burke, *An Account of the European Settlements in America*, 2:195-96.

ideology insofar as it was in harmony with primitive Christianity and valued morality over theology. Letter 4 is dedicated to Penn, who "might, with reason, boast of having brought down upon earth the Golden Age, which in all probability, never had any real existence but in his dominions."[2] Voltaire came to see Quaker ethics as an antidote to the inadequacies of contemporary French society. As Echeverria noted, this enabled him to prove that "dogma and ritual had nothing to do with happiness and virtue, and that freedom and toleration produced, not anarchy, but peace and prosperity."[3] In the *Essai sur les moeurs* Voltaire wrote:

> He [Penn] and his companions professed the same simplicity and equality which prevailed among the primitive disciples of Christ. They knew no other religious tenet but those which proceeded extempore from the lips, and which were all confined to the love of God and their fellow-creatures. They did not admit baptism, because Christ baptized no one. They had no priest because Christ Himself was the only teacher and pastor of His first disciples. Here I perform only the duty of a faithful historian, and shall further add, that if Penn and his followers erred in their theology—that inexhaustible source of misfortunes and disputes—they at least excelled all other people in the strictness of their morals.[4]

News about the Quakers soon spread to Italy as well, but, as the eclectic Neapolitan intellectual Raimondo de Sangro di San Severo noted in 1750, it was Voltaire who bestowed credibility on them: "Many discuss the *Quakers,* but we must note that it is especially Mr. de Voltaire who discusses their religion in volume IV of his works."[5] Still, Quaker doctrine met with some resistance in eighteenth-century Italy, as confirmed by

---

2. *The Religion of the Quakers*, in *The Works of Voltaire*, with notes by Tobias Smollett, revised and modernized new translation by William F. Fleming, and an introduction by Oliver H. G. Leigh, 42 vols. (Akron: Werner Company, 1905), 39:209.

3. Durand Echeverria, *Mirage in the West: An Image of the French History of American Society to 1815*, (Princeton: Princeton University Press, 1957), 27.

4. *Possessions of the English and Dutch*, in François Marie Arouet de Voltaire, *Works*, 22 vols. (Akron: St. Hubert Guild, 1901-3), 19:263.

5. Raimondo de Sangro di San Severo, *Lettera apologetica*, 141n. Castiglioni, however, was the first to make a distinction between the true Quakers and the branch of the so-called Shakers, which arose in America; see Luigi Castiglioni, *Viaggio: Travels in the United States of North America 1785-87* (1:90-91), 50: "Among them, that of the Shaking Quakers, recently arisen in America, deserves particular mention. The founder was an Irish woman, who, upon arriving in Boston and declaring herself the Chosen Woman, began to preach a new doctrine and very quickly formed a body of converts, who were persecuted by the

Genovesi: "The Spaniards laugh at the superstitious affectations of the Americans: the French at those of the Spaniards: the English at those of the French: and the Italians laugh at English Quakerism."[6] Suspicion of this religious sect was documented as well by Goldoni's *Il filosofo inglese* (1754), where the playwright assigned the role of *alazones* (impostors) to two London Quakers, Emanuel Bluk and Master Panich. Without ever mentioning the word *Quakers*, the playwright used a series of stereotypes to describe their egalitarian ideology:

Here is another species of strange philosophers.
They address all with thou, sovereign kings included.[7]
We all are born equal, what is in the world is ours.
Thus ought one not say, this is mine, this is yours.[8]

---

people and multiplied rapidly. The main point of their belief is that the end of the world sunken in wicked vices is approaching, and that God sent this woman to be the leader of the chosen people. This is how her followers, who must preach to men penance for the sins committed, call themselves. They summon to penance not only the living, but even the dead, with whom they say they have frequent conversations, as also with the angels and demons. . . . These religious exercises consist of laughing, weeping, singing, and jumping in a circle in the fields until they are utterly worn. . . . The founder of this new sect died two years ago, as the consequence, so they say of almost continuous drunkenness, from which it can be argued that she was indebted to beer and rum for the ecstasies in which she declared herself absorbed and for the principal points of her singular doctrine."

6. Antonio Genovesi, *Lettere accademiche*, 557.

7. " . . . un'altra specie è questa di filosofi strani. / Il tu lo danno a tutti; lo danno anche ai sovrani." *Il filosofo inglese* (act 1, scene 4), in *Tutte le opere di Carlo Goldoni*, 5:274. Vincenzio Martinelli (*Istoria del governo d'Inghilterra e delle sue colonie in India, e nell'America settentrionale* [Florence: Cambiagi, 1776], 86) noted: "In addition to bringing back the "thou" form of speech, Fox banished the childish embellishment of titles, and in his organization Excellency, Most Illustrious, even Highness and Majesty were dropped. Instead of Master, Servant, Slave—abject prostitution of flatterers, never heartfelt titles— they brought back to their genuine beginnings the words friend, brother. Their enthusiastic disdain reached such a height that they did not remove their hat even for the sovereign, so that a courtesan was entrusted with the task of removing it from their head. Those who want to know more, may read their history." Further documentation from the turn of the century on English Quaker customs is given by Luigi Angiolini in his *Lettere sopra l'Inghilterra, la Scozia e l'Olanda* (1790). In *Letterati, memorialisti e viaggiatori del Settecento*, ed. Ettore Bonora (Milan: Ricciardi, 1951), 1075-79: "Quaker men as well as women dress in a simple, though highly proper fashion indeed. They allow no decoration, lace, brilliant colors or metals. They do not remove their hats, nor do they curtsy to anyone, king included. . . . Their refusal to remove their hat, to greet or bow to anyone, forecasts pride and disdain for any difference in rank, and tends toward an equality which is in no case compatible with the prevailing customs of current society."

8. "Nati siam tutti eguali, quel ch'è nel mondo è nostro. / E dir non si dovrebbe; questo è mio, questo è vostro." Ibid. (act 3, scene 4), 300.

As emphasized by Del Negro,[9] these are traditional platitudes derived from various eighteenth-century sources (especially Moreri's *Great Dictionary*). Among these, the "custom of doffing their hats in greeting, substituting for it the handshake,"[10] suggested to Goldoni the scene where Emanuel Bluk scolds Jacobbe:

> EMANUEL.   Good morning (*to Jacobbe*)
> Greetings. (*removes his hat*)
> JACOBBE.   Your hat on your head.
> EMANUEL.   These ceremonies in a year's time
> Wear out hats and cause damage.
> JACOBBE.   If all had the same thought you have,
> The hatter's art would come to nought.
> EMANUEL.   No art is more useless than this:
> A cap, a piece of cloth, suffice to cover one's head.[11]

The general intent of the comedy however should not be understood as an anti-egalitarian polemic or a condemnation of religious fanaticism, but rather as a comic rendering of the contradiction between theory and practice that was inherent in Quaker philosophy. In any case, Goldoni indicated in *L'Autore a chi legge* that the two characters' choice of religious practice was not especially intended as a critique of English Puritans and that "in every religion, Body, Community, there are the good and the bad, therefore if the comedy's two impostors were in fact Quakers, they would have been among the bad ones, who nevertheless do not diminish the reputation of the honorable."[12]

The American Quaker's place in the theater of those years is further documented by several playful dramas and pantomime ballets, such as

---

9. See Piero Del Negro, *Il mito americano*, 56.
10. Luigi Castiglioni, *Viaggio* (2:37), 227.
11. EMANUEL: Buon giorno (*a JACOBBE*)
    JACOBBE: Vi saluto. (*si cava il cappello*)
    EMANUEL: In testa il tuo cappello.
    Queste son cerimonie, le quali in capo all'anno
    Consumano i cappelli, e apportano del danno.
    JACOBBE: Se tutti, come voi, avesser tal pensiero,
    L'arte de' cappellai si ridurrebbe al zero.
    EMANUEL: Arte non vi è nel mondo più inutile di questa:
    Una berretta, un panno, basta a coprir la testa.
    Il filosofo inglese (act 3, scene 6), 300.
12. *L'autore a chi legge*, ibid., 263.

Porta's *L'americana in Olanda*, which was staged at San Samuele's theater in Venice in 1778,[13] and Bertati's *I quacqueri* (1779). Like the "savage," the "American" character par excellence, the Pennsylvania Quaker was a fixed, one-dimensional figure. The American Indian had been and continued to be a symbol of naïveté and frankness, while the new "American character" based on the Pennsylvanian Quaker was to be a symbol of calm seriousness and stubbornness.

In his novel *Guglielmo Penn,* Francesco Soave embraced a clearly humanistic perspective, as he contrasted the pacific expansion of the Quakers in Pennsylvania to the barbarism of the conquistadors:

> Another Englishman, whose name shall live immortal in the memory of future generations, conducted himself in a very different manner in those unhappy lands that were a theater of European cruelty and plunder. Having been granted from Charles II, King of England, possession of that part of North America which later came to be called Pennsylvania, after his name and after the many woods which covered it, William Penn instead of torturing those poor people, as others had done, only cared to uplift them. By his humanity and frequent acts of charity, he became the eternal object of their admiration and love.[14]

Soave expressed the wish that Penn's fellow citizens should always "have before their eyes his inspiring example" for the eternal glory of "the Quaker republic."

Until the middle of the eighteenth century and even later, Pennsylvania, which, along with Virginia, was to Europeans the best known of the English colonies, continued to be called "Quaker country."[15] In *La donna*

---

13. Next to the protagonist, Zemira, the orthodox Quaker Monsignor Naimur made his appearance. Furthermore, there is evidence of a "Quaker" mask in eighteenth-century Roman and Neapolitan carnivals; see Giuseppe Massara, *Americani: L'immagine letteraria degli Stati Uniti in Italia* (Palermo: Sellerio, 1984), 32n.
14. Francesco Soave, *Novelle morali*, 2:88.
15. The association of Quaker with Pennsylvania (and often of Quaker to North American) is commonly accepted up to the eve of the American Revolution. As documented by Del Negro (see *Il mito americano*, 25) in 1784—a year after the Peace of Paris—a regatta was organized in Venice honoring Gustaf II, king of Sweden. In this yearly boat race, one of the state boats, called *The Americans*, featured sailors all dressed as savages. It was flanked by another state boat manned by Quakers, perhaps as a symbol of the "New American Republic."

che non si trova, Chiari was one of the first intellectuals to perceive the decline of Virginia's popularity and the rise of two new stars, New England and Pennsylvania. As Del Negro pointed out, this was a relevant change in perspective, inasmuch as it signaled the waning of the "plantation-colony and the rise of the trade colony,"[16] a change that resulted in widening the horizons of New America. Bridfield, a Philadelphia merchant who is the "good Quaker" character in *La donna che non si trova*, testifies to the positive evaluation of the Pennsylvanian heretics. But this was an isolated instance in Venetian intellectual society which was, as a rule, suspicious of English and American puritans. Even later, especially in his *Trattenimenti dello spirito umano* (1780), Chiari would continue to praise "the brotherly tranquility, the incredible harmony and peace"[17] of the state of Pennsylvania, founded as it was upon tolerance and the free circulation of ideas.

In the 1770s especially, with the expansion of information and the rise of a greater spirit of tolerance, there were enthusiastic defenses of the Pennsylvanian Quakers. In the *Summary* of Barbeau Dubourg's preface to Franklin's works, we read:

> At the turn of the last century, among the American savages almost overnight a city arose, whose boundaries have not as yet been enclosed and which expands daily in accordance with its initial plan. It is called Philadelphia. Its only fundamental law is brotherly love. Its doors are always open to everyone and although its founder expressly excluded two kinds of men—the atheist and the idler— it seems that this exclusion would be only temporary since, if an atheist existed in the rest of the universe, he would convert upon coming to this City where everything is so neatly ordered. Were a slouch to be born there, as he would constantly have before him three lovely sisters—opulence, science and virtue—all daughters of labor, he would quickly fancy them and would seek to win them from their father.[18]

---

16. Piero Del Negro, *Il mito americano*, 53.

17. Pietro Chiari, *Trattenimenti dello spirito umano sopra le cose passate presenti e possibili ad avvenire* (Brescia: Berlendis, 1780), 3:15.

18. *Compendio della Prefazione di Monsieur Barbeau Dubourg alla traduzione francese delle Opere del Dottore Beniamino Franklin* (Milan: Marelli, 1774), 9. The author of the Preface further observes (10): "Under the guidance of Pen's [*sic*] laws, Pennsylvanians enjoy all of life's sweetness and their number has grown one-hundredfold in less than a

But in these same years, Filippo Mazzei, in the chapter "The Quakers" in his *Researches on the United States,* suggested a curtailment of the idealized Quaker legend. Mazzei's intent in his *Researches* was to critique Raynal on the Quakers; he accused the abbé of rigidity insofar as he attributed arbitrary qualities to Penn's followers: "For no reason whatsoever the abbé claims the Quakers are disinterested. . . . [His] description of Quaker character . . . is no less exaggerated than his portrait of the Dunkers."[19] Although he gave credit to Quaker virtues, Mazzei introduced a note of realism (undoubtedly a product of his American experience) when he stated that Quakers also "have their share of human passions." For Mazzei, Pennsylvania was not the promised land, and Penn was not at all a disinterested benefactor; Quakers did not differ from other Americans. We should point out, however, that Mazzei was opposed to the "Protestant Jesuits," especially because they attempted a reconciliation with England during the revolution, thus hindering the American cause on account of sectarian interests.[20]

From Raynal's idealistic point of view—which Mazzei rejected—Penn's laws, based as they were on freedom and property, would guarantee the happiness and harmony of the people. Penn was credited with founding a haven of peace and brotherhood "with no war, no conquest, no effort," which could serve as a model to Europe. The abbé also praised the sect's renouncing of weapons:

---

century. In Philadelphia, all the fine arts are highly valued; people from every walk of life join to a deep love of science, a great simplicity of customs." Martinelli (*Istoria del governo d'Inghilterra,* 89) writes that "Pennsylvania can be called the land of brotherly love, because those who lack the resources to purchase are assigned land in accordance with the number of families." Furthermore, "all its just laws contribute to make of Pennsylvania a repository of that golden age Poets have represented with such fancy. This happiness however cannot last because Quakers, who constitute the majority of Pennsylvanians, will not defend themselves. In case of attack, they will either be defended by their neighbors acting in their own interest or, as they will not use force in self-defense, they will become the meek victims of their oppressors." On the idyllic condition of Pennsylvania, Antonio Genovesi (*Lettere accademiche,* 445) writes: "William Penn, the great father of Pennsylvania, a new kind of republic which even Aristotle could not conceive, had, as a Quaker, a better plan. One major law in Philadelphia rules that every lad having reached twelve years of age, be he noble or plebeian, must learn a trade. Thus, he will not be a burden to others; and should a rich or noble man have a reversal of fortune, he will not die a beggar nor will he weaken the ties of the body politic."

19. Filippo Mazzei, *Researches on the United States,* trans. and ed. Constance D. Sherman (Charlottesville: University Press of Virginia, 1976), 230, 231.

20. "The Quakers cannot justify the role they played during the Revolution, when they denied their own principles and used their religion to mask insidious politics" (ibid., 232).

But on the other hand, how shall we reconcile the strictness of the gospel maxims, by which the Quakers are literally governed, with those military preparations, either offensive or defensive, which maintain a continual state of war between all Christian nations? Besides, what could the enemy do, if they were to enter Pennsylvania sword in hand? Unless they massacred, in the space of a night or a day's time, all the inhabitants of that fortunate region, they would not be able totally to extirpate the race of those mild and charitable men. Violence has its boundaries in its very excess; it is consumed and extinguished, as the fire in the ashes that feed it. But virtue, when guided by humanity and by the spirit of benevolence, is revived as the tree under the edge of the pruning knife. The wicked stand in need of numbers to execute their sanguinary projects. But the Quaker, who is a good man, wants only a brother from whom he may receive, or to whom he may give assistance. Let then the warlike nations, let people who are either slaves or tyrants, go into Pennsylvania; there they will find all avenues open to them, all property at their disposal; not a single soldier, but numbers of merchants and farmers. But if these inhabitants be tormented, restrained, or oppressed, they will fly, and leave their lands uncultivated, their manufactures destroyed, and their warehouses empty. They will cultivate, and spread population in some new land; they will go round the world rather than turn their arms against their pursuers, or submit to bear their yoke. Their enemies will have only gained the hatred of mankind, and the execration of posterity.[21]

But many of Penn's faithful broke the mythical peace of Pennsylvania and took up arms in the Revolution. Castiglioni recalled that:

since the Quakers consider war the most horrible of evils, they always refused to bear arms, and if a few praised this opinion of theirs, the majority despised it as if coming from their lack of patriotism, fear, or cowardice. The younger Quakers were unwilling to put up with this accusation, and quite a few of them abandoned the Society in order to take up arms. This decrease in subjects had not yet altered the principles of their morality, until the multiplicity of disorders and

21. Raynal, *A Philosophical and Political History of the Settlements and Trade of the Europeans in the East and West Indies*, 6:29-30.

crimes, the natural consequences of a civil war, led astray many of these sectarians and changed the public sentiment, which previously held the very best opinion of them.[22]

On the other hand, a letter from Philadelphia, dated August 30, 1769, and published in the *Gazzetta di Milano*, documents the resolve to enfranchise the slaves. This letter was acclaimed by European philanthropists and "progressives":

Our Quakers gave an unusual proof of love for humanity. The majority of the residents of that colony agreed to free all their black Slaves. Of what use is it to protest against the tyranny of the British Parliament, if we also are tyrants and keep enslaved human beings who are similar to us, just because they have black skin and woolly heads? We want other Religious Societies to follow the example of their Brothers, the Quakers.[23]

Vincenzio Martinelli, the author of *Istoria del governo d'Inghilterra e delle sue colonie in India e nell'America settentrionale*, also praised the Quakers who, "not bearing to see [slavery] in a society which by law mandated freedom of action," did not force "those poor blacks under the yoke of slavery."[24] The issue of slavery contrasted with the libertarian, egalitarian aspirations of the insurgents, and was often a pretext for "traditionalist" condemnation of the lack of coherence in policy as it was seen to limit the effectiveness of the Revolution. This contrast between slavery and ideals of "independence" inevitably added complexity to the meaning of American "freedom." It highlighted its contradictions and provoked a series of polemical pieces from different sides.[25] The abbot Roberti, writing from a "traditionalist" perspective, which tended to underestimate and dampen the revolutionary fervor, asserted, in opposition to Raynal, that slavery had not completely disappeared in Pennsylvania. In support of his contention, Roberti described with compassion the current life of the blacks, who

22. Luigi Castiglioni, *Viaggio* (2:36-37), 227.
23. *La gazzetta di Milano*, 2:611.
24. Vincenzio Martinelli, *Istoria del governo d'Inghilterra*, 91.
25. Filippo Mazzei (*Researches*, 344) notes that "men who love justice and humanity are naturally surprised to learn that although the principles embodied in the new state governments proclaim liberty and equality, slavery still exists in the United States."

only have one hour in which to eat and their food consists of few roots with salt as sole condiment. They rarely enjoy the pleasure of a little meat, milk or lard, or a dried herring. When they come back at dusk from a day's labor in the fields, they are taken to the tobacco warehouses. Those who are slow are inevitably whipped on their naked back.[26]

At the end of the 1770s, Luigi Castiglioni's *Viaggio,* together with the chapter "The Quakers" in Mazzei's *Researches,* offered the only direct testimony from the Italian intellectual generation of the late eighteenth century about Philadelphia's Quakers, who, for "[their] simplicity of customs . . . ought to serve as an example to the other Americans."[27] Castiglioni rejected the traditional identification of Quakers with Pennsylvanians that had been generally accepted for an entire century. Yet he admitted that in Philadelphia "the customs of the people are not different from those of nearby cities, especially New York, except insofar as the Quakers are concerned, who make up most of the population of Philadelphia." Castiglioni went on to trace a brief history of the Quakers and their commendable customs:

> This sect, which originated in England shortly before the arrival in America of William Penn, began to spread among the lowest class of the people, who were very soon joined also by some of the more wealthy. A number of them arrived in America with William Penn and began by establishing complete freedom of conscience. The constant friendship that was seen to reign among the members of that Society, the beneficence that they exercised toward the poor of every faith, their honesty in business transactions, along with their exemplary customs and the patience with which they endured derision and persecutions, made them quickly the object of universal admiration and the model of good and useful citizens.[28]

He also observed the "lifestyle" of Penn's followers:

26. Quoted in Piero Del Negro, *Il mito americano*, 216. For references to the debate on slavery then taking place in Veneto, see 214-16.
27. *Viaggio* (2:166), 269.
28. Ibid. (2:35), 226.

Italy and the New America 117

The amusements of dancing, gambling, and music are forbidden, hence they spend the evening in family conversation; and during the hours of the days when they are not busy both men and women apply themselves to reading, so that their company is very pleasing and instructive.[29]

But Castiglioni perceived a certain decadence in these healthy customs, a decadence he attributed to the revolutionary maelstrom, insofar as Quakers had been corrupted by "the natural consequences of a civil war, [that] led astray many of these sectarians and changed the public sentiment, which previously held the very best opinion of them."[30] Although he admitted that there were some among them who preserved their earlier customs and did not follow the changes produced in the others by the "wretchedness of the times," he added:

The number of Quakers drops from day to day, since the young ladies marry persons of other sects, with the result that in the course of a few generations there will exist in America only the name of a Society to which Pennsylvania owns [sic] its flourishing countryside and Philadelphia its preeminence over the other capitals of the United States.[31]

Accordingly, keeping up with modern times involved a deterioration of Quaker philosophy and a loss of those simple customs that had been, and still were, the reason for the esteem Pennsylvania enjoyed among Europeans.

29. Ibid. (2:37), 227.
30. Ibid.
31. Ibid. (2:37-38), 227-28. In alluding to the weakening of Quaker orthodoxy, Castiglioni continues (2:36), 227: "They remained so long as they attracted to themselves the eyes of the multitude; but when the wonder produced by the novelty wore off, their fervor also ceased, and the simplicity of their manners was henceforth constantly altered. Contortions were given up, the pretension of being inspired was abandoned, and only the right common to all to speak up in their churches was maintained. Even the girls, upon seeing that their modest dress was no longer the object of admiration, strove to arouse the attention of the men by adopting dresses of richer fabrics and to show off their beauty by means of a studied simplicity. These modifications in their principles were not very important until the time of the Revolution, when they became greater and of greater consequence."

2. Benjamin Franklin's Image

The choice of Pennsylvania as a reference point for the evaluation of the New America was undoubtedly related to the popularity that Franklin enjoyed. Already in the 1750s, translations of his letters had begun to circulate, and from the very first, thanks to his plurality of interests, the celebrated Bostonian was officially accepted as a paragon of the Enlightenment. In 1754, Algarotti wrote to the Bolognese scientist Giacomo Mariscotti that

> from English America we not only get tobacco and indigo, but philosophical systems as well. From Philadelphia a Quaker sent us the world's most beautiful reflections and arguments on electricity. All of Europe's electrical scientists should take their hat off to this American.[32]

To most of the Italian public in the eighteenth century, Franklin's name was known particularly in connection with his successes in physics. Only later, when the English colonies would come to occupy first place in international events, did his name come to be associated with his political and philosophical work. His brilliant scientific career and his exploration of the "mysteries of nature was felt to be somehow a function of a more natural way of life and a confirmation of the idea that America brought out in its happy dwellers a simple yet profound wisdom, love for fellowman, and scorn for the corruptive frills of civilization."[33] Vincenzio Martinelli emphasized that, to Franklin, "the Universe is indebted for the most useful discovery ever made by Philosophy throughout the centuries," and that "a Poet could state without exaggeration, that this excellent Philosopher taught the art of snatching the thunderbolts from the hands of Jupiter."[34] The image of the scientist and inventor influenced contemporary literature. Parini alluded to the discovery of the lightning rod in *La recita dei versi:* "Another strips Jove's right hand of thunderbolts . . ." ("*A Giove altri l'armata / destra di fulmin spoglia . . .*") (lines 19-20). And the

---

32. Francesco Algarotti, letter to Signor Abate Taruffi of June 23, 1755, in *Opere* (Venice, 1792), 9:105.
33. Antonio Pace, *Benjamin Franklin and Italy* (Philadelphia: American Philosophical Society, 1958), 121.
34. Vincenzio Martinelli, *Istoria del governo d'Inghilterra*, 94.

Milanese Luigi Bossi was inspired by Franklin in his brief poem, "The lightning rods" (1776) where street lighting was praised:

> Your mind, excellent Franklin,
> The wise Goddess had enlightened,
> And by her powers where before
> The only known electric fire
> Was that which the thunderbolt
> Endowed with evil power,
> You she did show the secret whereof I speak.
> She alit on Philadelphia and from the Tower
> Showed you how the thunderbolt to unchain.[35]

Toward the end of the 1770s the literati's admiration for Franklin's personality shifted to his philosophical and political qualities, and the image of the inventor was replaced by that of the "American philosopher" and statesman. Giuseppe Compagnoni, author of *Storia dell'America* (1828), in 1777 asked Franklin's authorization to dedicate to him a poem on the Revolution, entitled "Washington." The Tuscan poet, Giovanni Fantoni, a contemporary of Alfieri, in his Anacreontic ode "A Palmiro Cidonio" (1778), described Franklin as the "new Brutus," defender of Pennsylvania's freedom:

> The Tyrants' yoke is shaken
> by the despised American
> whom the new Brutus from Pennsylvania
> taught how to triumph.[36]

Franklin became a symbol of freedom for the New World, as would also be clear in Alfieri's odes to *America libera*.

---

35. Quoted in Antonio Pace, *Benjamin Franklin and Italy*, 244. Here we must recall Vincenzo Monti's ode *Al signor di Mongolfier* in which there is a reference to the lightning rod: "From heaven you seized the thunderbolt / which now defeated / fell before you / and with broken wings / gently touched at your feet" ("Rapisti al ciel le folgori, / che debellate innante / con tronche ali ti cadde, / e ti lambir le piante.") in *Opere*, ed. Manara Valgimigli and Carlo Muscetta (Milan: Ricciardi, 1953), 739, lines 117-20. The Jesuit Giuseppe Maria Mazzolari in 1767 also composed a poem in Latin modeled after *De rerum natura* by Lucretius, dedicated to electricity (*Electricorum libri*; 1767).

36. Giovanni Fantoni, *Poesie* (Bari: Laterza, 1913), 22, lines 8-11.

Franklin's relationship to the New World had been seen as accidental at first (he was an "Englishman in America," not an "American"); only after the 1770s did his persona undergo a process of "Americanization"[37] and become the symbol of the first modern political system. This shift in perspective must be considered together with the consolidation of a political-cultural identity for the English colonies.

In 1774 the publisher Marelli published in Milan *Scelta di lettere e opuscoli* by Franklin, "a first-class literary figure" and a "person devoted to the common good."[38] The selection included mostly letters on scientific arguments (there were also two on music).[39] It opened with a translation of Barbeau Dubourg's *Summary* of the French edition of the writings of this "American philosopher." The author of the *Summary* noted:

> Born with a sensible spirit and raised among Quakers, he was able to reject its strange aspects; but where would he have been able to acquire a taste for frivolity? Dedicated uninterruptedly to the service of his Country, he was always loved and respected by his fellow citizens, being the spirit of their councils at home, and the chargé d'affaires of their interests abroad. Both at home and abroad he always fulfilled their wishes and in exchange was always able to inspire in them what he desired for the common good.[40]

Luigi Castiglioni as well, after praising the Philadelphia Philosophical Society (1769) and other American cultural institutions, contributed to Franklin's glorification in the following portrayal:

> Thus these, like other societies founded for the public welfare, were promoted by the celebrated Benjamin Franklin, to whom America owes so much, and who in his advanced old age continues to be

---

37. See Piero Del Negro, *Il mito americano*, 242.
38. *Scelta di lettere e di opuscoli*, 4. The translator stresses that the "ambition to make known and circulate the beautiful, new, and useful teachings scattered especially in his letters, could earn me a kind compassion for the possibly excessive courage I have shown in publishing a translation from a language, English, whose properties and subtleties I know not sufficiently (3)."
39. It is a recurrent theme in Franklin's writings, as evidenced by the letter he sent to the physicist Giambattista Beccaria of Turin ("The Harmonica." Letter from Mr. Benjamin Franklin to Father Giambattista Beccaria, Royal Professor of Physics at the University of Turin, translated from English into Italian [1769]).
40. *Scelta di lettere e di opuscoli*, 12.

useful to his country both with political discussions and with literary productions always directed to the advantage of humanity. His merits in the sciences are too well known in Europe for me to recall them now. . . . His face is sincere and venerable, his manner friendly and courteous, and his conversation always instructive. Although he has been employed for many years in public office, he has not thereby increased his wealth, and his neat but simple dress harmonizes perfectly with his character and his writings. In short, he can be said to be one of those rare respectable philosophers who behave according to their pronounced maxims.[41]

Castiglioni proceeded to narrate the life of the acclaimed statesman and praised his unfailing intuition when, at the time of the reform of Pennsylvania's constitution, he stated that

those laws which were excellent during the turmoils of war could be harmful in peace, and that one should do as the good gardener who, in order to have many fruit from a tree, condemns and cuts those very branches at first kept by him with all care in order to make it grow from the roots.[42]

In opposition to the theory of the degeneration of "savages" and settlers held by the naturalists of the time, Castiglioni claimed that

without having been in America, knowing the names of Washington and Franklin is sufficient to reveal what basis such a strange assertion has. But if to these more famous men one wants to add the others who distinguished themselves in the arts and sciences, as well as in war, the catalogue of the illustrious men of the United States would be a large one.[43]

There followed a list of personalities such as Lincoln, Madison, and Jefferson, to show once and for all the arbitrary character of the theories of Buffon and De Pauw on the inferiority of "savages" and of those Europeans who had moved to America. As we have seen, it was at about the same time

41. Luigi Castiglioni, *Viaggio* (2:38-39, 41), 228, 229.
42. Ibid. (2:41), 229.
43. Ibid. (2:160-61), 267.

that Gian Rinaldo Carli also rejected the theory of American degeneration. He forwarded two copies of the edition of his *Lettere americane* (1781-83) to Franklin (one copy was addressed to the Philosophical Society). Carli's work opened with a dedication by Isidoro Bianchi to Benjamin Franklin, "a competent judge of this book's merit," where the point was made that in Italy it was Carli who first "gave us the most dignified and adequate idea of that vast continent."[44] America, as perceived by Europeans through Franklin's writings, is governed by a new work ethic and a new reverence for success and riches. There, "those who are industrious . . . have no need to fear scarcity" and "hunger turns to look at the door of the hard-working man, but dares not enter."[45] Personal virtues are valued in the New America, as emphasized in *Information to Those Who Would Remove to America:*

> Much less is it adviseable for a Person to go thither who had no other Quality to recommend him but his Birth. In Europe it had indeed its Value, but it is a Commodity that cannot be carried to a worse Market than to that of America, where People do not enquire concerning a Stranger, *What IS he?* but *What can he DO?*[46]

In contrast, during roughly the same period, Crèvecoeur's *Lettres d'un cultivateur américain* evoked a pastoral image of America. It was the pragmatism of the "wise man from Philadelphia" that released the New World from the myth of Arcadia, and invited eighteenth-century intellectuals to take a new look at the American myth and to evaluate the social and political system of the United States realistically:

---

44. *Dedica al Dottor Beniamino Franklin, Lettere americane*, vol. 1.
45. *Il povero Ricciardo e la costituzione di Pensilvania, italianizzati per uso della Democratica Veneta Restaurazione* (Venice, 1797), 10-11. *Poor Richard's Almanac* published in Philadelphia from 1733 to 1758 was tailored along the lines of *Poor Robin's*, an English almanac. Several fictitious characters, such as Prince Richard Sunders, appeared in Franklin's almanac contributing witty remarks and pieces of wisdom. On *Povero Ricciardo*, Antonio Pace is enlightening; see his *Benjamin Franklin and Italy*, 205-34.
46. *Information to Those Who Would Remove to America*, in *Writing*, 976-77. Castiglioni supports Franklin's advice (*Viaggio* [2:159]), 266: "Emigrations from Europe formerly contributed a great deal to increase the population of those regions, but later, when they were composed of lazy and wicked people, they were more harmful than useful, because emigrants, as Franklin rightly asserts, should be industrious individuals and skillful in some art or craft in order to succeed, since the notion that to become rich all one needs to do is to go to America is completely false."

In short America is the Land of Labour, and by no means what the English call *Lubberland,* and the French *Pays de Cocagne,* where the Streets are said to be pav'd with half-peck Loaves, the Houses til'd with Pancakes, and where the Fowls fly about ready roasted, crying, *Come eat me!*[47]

A quick survey of Franklin's myth in the last three decades of the century indicates that the fame which the acclaimed Pennsylvanian enjoyed with the Italian public at large was especially due to a wide circulation of his moral and political writings, rather than his scientific writings. He "who stole the heavenly thunderbolt" became "father, counsellor, soul, mind / of an emerging freedom"[48] and a "demigod" of the New America.

3. Revolution and Vittorio Alfieri's *America libera*

In a letter sent from London in 1776 to his brother Amedeo, Baretti chose to "satisfy" the latter's "curiosity" on the issue of the "current raging dispute between England and its Colonies."[49] Baretti looked at the

47. Ibid., 978.
48. "Rapitor del fulmine celeste . . . padre, consiglio, anima, mente / di libertà nascente." Vittorio Alfieri, *L'America libera,* in *Opere di Vittorio Alfieri,* ed. Francesco Maggini (Florence: Le Monnier, 1933), 305, ode 4, lines 9-10. The ode to "America the free," which extols General Washington opens with an invocation to Franklin: (lines 1-16): "You, who stole the heavenly thunderbolt / Already since your young years / Now more daringly and with no less ingeniousness / From the hands of an earthly undeserving Jove / Thunderbolts inimical to the good you snatched / That caused greater misery / And reigned over the strong; / You, FRANKLIN / Still living seated with the demigods / And father, counsellor, soul, mind / Of an emerging freedom, / Be guardian to my song; in you I place / Hope, that hidden / Drama of ethereal flame all of which you hold / May now breathe in my bosom; / So that, if praise should no longer reach you / I may boldly look into your reflection." ("Tu, rapitor del fulmine celeste / Già fin da' tuoi verdi anni, / Ch'or con più ardire, e non minore ingegno, / Apportatrici di più lunghi affanni / Saette ai buoni infeste / Tolte hai di man di terren Giove indegno, / D'aver sui forti regno; / Tu, vivo ancor fra' semidei già posto, FRANKLIN, padre, consiglio, anima, mente / di libertà nascente; / Tu mi sii scorta al canto; ho in te risposto / Speme, che di nascosto / Dramma d'etereo foco, / Ond'hai tu il tutto, entro il mio petto or spiri; / Si che, se laude in te più non ha loco, / Nel tuo secondo audacemente io miri.")
49. *Epistolario,* in *Opere,* ed. Franco Fido (Milan: Rizzoli, 1967), 1055. Earlier, in 1769, the *Gazzetta di Milano* whose editor was Giuseppe Parini, had published a series of

dispute from a decidedly pro-English perspective, granting to Parliament the full right of taxation of the colonies.[50] He was appalled that even in England there could be people who supported the Americans' position and endeavored with all their power to further their cause, to the "detriment of their own fatherland." Such foolish backing of the rebels was due to a mistaken interpretation of the "word freedom, which was never understood correctly by a bestial and most ignorant rabble."[51] For Baretti, the very ideological motivation for the revolt was contradictory, insofar as Americans fought to free themselves from a state such as England, an "avowedly liberal" state. Nevertheless, although he was an unconditional admirer of British political institutions and recognized the military and naval superiority of England,[52] he objectively assessed the factors that

---

letters on the "American disorders." In a letter mailed from London on January 17 we read (2:73): "It looks as if the disturbances and unrest are growing in North America as well as in the West Indies, as the local administrations have been suspended since, in accordance with instructions forwarded to the governors, provincial assemblies have been suppressed until such time as the Court and Parliament will have determined a way to end the current dispute." Again, concerning the internal opposition in the English Parliament: "To the disturbances internal to the kingdom are now added those of our American colonies where, according to an express communication to the Court, the news is quite unpleasant. Apparently, serious riots occurred between the inhabitants of Boston and the military stationed there; and other events as well." We should recall here the translation of the *Lettere istoriche curiose e interessanti sopra gli affari correnti d'Africa, e d'America* (Venice: Colombani, 1775) where the letters about America all deal with the colonial events. In letter 49 dated September 3, 1775, the intentions of the Americans are clarified: "We fight neither for glory nor for a desire to achieve glory. On the contrary, we present humankind with a spectacle worthy of their attention, that of a people attacked by foes, who were not provoked and who cannot accuse us of any crime. They glorify themselves for their privileges; they take pride in being a civilized people; yet the sweetest conditions they offer are *slavery* or *death*. In our fatherland we have taken up arms to defend that freedom which is our birthright, and which we had continuously enjoyed until the latest attacks against it."

50. "Americans . . . want . . . to establish an American parliament or assembly chosen by their votes, and they want this body, instead of parliament, to have the authority to tax them: that is, they only want to pay what pleases them, which amounts to saying that they absolutely do not want to concur in supporting that government to which they owe all they have; that if England had not, of its own expense, discovered America and given it to them, and therefore supported and defended it, what the devil would they have?" (ibid., 1059).

51. Ibid.

52. "All the principal American cities lay along the seacoast. What will prevent the English from setting them on fire, one after the other, thus reducing their inhabitants to the most extreme conditions? The English will say: American gentlemen, if we must be friends, you must submit. If you refuse, you are our enemies and as such, what else can we do but burn all the cities, ruin and uproot you? Up to now we did not do you much harm and let you toddle about because at the beginning of every war we are never armed; today, however, we all fully armed and come to you with all our might. Either we set you on fire and annihilate

might lead to a British defeat and the possible international repercussions of such a war:

> Let us spend two words on the obstacles that could arise. France is always jealous of the powerful military strength of this kingdom which, through its colonies, was able for some time to maintain a decidedly large number of sailors, its main asset. Just recently Spain was highly offended by the attempt made to block the Strait of Magellan. Both must be desirous of taking revenge for the many damages sustained in the past war [the Seven Years' War]. Holland is quite jealous and envious of our huge trade. Prussia is not willing to be our friend and yearns to become somehow a maritime power.[53]

Along with these inevitable international repercussions, the disastrous effects of internal conflict also were evaluated:

> With all these dangers before their eyes, nine Englishmen out of ten, instead of showing solidarity with each other, rip each other apart with cruel words and fiery writings. Some want it hot, some want it cold, they are full of rancor against each other. Those few who speak wisely and for the common good are not at all listened to. Disagreement reigns in all their assemblies and is more triumphant than it was in Agamemnon's camp.[54]

Despite this pessimistic outlook, Baretti favored a definitive agreement between opposing parliamentary factions as a condition for military victory: "Yet, who knows? Perhaps everything will go well for England, a country as rich in valorous souls as it is in money. Perhaps, faced with greater and closer dangers, they will put a stop to animosities and will

---

you, or you must surrender and let us impose on you those laws which we judge will be able to contain you in the future. What choice do you think the Americans will make, left with this inevitable alternative? Will they want to be burned and destroyed?" (ibid., 1062).

53. Ibid., 1068.

54. Ibid., 1069. "Abysses everywhere. On one side, fear and indolence; on the other side, stubbornness. Meanwhile, expenses rise, and taxes and fees multiply. Only God knows how high they will rise. In addition, the general debt is mounting and its interest must be paid punctually through new taxes and fees. This one internal obstacle works against the happy outcome of our plans" (ibid., 1067).

suddenly all come together, thus healing all evil, because a unanimously united Parliament will make the world tremble."[55]

In November 1777 Baretti was strongly convinced of an imminent triumph of the British forces, and he wrote to Francesco Carcano, who had previously accused him of being "partial to the English," that "the power of the English nation is endless and that . . . if it does not defeat America this year, it will certainly defeat her the following year."[56] But just one month later, his letters to his brothers, dated December 5 and 12, revealed that he had changed his mind about the outcome of the war, as he acknowledged that "America will escape their hand, as it counts on too many people, large and small, who here openly side with her and want to see her acquire independence from England by any means."[57] As Fido pointed out, Baretti was one of the first Italian intellectuals to develop an interpretation of the American war and assess its causes and consequences.[58] But we must wait until Chiari for the Revolution to take its place in the sphere of fiction, and then only in a background role. Chiari, always willing to utilize current events as a backdrop for his novels, published his novel *La corsara francese della guerra presente* in the last two issues of his *Trattenimenti dello spirito umano sopra le cose passate presenti e possibili ad avvenire* (11-12; 1781). In the space of twenty years, a period from the Seven Years' War to the American Revolution, the novel's heroine would face incredibly complicated adventures that would take her from the Canadian forests to Boston and Philadelphia. Although he gave no space to political events, Chiari still made clear his support of the insurgents' cause and his sympathy for the emerging republic.[59]

Alfieri's odes to *America libera*[60] were undoubtedly the "cradle" of the Italian literary myth of Revolution and of a New World synonymous with freedom and democracy. Alfieri's enthusiasm for the American cause was especially clear between 1777, the year in which he wrote the essay *Of Tyranny* and 1786, when he completed the third book of *The Prince and Letters,* which contains interesting observations on the political events of the colonies. In this ten-year period, the circulation of news from overseas in Italy was documented not only by propaganda in magazines

---

55. Ibid.
56. *La scelta delle lettere*, ed. Leone Piccioni (Bari: Laterza, 1912), 130.
57. Letter of December 12, 1977; ibid., 289.
58. See *Epistolario*, 289.
59. On *La corsara francese*, see Piero Del Negro, *Il mito americano*, 202-3.
60. (Asti: Kehl, 1784).

and periodicals, but particularly by certain exemplary texts on English America, such as Raynal's *History,* the moral-political works of Benjamin Franklin and Vincenzio Martinelli's *Istoria del governo d'Inghilterra e delle sue colonie in India e nell'America settentrionale.*

Although it was his sympathy for the revolutionary events in general that incited him to compose the five odes of *America libera,* Alfieri's interpretation of the Revolution represented a unique example in the literary generation at the turn of the century, in that he identified in the war of independence completely new values and original impulses. Inevitably however, his understanding of the Revolution must in some way be situated and assessed in the context of the aversion to tyranny that Alfieri developed during these years of the colonists' rebellion against England. An understanding of the odes must therefore begin with the definition the poet from Asti gives to tyranny, and his distrust of enlightened reform.

The treatise's two books are founded on two extreme beliefs: reciprocal fear (of the tyrant by his subjects and vice versa) is the primary element on which tyranny is founded; the second is that a free man is faced with no solution other than the murder of the despot, suicide, or isolation. Although he accepted Montesquieu's distinction of powers, Alfieri rejected the latter's distinction between "despotism" (the authority of an individual who rules alone, without laws) and "monarchy" (the authority of an individual who rules alone, but through laws). For Alfieri any form of government that has the prerogative of repressing the free will of the individual must, by definition, be considered a tyranny. He specified:

> Tyranny is the name that must be applied without distinction to any government in which he who is charged with the execution of the laws may make, destroy, break, interpret, hinder, and suspend them, or even only evade them with assurance of impunity. And so, in any case, the lawbreaker, whether he be hereditary or elective, usurper or legitimate, good or bad, one or many, who has sufficient force to do this is a tyrant; every society which accepts him is a tyranny; every nation which endures him is servile. And vice versa, that government must be considered a tyranny in which he who is charged with creating laws can execute them himself.[61]

61. Vittorio Alfieri, *Of Tyranny,* trans., ed., and intro. Julius A. Molinari and Beatrice Corrigan (Toronto: University of Toronto Press, 1961), book 1, chap. 2, p. 11.

In rejecting any effective evolution of enlightened despotism, Alfieri conceived rigid, extreme concepts exalting an aristocratic notion of "liberty" understood as a "divine incomparable flame which in only a few breasts burns purely in all its vastness, and which by those few alone is faintly kindled and kept alive with difficulty in the frozen hearts of the majority."[62] Furthermore, he stated: "the first of all remedies against tyranny, silent and slow though it may be, is always the consciousness of it," thus expressing the need for a period of reflection preparatory to rebellion that arises with "energy, boldness, and (so to speak) a sacred rage to unmask, combat, and destroy tyranny."[63]

For Alfieri, the thrill of revolution is not in the reconstructive phase when a new form of government is founded, but in the initial, destructive phase when old institutions are demolished. From this point of view, the American Revolution was an explicit attack on despotism, an effort to establish an "English freedom," without the compromise of monarchy. In a page of *The Prince and Letters* Alfieri pointed to the English and Americans as an example of a modern free people, comparable to the Romans among ancient people:

> If in these two peoples, the modern English and American, and the ancient Roman, I investigate causes of their liberty and hence of their progress, happiness, virtue, and greatness, I invariably find the principal one to be a full cognizance of their own rights. Rights which were bestowed by nature upon all men, but which in a principality, a state contrary to nature, were degraded, usurped, bartered, and corrupted. In Rome tribunes guarded these sacred rights, in England the House of Commons, and I do not know yet who will watch over the nascent liberty of America: although, as she does not have nobility or clergy, vigilance will be much less necessary: since it is never the community that seeks to prejudice the rights of the community.

On this observation Alfieri built his belief that "liberty is born and promulgated, preserved, and defended, principally by those men who, by teaching peoples their rights, provide them with the necessary means of

---

62. Ibid., book 2, chap. 8, p. 100.
63. Ibid., 99.

defending them. Moreover, liberty represents the only true life of a people; for we find it to be the source of all great things accomplished by men.[64] In attempting to repress the settlers' rebellion, the English had betrayed the ideal of independence that had inspired two revolutions in the previous century and persuaded progressive Europe to recognize England as a guide toward freedom:

> Englishmen, care you no more for honor?
> You, who for so long
> Had meant for freedom to exist,
> By unjust, absolute desires are trying
> To now be enslaved?[65]

Again, an epigram from 1783 reads:

> The English, being already free, now sell themselves:
> The Gauls wake up and strive for themselves:
> The miserly Batavians know not what they are themselves:
> The troubled Spaniards boast about themselves:
> What is this? What is this?
> America laughs: it no longer has a king.[66]

Alfieri had come to think of the English as "enemies of freedom." An English victory would mean the dissolution of constructive libertarian opposition to European despotism:

---

64. Vittorio Alfieri, *The Prince and Letters*, trans. Beatrice Corrigan and Julius Molinaro, intro. and notes by Beatrice Corrigan (Toronto: University of Toronto Press, 1972), 150. In *Of Tyranny* Alfieri states (book 1, chap. 2, p. 13): "In this class [tyranny] I reckon all the present kingdoms of Europe, with the single exception so far of England." In the first book *Of Tyranny* there is an interesting reference to New America, in the chapter "Of Religion" (42): "In time, its excess of abuses forced some peoples who were more wise than imaginative to curb it, stripping it of many harmful superstitions. And these people, later distinguished by the name of heretics, thus opened once more a path for liberty, which was born anew and flourished admirably among them after she had long been banished from Europe; this is proved to us by the Swiss, by Holland, by many cities of Germany, by England, and by new America."

65. "Angli, a voi nulla il vostro onor più cale? / Voi, che a si lunga prova / Già intendeste che fosse libertade / Di voglie ingiuste ed assolute, a prova / Schiavi or vi fate?"; ode 1, in *Opere*, 290, lines 33-37.

66. "Gli Angli, già liberi, or vendon sé: / I Galli svegliansi e fan per sé: / Gli avari Batavi non san di sé: / Gl'Ispani torbidi millantan sé: / Che n'è, che n'è? / Ride l'America: non ha più re" (ibid., 189).

In our own era, by driving out royal authority while still retaining her kings under the infrangible shield of laws, England rose in power and glory in less than a century; and we see her in our day confronting alone the many stronger European monarchies aligned against her, often vanquishing them and so far never vanquished. Consequently in the recent war against America nearly nine million Englishmen were seen facing twenty or more million Frenchmen, ten or so million Spaniards, and five or six million Dutch or Americans. A political miracle which cannot be explained except by admitting that one free man is worth at least six slaves. Yet since the Americans were fighting for their liberty, they were not conquered in their war against the English, who in America assumed the role of slaves and tyrants rather than that of free men.[67]

Having postulated a correlation between England and despotism, Alfieri went on to give a general definition of the Revolution as opposition to tyranny, and consequently anti-English. The fact that he was removed from the war made this idealization easier, as a radical alternative to the decay of European political institutions. We must agree with Bairati that the type of revolution that Alfieri accepted as a model of freedom, must somehow be "removed in space like the American [Revolution], or projected into the future of prophecy, like the Italian [Revolution]; it cannot however be associated with the misery and hardship of experience and real life, like the French [Revolution]."[68] Alfieri saw the American insurrection as a "people's" revolt with no class distinction, as opposed to the French Revolution a revolt of the "lowest classes." It is essential to distinguish between "people" and "lowest classes" in order to understand Alfieri's different attitudes with respect to the two revolutions of his times:

> May I explain once and for all that when I say PEOPLE, I only mean that mass of citizens and peasants of more less moderate circumstances, who possess private resources or trades, and have wives, children, and relatives: but I never include that more numerous but much less worthy class of indigents of the lowest populace. No form of government, not even pure Democracy, should or can have any regard for those individuals other than to see that they never lack

---

67. *The Prince and Letters*, book 3, chap. 10, p. 149.
68. Pietro Bairati, *Alfieri e la rivoluzione americana*, in *Italia e America dal Settecento all'età dell'imperialismo* (Venice: Marsilio, 1976), 68.

either bread, justice, or fear, accustomed as they are to live from day to day, indifferent to any form of government since they have nothing to lose, living in cities mostly, and consequently very corrupt and unprincipled. For if any of those three things is lacking, every good form of society may be overturned or even completely destroyed by them.[69]

To Alfieri, the American revolutionaries are, for the most part, farmer-soldiers:

> Every peasant into bold warrior turned
> For the great cause, I see;
> And I see the rustic hoe and plowshare
> Into shiny saber made, rotating
> Being plunged into the oppressor.[70]

As Mauzi[71] pointed out, Alfieri's idealization of rustic life led him to condone rebellions and riots that, in another context, would be clearly considered subversive. The image of New America and the Revolution received by eighteenth-century Europe was primarily rural. This simple—hence genuine—farmers' life of the settlers was praised in several turn-of-the-century texts, such as the *Lettres d'un cultivateur américain* by Crèvecoeur, Mazzei's *Researches on the United States,* and Castiglioni's *Travels in the United States of North America.* As Carlo Botta would write in his *History of the War of Independence of the United States of America,* the settlers' propensity for freedom was a result of life on the farm, and a direct contact with nature (see Chapter 5): "Finding all his enjoyments in rural life, [the settler] saw spring up, grow, prosper, and arrive at maturity, under his own eyes, and often by the labor of his own hands, all things necessary to the life of man; he felt himself free from all subjection, from all dependence."[72]

69. *Of Tyranny*, book 1, chap. 7, p. 39n.
70. "Ogni bifolco in pro' guerrier converso / Per la gran causa io miro; / E la rustica marra e il vomer farsi / Lucido brando, che rotante in giro / Negli oppressor fia immerso" (ode 4, in *Opere*, 292, lines 113-17).
71. See Robert Mauzi, *L'idée du bonheur dans la littérature et la pensée françaises au XVIIIe siècle* (Paris: Armand Colin, 1967), in particular the chapters "Bonheur et condition sociale" and "L'immobilité de la vie heureuse."
72. Carlo Botta, *History of the War of the Independence of the United States of America*, trans. George Alexander Otis, 2d ed., in 2 vols., revised and corrected (Boston: Harrison Gray, 1826), 1:14.

In Alfieri's view, the American Revolution was a "farmer's" revolution and was an authentic war for independence, while the French Revolution was essentially an "urban" phenomenon. In *Misogallo,* while censuring the "plebeian" character of the 1789 revolution and the deterioration of the ideals that had inspired it, the poet would point to the freedom of the New World as an alternative to French demagogy. *Dialogo tra un libero ed un liberto* (1794), a dialogue between the "free" American and the French "freedman" embodied the two nations' conflicting ideologies:

FREEDMAN: Although I never saw you in my days, your frank look and your manly behavior reveal from the first that you are a free man.

FREE MAN: In fact I take pride in being so, by birth and inclination.

FREEDMAN: Were you perchance born in English America?

FREE MAN: Yes, just so; from my early years I was a soldier for my motherland; and at last I was greatly comforted in seeing reestablished and strengthened that first freedom, under whose auspices our colonies had been founded, but which the British government had later unjustly violated. . . .

FREEDMAN: I would sooner believe that you come from the Moon, than from America. Don't you know that no other people except us are left in Europe?

FREE MAN: You, meaning the French? Since I never read public papers, as I have no time to waste, what you say is news to me, nor did I ever know that you were a People.

FREEDMAN: What? While the whole world resounds and trembles with our victories and conquests, you know not that the French have become a true, great People?

FREE MAN: I knew that the French, subjects of a de facto absolute King, were sending opportune aid to my country so as to remove her from England's property. And, to tell the truth, I inwardly blushed (as did many other Americans) in thinking that the slaves of an absolute King were to be our tools to freedom against a motherland who, although unjust toward us, was herself also free.[73]

---

73. *Dialogo di un uomo libero e di un liberto,* in *Scritti politici e morali,* a cura di Pietro Cazzani (Asti: Casa dell'Alfieri, 1951), 169–72.

In the American "people's" revolution, born of freedom and directed toward its permanent attainment, Alfieri's tragic and aristocratic temperament came to identify exceptional men as the heroes of independence: Franklin, Lafayette, and especially Washington. Already the first book of *The Prince and Letters* listed Washington among the "few other great men who conceived or carried out important revolutions" such as "Junius, Brutus, Pelopidas, William Tell, William of Nassau,"[74] and in the fourth ode he exhorted him to unmask "the enemies of freedom":

> Come forward, WASHINGTON: the time has come
> That you will show freedom's traitors
> How they shall pay for their offence.
> No other memorable warrior's feats
> Will stand before this one.
> Already you face the foe
> To press on him his last sorrows.
> Oh victory, worthy of your human heart![75]

This is neither transitory enthusiasm nor rhetorical gratification; in 1788 he dedicated *Bruto primo* to Washington, that "most famous, most free of men" and forwarded to him a copy of *America libera*,[76] in the certainty that "only the name of America's liberator can stand next to the tragedy of Rome's liberator."[77] The colonies' war for freedom became a model for the rebirth of the spirit of Rome, and for a consequent rebirth of future Italian generations. Implicitly, "America" echoed for Alfieri the idea of liberty, and therefore revolution, at least in its first stage, the struggle

---

74. *The Prince and Letters*, book 1, chap. 8, p. 22.

75. "Esci, WASHINGTON, esci: ecco l'istante, / Ove scontar le offese / Ai traditor di libertà farai. / Tra le guerriere memorande imprese / Nulla starà davante / A questa tua. Già incontro all'oste vai, / Recando ultimi guai. / Oh dell' uman tuo cor vittoria degna!" (ode 4, in *Opere*, 305, lines 113-20).

76. See Franco Fido, *A proposito di un manoscritto dell' "America libera,"* in *Giornale Storico della Letteratura Italiana* 149 (1972), 473: "We do know that at an undetermined date between 1788 and 1789 (that is, during the period in which the letter dedicating the tragedy was written) he gave a copy of Kehl's edition of *America libera* to John Paradise for him to deliver to Washington. Paradise, an English polyglot scholar, . . . had been Washington's guest in Mount Vernon at the end of 1787, but after his return to Europe in 1788 he no longer had the occasion to go to the United States. Alfieri's book therefore was entrusted to the Milanese knight, Paolo Andreani, as documented in a letter from Paradise to the American president of April-May 1790."

77. *Lettere*, in *Opere*, 160.

between independence and tyranny. But the participation of European "tyrants" who offered their "despotic sword" to Americans, not so much in order to free them from slavery, but for selfish, utilitarian purposes, was a mockery of the original revolutionary principles. This belief is especially clear in the last ode, *Pace del 1783*,[78] where it is expressed in an explicit attack on "despotism":

> Alas! But over the vast plains
> Of the ocean, that divides us from
> America, what powerful proud
> Grim blasphemous daemon travels
> Over immense black wings open to the wind?
> It moves from Europe and boldly
> With just the movement of its wings
> It halts the throbbing storm
> That makes us safe and free.
> . . . .
> Alas, who are you, who force to guilty trembling
> Even the most iron-like hearts?
> Only a chosen few
> Whose thirst you quench with blood and feed with gold,
>
> [You] Call trembling to your deadly board,
> And allow them to gorge on others' tears?
> You I do recognize and in vain
> With your crooked eyes
> You signal and threaten me not to say your name:
> You are that evil monster, who was given life
> By fat ignorance, and scrawny
> Fear, who the most sublime flame
> Ices with its dreary face.
> Your name is DESPOTISM; you only
> Guard our wretched shores
> Where in death we live.[79]

---

78. Giovanni Fantoni also composed an ode on the occasion of the end of the war, *Per la pace del 1783* (see *Lirici del Settecento*, 706-7).

79. "Ma, oimè! qual sorge sull'immenso piano / Dell'ocean, che parte / Dall'America noi, fero possente / Sovra negre ali immense all'aura sparte, / Torvio genio profano? / D'Europa ei muove, ei baldanzosamente / La tempesta fremente / Che a noi salvezza e libertade apporta,

Italy and the New America   135

The final ode of *America libera* was composed in Venice in 1783 on the occasion of the peace treaty between England and America.[80] Chronologically detached from his earlier poems, this ode reveals a shift in Alfieri's interpretation of the events overseas. The poet claimed to have written the remainder of the odes "in one breath," but in a letter to Marchioness Alfieri di Sostegno dated May 21, 1783, he touched on the difficulty of composing the last ode and, in general, on a crisis in creativity, which most probably coincided with a waning of his revolutionary enthusiasm: "The poems about America need an addition on the achievement of peace, a kind of short poem. As my spirit is perturbed however, I am unable to compose these additional verses. Everything is thus suspended while I wait for inspiration or for evidence that I cannot proceed. But the additional poem will certainly be written."[81] After the success of the revolution, Alfieri seems to have lost interest. As Fubini pointed out, he "shows that he cannot glimpse in the war of which he sang, the heroic war of which he dreamed . . . nor could he glimpse in the peace which sanctioned America's Independence, that more just order in which he had hoped":[82]

> Why do I now sing of peace?
> While half the herd
> Now knowing why, remains in arms;
> Trembling the other half, unsure even of bread
> Stands still and amazed?
> Is it freedom, that now there protects
> He who here absolute rules?
> Was this a war, where foes

/ Arresta ei sol col ventilar dell'ale. / . . . / Oh! chi se' tu, che a rio tremor costrigni / Anco i cor più ferrigni? / E soli eletti pochi, / Cui di sangue disseti, e d'oro pasci, / Tremanti a tua feral mensa convochi, / E satollar del pianto altrui li lasci? / Tu se' colui, ben ti ravviso e indarno / Cogli occhi torti cenno / Minacciando mi fai, che il nome io taccia: / Tu sei quel mostro rio, cui vita dienno / Pingue ignoranza, e scarno / Timor, che il fuoco il più sublime agghiaccia / Con sua squallida faccia. / DISPOTISMO t'appelli; e sei custode / Tu solo ormai di nostre infauste rive / Dove in morte si vive" (ode 5, in *Opere*, 308-9, lines 49-57 and 75-90).
   80. "Then when I was in Venice and heard that peace was published and established between the Americans and England and that they had secured their complete independence, I wrote the fifth "Ode to Free America," with which I brought that lyrical poem to completion" (*The Life of Vittorio Alfieri, Written by Himself*, trans. Sir Henry McAnally [Lawrence: University of Kansas Press, 1953], 189).
   81. *Lettere*, 20.
   82. Mario Fubini, *Ritratto dell'Alfieri* (Florence: La Nuova Italia, 1967), 94-95.

Searched and never found each other
This, the most atrocious woe?
They have done well: can a lowly herb
That, infused in boiling water, smells
Be a reason for man's death;
Drunk, it weakens body and soul?
Of the lowest infamous Indian shore
America will be poorer and its slave.[83]

The loss of faith in the regenerating energy of revolution was a consequence of the inevitable conflict between ideal principles and the contingencies of political life. America as a "land of freedom" was a metahistorical image destined to be a term for ideal comparison in an equation that is to be resolved only ideologically, not historically or politically.

4. Filippo Mazzei, Witness to Revolution

The Florentine Filippo Mazzei was a prominent personality of the eighteenth century who contributed significantly to the dissemination of ideas on the New America. A physician, farmer, and diplomat, he should be remembered not as a thinker, but above all as a "communicator . . . of a new intellectual climate from the Old to the New World."[84] In the past fifty years American as well as Italian historians[85] have traced the political

---

83. "Che canto io pace ormai? Fia pace questa, / Mentre in armi rimane, / Né sa perché, l'una metà del gregge; / Tremante l'altra, e dubbia anco del pane, / Stupida, immobil resta? / Fia libertà, quella che or là protegge / Chi assoluto qui regge? / Fu guerra questa, ove il cercarsi ognora / L'osti fra lor, né il ritrovarsi mai, / Fu il più atroce de' guai? / Ben fèro: esser cagion perché l'uom mora / Può un'erba vil, che odora / Infusa in bollente onda; / Bevuta, i corpi al par che l'alme snerva? / Pur dall'ultima d'India infame sponda / Va l'America a far povera e serva" (ode 5, *Opere*, 309, lines 97-112).

84. Alberto Aquarone, introduction to *Memorie della vita e delle peregrinazioni del fiorentino Filippo Mazzei* (Milan: Marzorati, 1970), 1:15.

85. Here we limit ourselves to listing the most significant bibliographical contributions on Mazzei: Richard Cecil Garlik, *Philip Mazzei, Friend of Jefferson: His Life and Letters* (Baltimore: Johns Hopkins University Press, 1933); Howard R. Marraro, *Philip Mazzei, Virginia's Agent in Europe: The Story of His Mission as Related in His Own Dispatches and Other Documents* (New York: Public Library, 1935); Angelina La Piana, *La cultura americana e l'Italia* (Turin: Einaudi, 1938); Edoardo Tortarolo, *Filippo Mazzei e la rivoluzione americana: Alcuni documenti inediti*, in *Rivista storica italiana*, 93 (1981): 186-200 and *Illuminismo e rivoluzioni: Biografia politica di Filippo Mazzei* (Turin: Angeli, 1985).

biographies of Mazzei, stressing the role of his revolutionary experience in his intellectual formation. But a reconstruction of Mazzei's activities during his American sojourn is difficult, due to the lack of available documents; in fact, the greater part of his writings from Virginia were lost, so that any research must be based on documents kept by Mazzei himself, his correspondence and autobiography. A starting point for the study of his American period are the "American" pages of his *Memoirs,* written in 1810 in Pisa, where Mazzei, then almost eighty years old, had retired from political life, and published in Lugano in 1846 by Gino Capponi. To the anonymous reader to whom the autobiography is dedicated,[86] Mazzei confessed that he had to resort to memory for the "more interesting times" of his life, having left his papers in Virginia and Poland:

> You have asked me more than once to write the story of my life. I have always pointed out that this would be a most arduous task for one who is almost eighty years of age. And furthermore, I do lack material concerning the most interesting period, that is, from 1772 to the middle of 1792. During these years I was very active, first in the state of Virginia, as a worthy citizen of my adopted country, then as envoy from that state to Europe, still later as envoy from King Stanislaus of Poland, and finally as chargé d'affaires from that King and his Republic to the Court of France. I left the data relative to the first part of this period in Virginia in 1785, intending to return there within a year; I left that relative to the second part in Warsaw in July, 1792.[87]

Although the memoirs of an octogenarian may not always lucidly record events and ought not in any case be construed as objectively factual for the purposes of historical reconstruction, they are indispensable in this case if we want to retrace Mazzei's American voyage from "farmer" to theoretician of the independence.

Born into a well-to-do bourgeois family in Poggio Cajano in 1730, Filippo Mazzei wanted to become a physician. But in 1750, as a result

---

86. According to Ciampini the autobiography was dedicated to Giovanni Carmignani, professor of criminal law at the University of Pisa and a friend of Mazzei in the latter's late years; according to Pace, it was dedicated to Giovanni Fabbroni, an economist and agronomist in the circle of the Grand Duke Leopold of Tuscany.

87. Philip Mazzei, *Memoirs of the Life and Peregrinations of the Florentine Philip Mazzei, 1730-1816,* trans. Howard R. Marraro (New York: Columbia University Press, 1942), intro.

of a disagreement with his brother concerning their father's inheritance, he moved to Leghorn, intending to embark for the Spanish or Portuguese colonies in America. Swayed from this voyage by his father's friend, the marquis de Silva, consul of Spain, he returned to the Tuscan city for another two years. In 1753 the spirit of adventure that would accompany him all his life enticed him to follow a physician friend to Smyrna. Then, toward the end of 1755, wanting to "see more of the world," he left Turkey for London, where he lived for the next twenty years. At first he worked as a physician, then as a teacher of Italian, and finally as a merchant, exporting farm products from Tuscany to England. In 1767, he bought for Leopold, grand duke of Tuscany, two "stoves" from Benjamin Franklin, who was then in England as agent for Pennsylvania. With Franklin he met the Virginian Thomas Adams and several other American gentlemen. As he reported in his *Memoirs,* through his association with London's "American" circle he became interested in events taking place in the colonies. He also developed the idea of traveling to Virginia in order to introduce new farm cultivation such as grapes and olives:

> For some time my new American friends, especially Dr. Franklin and Mr. Thomas Adams, had been advising me to go to live among them. I was afraid their government was but a poor copy of the English system and that the basis of their liberty was, as a consequence, even less solid. But Franklin and Adams assured me that in America there was no aristocracy, that the eyes of the people were not dazzled by the splendor of the throne, that the head of every family could cast a vote in the elections and could be elected to office, that the colonies had their own municipal laws, and that they had adopted only those English laws that fitted their needs.[88]

Unswayed by the "Anglomania" of those years, Mazzei did not consider himself an unconditional admirer of British political institutions; his basic

---

88. Ibid., 173. Mazzei recalls: "I struck up a friendship with Franklin and, through him, with various other persons from the colonies, which now form the Republic of the United States. One of these persons was Mr. Thomas Adams, a Virginian, who, being a close friend of Jefferson, made it possible for Mr. Jefferson and me to know a great deal about each other some years before we actually met. There was a lady from Virginia in London, married to a Mr. Norton, an important English merchant in the city, who invited all the Virginians to dinner every Christmas. Mr. Adams took me to one of these gatherings, and this was probably the reason, or at least one of the chief reasons, that I came to know rather intimately more inhabitants of the colony Virginia than of all the others put together."

mistrust of the English, together with other factors, including psychological ones,[89] persuaded him to move to Virginia in 1773. His decision to leave England provoked the indignation of his friend Antonio Chamier, who wrote in an attempt to dissuade him: "I never expected such a resolution from a man of sense, as you are. You will leave a place, where you have so great a number of excellent friends, that no foreigner ever had, to go in [sic] a country, where, if you breack [sic] a chair, you will find nobody to mend it for you. I wish at least, that the little, dirty, tricking knavery of America, may prove less interruption to your comforts of life, than the plain dounright [sic] roguery of this country."[90] But Mazzei had already decided to leave, with ten peasants and the rural implements necessary to his mission. Then, when he was about to embark, a problem arose:

> When I had everything ready to leave, I could not find the group of ten farmers who were to accompany me. A certain Masi, from Ponte a Rifredi, who, I learned, had been to one of the French islands in the Antilles, had told the man who had procured me the other nine, that in America the stars fall from the sky and burn the laborers in the fields. I imagine he was referring to those meteors which appear like comets falling from the sky and which the common people call stars. They are very common in those hot regions, and, as ignorant travelers are inclined to exaggerate, he added the bagatelle of their burning the workers in the fields. But he had said *America*

---

89. In his letter to Adams dated July 23, 1773 (*Philip Mazzei: Selected Writings and Correspondence*, ed. Margherita Marchione [Prato: Cassa di Risparmi e Depositi di Prato, 1983], 1:46) Mazzei points to economic problems: "My dear Friend, I have been disappointed and ill-used by the European Friends and Acquaintances, I have been plundered, they have been the occasion of my throughing away a great deal of money without purpose, which would be impossible to explain to you in a letter, however I have three constant friends that I cannot loose, Honesty, Industry and Courage. If I should not be able to carry my other riches with me to Virginia, but these three friends I shall be contended [sic]. The only thing I have to fear in coming to you proceeds from your too great friendship, which makes you consider more than I am worth, and I plainly see by your letter that you have prejudiced your friends a great deal too much in my favour." Again, on August 6 of the same year, he wrote to Adams (1:48): "I have told you my present situation, and I am last to give you a hint of disappointments and misfortunes that have reduced me very low; but I would not have you be in the least uneasy about me. I hope that you believe that I speak from my heart. Know then, my dear Friend, that I want no courage, that I want nothing else but to be in Virginia, that I could not bear the idea of being obliged to any body for my subsistence, and nobody shall be happier than I shall if even I should be left without a farthing as long as I shall be able to get my bread in any honourable way whatsoever."
90. *Memoirs*, 173–74.

not without reason, for the French call the Antilles, as well as the continent, America.[91]

The legend of the dangerous American stars had frightened the farmers away. Mazzei had to collect another crew, this time composed not of technicians, but of adventurers such as a "fruit vendor's boy" and a tailor.

Upon arriving in "Williamsburgo" ("Williamsburg might really be called a township rather than a city, although the governor's palace, the Assembly Hall, the college, and the court were located there"),[92] he was received by Washington. Here, together with Washington, Jefferson, and other personalities of the time, he started to work on his plan for a farming cooperative. After several months in Virginia, Mazzei was impressed by the democratic and egalitarian spirit of the New America's freedom of expression ("in those lands, a difference of opinion in no way lessens friendship and esteem")[93] and by the education of the settlers. He noted, in fact, that there was "[no one] in that country who could not read and write. In the homes of all those who work in the fields, or who practice some mechanical trade, one finds books, inkwells, and writing paper. Not infrequently they also know arithmetic."[94] These general remarks, however, do not recur often in the *Memoirs'* "American" pages, which are instead filled with political anecdotes and farming details.

Mazzei's original plan was to initiate direct commercial exchanges between Tuscany and Virginia; soon, however, revolutionary fervor stirred him to write political articles as an impassioned theoretician of independence. Although the resistance movement against the English parliament's jurisdiction over the colonies was already under way when Mazzei landed in America in September 1773, the American public was not yet convinced of the necessity of separation from the British crown. When conflict reached the acute phase of armed struggle, Mazzei devoted himself completely to the cause of colonial independence. In his *Memoirs,* he claimed credit for steering Jefferson and other Virginians toward a policy of complete autonomy, discouraging them from any compromise with England. He was firmly convinced that independence could never be achieved so long as England was still thought to represent political and institutional perfection:

91. *Memoirs,* 186.
92. Ibid., 189.
93. Ibid., 277.
94. Ibid., 213.

The conduct of the Cabinet at St. James's made it perfectly clear that if the colonies did not wish to run the risk of being its victims, they had to arm themselves, with the inevitable result either of achieving complete liberty or of suffering under the most oppressive slavery. If they succeeded in attaining their liberty, they had to be prepared to establish a good government. This could be accomplished only by removing the prejudices of those people who were accustomed to look upon England as a model of perfection.[95]

Mazzei was convinced that the Revolution would not succeed unless a consciousness-raising campaign could persuade the people to reject the English model. He wrote of his participation in this "attempt to enlighten people"[96] in his *Memoirs*: "To achieve our aim [independence] it was not only necessary to write articles, but also to encourage discussions, which would give us an opportunity to combat the prevailing prejudices and to point out saner principles."[97] He published revolutionary tracts under the pseudonym "Orlando Furioso"; as he told James Madison, they were written to promote "the interests of our country" and to show "in the brightest light the justice of our cause."[98] Two articles of revolutionary propaganda that Mazzei recalled having written for the "Virginia Gazette" between 1774 and 1775 (first in Italian, together with Jefferson, who translated them, and later directly in English) would fall into this category, but there is no documentary evidence for them.

95. Ibid., 204. Mazzei recalls that "the majority of the inhabitants, however, were convinced that the English nation would never permit its government to force the colonies to a separation, and, since the desire to remain united to the country of their forefathers was still strong, everything was done to achieve this."
96. Giovanni Schiavo, *The Italians in America before the Civil War*, 164.
97. *Memoirs*, 204.
98. Letter to James Madison dated March 13, 1782 (in Margherita Marchione, ed., *Philip Mazzei: Selected Writings and Correspondence*, 1:338). In his *Memoirs* Mazzei recalls he had written several articles of propaganda, but neither the *Frammenti di scritti pubblicati nelle gazzette al principio della rivoluzione americana da un cittadino della Virginia*, nor other pamphlets could be traced. We mention however *Ragioni per cui non può darsi agli Stati Americani la taccia di ribelli, Riflessioni tendenti a prognosticar l'evento della presente guerra, La giustizia della causa Americana*, and other writings of a primarily economic nature. In a letter to James Madison dated March 13, 1782 (ibid., 1:338), he refers to his political articles: "I would like you to see them. I sent two copies: if both of them should arrive safely, you might ask to have one sent to you. The first, written at the beginning of last year, is entitled, *Reasons why the American States cannot be accused of having rebelled*.... To the second, written during the following April, I gave the title, *Reflections tending to predict the outcome of the present war*."

Thanks to his intimate relationship with Jefferson (they enlisted together in the county army) and other political figures, Mazzei was able to contribute to legislative policy in several ways. One hotly debated issue at that time was slavery. Although he agreed with Jefferson that, from an ethical point of view, retaining slavery contrasted with the colonists' enthusiasm for freedom, Mazzei disagreed on a practical level. Jefferson favored an immediate abolition of slavery, while Mazzei and Mason underscored the necessity of psychologically "preparing" slaves for freedom. A page in the *Memoirs* summarizes the different points of view on this issue:

> Jefferson said that he did not believe in palliative remedies, but rather in getting at essential causes; that he himself would have proposed the total abolition of slavery, in the name of humanity and justice. He said, further, that to keep in a state of slavery human beings who are born with rights equal to ours, and who do not differ from us save in color, is not only a barbarous and cruel injustice, but also a shameful act, especially since this people braved everything for our liberty. He concluded by saying that it would be preferable to run the risk of having to till the soil with our own hands. . . . Mr. George Mason and I were the only dissenters against the immediate abolition of slavery. I said that I wished ardently to see the plan put into execution as soon as possible, that is, as soon as circumstances permitted, but that, under the conditions then prevailing, such a step seemed too risky, since the number of colored people exceeded our own by two to one. Moreover, the benefit would seem even greater, in my opinion, if the slaves knew that their masters were inclined to bestow freedom on all those who deserved it because of good conduct; whereas, by freeing them universally and unexpectedly, we might run the risk of their believing the act to be caused by fear, instilled by the circumstances. Mr. George Mason said much more, pointing out the necessity of educating the Negroes before taking such a step and of teaching them to make good use of their liberty. "We all know," he said, "that the Negroes consider work a punishment." And he called attention to the fact that the first use they would make of their liberty (having had no previous education) would be to do nothing and that they would then necessarily become thieves.[99]

---

99. *Memoirs*, 221-22. Mazzei continues: "Everyone was convinced (and Jefferson first of all) by the reasons presented by Mr. Mason and myself. Wherefore it was agreed that

Mazzei proposed a moderate, nontraumatic solution, fearing that a sweeping emancipation of the slaves would lead to anarchy in the infant state. Just as he had previously insisted on "enlightening" Americans in preparation for the Revolution, he now considered acculturation of the blacks a necessary preparation for emancipation, so that they might make good use of freedom.

In 1779, having been appointed agent for Virginia, Mazzei was dispatched to Europe with the task of obtaining loans to continue the war. This diplomatic mission was to fail, mainly due to Grand Duke Leopold's indifference to the American cause. As witnessed by the many articles and by his correspondence,[100] Mazzei was at that time actively involved in propaganda favoring "unlimited independence for America"; he sought to "enlighten" Europeans on the events that were happening overseas. His mission was not only to secure financial support for the war, but also to secure Europe's support of the war's ideological principles. In a letter from 1782, written while he was on a mission to Florence to try to persuade the grand duke to initiate trade relations with Virginia, he stated that "the ill-considered assertions that England will never recognize American independence, no matter what the cost, come from minds stirred up by passion or paltry politics, for it can easily be seen that such a step, however hard it may be, is equally inevitable."[101] England's stubborn insistence on turning back the irreversible process of a revolution for freedom seemed blindly utopian to him, and convinced him that "all Europe together could not now take their independence from the Americans."[102]

---

the two aforementioned laws, disapproved by the King of England, should be proposed and that word should be passed about that another law would be prepared, which would force the masters to send the colored children to the public schools in each county, to learn reading, writing, arithmetic, and how to make the best use of liberty, which the masters had decided to grant to those who earned it by right conduct." In the *Researches* as well Mazzei stressed the contrast between independence and slavery in the following passage: "Men who love justice and humanity are naturally surprised to learn that although the principles embodied in the new state governments proclaim liberty and equality, slavery still exists in the United States (*Researches*, 4:344)."

100. Together with her recent selection of Mazzei's letters, see the English edition of Mazzei's writings, also edited by Margherita Marchione, *Philip Mazzei: Jefferson's "Zealous Wig"* (New York: American Institute of Italian Studies, 1975) and *Philip Mazzei: My Life and Wondering: The Story of an Eighteenth-Century World Citizen* (Morristown: American Institute of Italian Studies, 1980).

101. *Philip Mazzei: Selected Writings and Correspondence*, 1:375.

102. Ibid., 376. Mazzei in these years stressed the distinction between "liberty" and "anarchy" denying the European conviction according to which America was in the throes

When the war ended, and England permanently relinquished its rights to the colonies and opened peace negotiations in 1783, Mazzei returned for his last stay in Virginia. He left in 1785, although he intended to return before long. He moved to Paris at a time when Jefferson was ambassador to the United States. It was Jefferson who introduced him to the literary and scientific personalities of the time, such as Marmontel, Morellet, Lavoisier, the duke of Rochefoucauld and the Condorcets. In this cultural climate he composed his *Researches,* with the intention of offering "a complete, impartial description" of the new republic. This work was translated into French by Faure, a young lawyer, and published in Paris by Froullé in 1788; in his letter to Madison of August 14, 1786, Mazzei referred to a Tuscan original (which has unfortunately been lost): "[The work] will make up two octavo volumes, and will have to be translated into French, and printers take their time. Those who understand Italian, would like the original, which I do not think can be printed even next year. The American translation will probably precede it."[103]

His friends, and especially Jefferson, encouraged him to write his *Researches* as a polemical response to Raynal and Mably's studies on the New America:

> Abbé Raynal had for a long time been getting on my nerves, and Abbé de Mably's *Observations* on our governments made my blood boil as soon as I saw it and heard it had made a bad impression. It was easy to see that the source of the evil was the author's fame, which had led most people, who do not like to take the trouble of thinking, to take his dreams as axioms. Some confutations of his insolent and stupid booklet that I wrote for the press moved several worthy persons to wish that Europe would be undeceived more effectively than through that medium. The little I had done had led

---

of a state of chaos caused by the war; this tale will later give him the opportunity to develop his conception of freedom, and to assert in his *Researches* that "differences in approach lead to arguments, and the opposing parties are often excited in proportion to their zeal for public welfare.... These debates instruct the inhabitants, teach them to reason, and put them on guard against anyone who might try to upset public tranquility in order to satisfy personal ambition" *(Researches,* 4:298). After the Revolution, Jefferson wrote that "all those who lack courage prefer the calm of despotism to the stormy sea of freedom" and pointed out that independence, once achieved, can be maintained only at the cost of "ongoing struggle and dangers" ("Articolo di lettera di Tommaso Jefferson ad N.N. suo concittadino e amico in Toscana," April 24, 1796, in *Memorie,* 2:495).

103. *Philip Mazzei: Selected Writings and Correspondence,* 1:530.

M. de Marmontel, Abbé Morellet, and other luminaries to believe that I could do the rest. So, I began to write a thoroughgoing refutation. A huge amount of notes, consisting of historical reports, reflections, discussions, etc., induced my friends to wish I would treat the topics separately. The greatest mathematician and most vigorous writer in France, the Marquis de Condorcet, said that I did the two Abbés too much honor by making them the heroes of my poem.[104]

The four volumes of the *Researches* are devoted to a defense of the new republic. The first book is a history of the various states and covers the historical and constitutional aspects of the country; the second and the third book are refutations of Mably and Raynal; the fourth covers different topics such as slavery, anarchy, the Indians, and so forth. Mazzei set out to evoke the "true spirit of the Revolution":

> Since European attention was focused on the American Revolution, a number of writers hastened to treat such an interesting subject, and as each was eager to be first, he published his book before he could obtain adequate information. . . . My principal object is to give a precise and accurate account of the situation in the thirteen United States, especially with regard to their governments, and I shall refer to those historic events which may shed light on the subject.[105]

In his *Observations sur le gouvernement et les lois des Etats Unis* (1784), pedantic old Mably had drawn a distorted picture of American political institutions. Mazzei recalled meeting him in Paris, upon his return from Virginia:

> I had heard of these observations before my return to Virginia. I had met the author casually at the home of Shallux, the banker, in the Place Vendôme, at which time he had struck me as the greatest pedant I had ever known. He was very old. Two other abbots of about the same age were there at the same time, one of them was the banker's brother, and the other a certain Arnauld from Provence. These men were both very ignorant, and they exalted Mably as

---

104. Letter of August 14, 1786, to James Madison, in ibid., 530.
105. *Researches* (1:1), 4. The only modern edition of Mazzei's *Researches* is in English: *Researches on the United States*, trans. and ed. Constance D. Sherman (Charlottesville: University of Virginia Press, 1976).

if he were a Solon or a Lycurgus, and he preened himself before their flattery.[106]

After reading the Abbé's work, Mazzei wrote: "I decided to write some observations about it in a style calculated to make my friends laugh. I wrote about a dozen of these, which I read to Marmontel. He laughed at them, but said that the work should be refuted seriously, because the Abbot was generally believed."[107] Mably's *Observations* is not a systematic work, and at the beginning of his *Réponse aux observations de l'Abbé de Mably* (certainly identifiable with the "serious" remarks that Marmontel had suggested he should write), Mazzei remarked: "The lack of clarity and precision in his book makes it impossible to refute it in an orderly fashion. We have to quote the text to keep from being accused of partiality."[108] Accordingly, Mazzei went on to quote from and comment on the passages in Mably that could be more easily refuted. He attacked Mably's method (his recurrent comparison of American events to utopian classical models of a republic) and his too-theoretical point of view (his initial rather stiff and schematic concept of "society").

In his insistence on viewing America's social structure from a European perspective, Mably predicted that different classes would emerge in the United States. Mazzei pointed out that the structure of American society was radically different: it was mobile, there were no obstacles to prevent the "citizens' climb," and it was a continuum, with no "stiffening" of class distinctions.[109] Mazzei criticized Mably's failure to take into consideration

---

106. *Memoirs*, 293.
107. Ibid., 293-94. Mably would die a few days after the publication of Mazzei's *Researches*. In his *Memoirs*, Mazzei remembers a funny episode of "spiritism" (300): "The evening before publication, a letter was brought to me by a public messenger. It was dated 'From the other world, January 20, 1788,' and signed 'Abbot Mably.' The abbot had died shortly before this time. It was written in an unknown hand, but I recognized Gallois' style and addressed my reply 'To the Irreverend Abbot Mably in the Other World.' At dinner I saw that my fellow guests were watching furtively, trying not to laugh, and I pretended not to notice anything. When dinner was over, before getting up, I pretended to have remembered something and said: "By the way, would you have thought that the Abbot Mably would have had the courage to write me a letter of reproof from the other world? But I answered him as deserved. Gallois, please read Mably's letter; then I shall read my reply. . . . These two letters amused several friends, especially Marmontel and Condorcet. The latter's wife found Gallois' phraseology a bit too strong hence she refused to believe that he was a true friend."
108. *Researches*, 2:116.
109. For the relationship between Mazzei and Mably, see Edoardo Tortarolo, *Illuminismo e rivoluzioni*, 119-39.

the substantial "diversity" of post-Revolutionary America as compared to Europe: "The author was wrong in comparing our people to the populace of other nations, for Americans differ from all others."[110]

Mazzei again argued with Mably on the latter's interpretation of the American Constitution. For example, he remarked on the Abbé's opposition to freedom of the press, which he considered a dangerous breeding ground for anarchy:

> The author [Mably] calls himself a zealous partisan of the republican form of government, but the principles he advocates are diametrically opposed to it. Nothing is more important for this kind of government than freedom of the press. It is essential to extend useful knowledge, to correct abuses, to lay bare governmental vices, to ascertain the wishes of the people, and to prepare them for needed reforms.[111]

Mazzei pointed out that denying freedom of the press could have dangerous psychological effects, since censorship would encourage malicious curiosity and a sense of the forbidden: "Prohibition would not only encourage temerity but would embolden malice and ignorance. As soon as anything is forbidden it appears good, and prohibition causes the worst books to be sought avidly."[112]

Another adversary to be refuted was Abbé Raynal who, after the success of his *Philosophical and Political History*, had published two studies on the American revolution.[113] In his *Memoirs* Mazzei reminisced that he had already heard in Virginia about the "great commotion" occasioned by Raynal's best-seller:

> Before I had been given my commission by the state of Virginia, I had heard there of a book by the abbé Raynal which was creating a great furor, especially because of its pompous title: *Histoire*

---

110. *Researches*, 2:125.
111. Ibid., 2:133.
112. Ibid. Another topic on which Mazzei disagreed with Mably was the question of the slaves. Mazzei pointed out that there is identity between slave and black, which the Abbé ignores (ibid., 2:121): "The word *slave* has never been used either in this connection or in speaking of the criminals brought from England before the Revolution, and contracts dealing with servants or apprentices are the same as they have always been."
113. *Révolution de l'Amérique* (London: Locker Davis, 1781) and *Tableau et révolutions des colonies angloises dans l'Amérique septentrionale* (Amsterdam: La Compagnie des Libraires, 1781).

philosophique et politique des établissements et du commerce des Européens dans les deux Indes. After my arrival in Paris I had met the author casually. There was some talk of a new enlarged edition of this work, to be published in Geneva, and he was in search of subscribers to pay a louis in advance and a half-louis on receipt of the work. I subscribed, paid the louis to the man himself, and left it to a friend of mine to receive the work and pay the half-louis. On my return, my friend had received it. I had no time to read the seven volumes so I limited myself to what was said about European settlements in North America. I soon saw that not only was there very little truth, from beginning to end, but also that in speaking of the dissensions which arose between the English colonies and England, of the war these brought on, and of the conduct of both parties, he did not always lie through ignorance. I deemed it proper to expose him, therefore, and decided to publish in a single volume the refutation of both the abbés [he was also referring to Mably], adding only what I supposed would not find disfavor. I consulted Jefferson on this project, and he agreed.[114]

Mazzei argued against Raynal's penchant for "fable-like stories" that resulted in a distortion of historical reality, and in unreliable information on the geography and economy of the United States. He contrasted the French Abbé's "adventure novel" observations, such as the supposed degeneration of plants and animals, along the lines of Buffon and De Pauw, with his own American experience. In fact, as Gerbi noted, the sources for Mazzei's *Researches* are "not of course the Jesuit missionaries, nor the armchair naturalists, but the years spent in working the earth of Virginia, arranging exchanges of products and supporting the cause of the insurgents, finding money to lend to and men to work for the United States."[115] As his rebuttals shifted from naturalistic to political themes, Mazzei criticized Raynal for his axiomatic reasoning, which led him to frame events within inflexible schemas, relating them to predetermined categories. Raynal's lack of flexibility and of a sense of history prevented him from investigating the causes and effects of the Revolution, which he understood in an overall sense as a colonial war against the British crown. For Mazzei, this was a simplistic understanding of the American

---

114. *Memoirs*, 1:295–96.
115. Antonello Gerbi, *The Dispute of the New World*, 272.

Revolution as a struggle against England for freedom, rather than as an economic, social, and intellectual transformation in world history.

Although they were to be one of the main sources for Carlo Botta's *History of the War of Independence of the United States of America*, the *Researches* did not meet with the success Mazzei expected among the contemporary public, especially because the book was competing with works by renowned historians of the latter part of the eighteenth century such as Mably and Raynal.[116] Although they do not constitute an original contribution, insofar as they contained no masterly thorough critique and simply "recycled" information that was already part of the historical and geographic body of information on America, they do constitute an overall problem-focused assessment of Philip Mazzei's experience during the years of the Revolution.

After publishing the *Researches*, Mazzei began the last phase of his political activity, taking up service with the king of Poland, with the task of keeping him abreast of the revolutionary upheavals occurring in Paris. Even if observing from afar, he still followed the events of his "adoptive fatherland." A few days before he left Virginia, not knowing he would never return, he had written to Madison: "America is my Jupiter, Virginia my Venus. When I consider what I felt on crossing the Potomac, I am ashamed of my weakness. I do not know what will happen as I lose sight of Sandy Hook. I am well aware that no matter where or in what situation I may be, I shall never tire of exerting myself for the prosperity of my dear adoptive country."[117]

5. Luigi Castiglioni's *Travels in the United States of North America*

In April 1785, the Milanese botanist Luigi Castiglioni (1757–1832), a nephew of Pietro and Alessandro Verri, decided to embark upon a long voyage to North America for scientific purposes. This experience, exceptional for an Italian of his time, resulted in the two volumes of his *Travels*

---

116. For a synthetic view of the *Researches*'s success, see Edoardo Tortarolo, "Le risposte alle 'Recherches,' " in *Illuminismo e rivoluzioni*, 139–44.
117. Letter of June 3, 1785, to James Madison, in *Philip Mazzei: Selected Writings and Correspondence*, 473.

in the United States of North America in the years 1785, 1786 and 1787, published in Milan by Marelli in 1790. One of the voyage's purposes was to study plants suitable for Europe's climate. But Castiglioni's interest in the New World was not exclusively botanical, as he stated in the preface. He was curious to see the republic born from a revolution:

> The Revolution which had taken place in the last few years in North America is one of the most memorable events of this century and may in time produce important consequences for Europe. No wonder, therefore, if after such an epoch reports on things having to do with the United States are more sought after than before and that various travelers have visited this country hitherto little frequented by them. Among these, I too was moved by curiosity to see the political birth of a Republic composed of diverse nationalities, scattered over vast provinces far removed from one another, and varied in climate and products.[118]

Castiglioni's journal is in all probability the only late eighteenth-century account by an Italian traveler to the United States. It is truly a journal, as confirmed by the direct influence of the "voyage" on the development of the plot and, by a chronicle-type rhythm that is clear from the start of the book: "On April 13, 1785, I went aboard the 250-ton American vessel *Neptune*, which was to sail from Deal for Boston in Massachusetts."[119]

The *Viaggio* is divided into *capi* or chapters, each dedicated to a state Castiglioni visited. It begins with details of the crossing and a description of the moonlike spectacle of Greenland: "The endless expanse of snow-covered icebergs occupying the entire surface of the ocean as far as the eye could see, the glow of the atmosphere reflecting the whiteness of the snow, and the quantity of sea dogs which, coming out of the water, walked tranquilly about on those reefs of ice, offered to our eyes the horrors of a completely new solitude."[120]

---

118. *Viaggio: Travels in the United States of North America* (1:v), 3.
119. Ibid. (1:1), 5. Castiglioni was decidedly in favor of independence; he stated that if "the Americans had not attempted the Revolution, they would have remained always at the same level of mediocrity, in fact they could only have deteriorated." Ibid. (2:166), 269.
120. Ibid. (1:5), 7. Seeing the glaciers reminded Castiglioni of Captain Cook's travels: "Everything about me reminded me inevitably of the trip of the renowned Captain Cook, who sailed for a long time in the frozen seas near the poles; and the use he made of the water obtained from ice (which was found to be not only sweet to the taste, but even healthful)

After landing in Boston, Castiglioni began the adventurous itinerary that would take him from New England to Canada and to Georgia. After a description of the bay of Cape Cod, whose "pleasant islets" and coves reminded him of the places "described by the poets as the habitat of the Naiads and Nymphs,"[121] then of Boston and Harvard College,[122] he went on to describe the "true customs" of the "Massachusettese":

> Frank in their personal relationships, they reveal themselves as affable and courteous, and they do not abuse strong liquors as much as the inhabitants of the South. The women, too, are generally of

---

persuaded me to try the same experiment" (ibid., 1:6), 7-8. Alfieri also was struck by the desolation of the Arctic lands. In his autobiography he recalled the crossing of the Baltic Sea on his voyage to Russia (*The Life of Vittorio Alfieri*, 91-92): "When I reached Grisselhamna, a little Swedish port on the east coast, right opposite the entrance to the Gulf of Bothnia, I came upon winter again. It seemed that I had been of set purpose speeding to catch up with it. The greater part of the sea was frozen over and the passage from the mainland to the first of the five small islands . . . proved, owing to the complete immobility of the water, impossible at that moment for any type of boat. . . . All that mass of little floating islands gave a most strange appearance to that repelling sea; it seemed rather a piece of land unhinged and set loose than a tract of water." In any case, Castiglioni could not have been acquainted with Alfieri's *Life*, which would be published only in 1804.
121. Ibid. (1:11), 11.
122. "Cambridge boasts the oldest university in the United States of America, founded in 1636 under the name of Harvard College. Since that time more than 3000 persons have received their degrees there. The building, made of brick, is very large, and 100 self-supporting students live there. There are six professors: one for theology, one for mathematics and natural philosophy, another for oriental languages, a professor of anatomy and surgery, one of theoretical and practical medicine, and finally, one for chemistry and materia medica. There are, moreover, four teachers called tutors for the English and Latin languages, and geography. The library is furnished with about 10,000 volumes, among which are the ancient classical authors and the most renowned of modern philosophers, in addition to an adequate collection of curious and handsome books. . . . On the first day of classes and on graduation day there is a public test of the progress that the students have made in the sciences, and on those days there is a competition among the most distinguished inhabitants of Boston and many from the most distant parts of the state. The ladies (who in America do not disdain attending scientific disputations) likewise assemble there and perhaps by their presence increase in the students the desire to win the approval of the gathering. That same evening, and on the two subsequent ones, there is a public ball, at which the young people seek relief from past occupations in dance and gallantry" (ibid., 1:32-33), 23. Castiglioni mentioned other colleges, including Princeton (see 2:56-57, 235) and Providence College "quite a vast building situated to the east at the top of the hill" (2:97), 255. He also briefly mentioned Dartmouth College in the chapter on New Hampshire (1:110), 60: "[In New Hampshire] the sciences are not much cultivated owing to the lack of institutes, so that the well-to-do send their children to the college of Cambridge in Massachusetts. There is, of course, a college at Dartmouth, too, near the Connecticut River; but apart from the fact that it was founded for the education of the Indians, its income

fair and refined features, of ruddy and healthy complexion. But their beauty does not last for many years as in Europe, and for the most part they have bad teeth and thin hair. Before marrying they delight in pastimes, but without slighting their housework, at which they keep themselves very busy. They also amuse themselves with music and reading, and they possess a natural vivacity and openness unspoiled by the refinements of gallantry. They marry at between 15 and 18 years of age and then abandon every form of amusement, concerning themselves henceforth only with domestic matters, thus serving as the basis for family happiness by the training they give their children and by their attachment to their husbands, toward whom they maintain the most meticulous loyalty, which not infrequently is not so scrupulously reciprocated. Their winter diversions are sleigh runs in the country, and dancing, which they love so much that they give it up only in old age. During the summer they substitute walking, fishing, horseback riding, and, finally, tea parties after dinner, which resemble our *conversazioni*.[123]

He approved of these "Massachusettese," who, unlike all other Americans (former colonists and "savages" as well), drank alcohol in moderation. In Massachusetts, he writes: "the most common beverages are cider, spruce beer, . . . and toddy, which is rum mixed with water. But at the tables of the well-to-do they drink Madeira, port, and Bordeaux wines. Before sitting at table punch is served in a large porcelain or silver jug, and the guests drink in turn from the same bowl, beginning always with the master of the house. It must be said, however, that although these liquors are used freely, they are very seldom abused, with the result that drunkenness is less common there than in the other cities of North America."[124]

Progressing toward the South of New England, Castiglioni, made numerous stops, including the island of Nantucket,[125] and eventually

---

is too small and its location too inconvenient and remote to keep teachers and to house students there."
123. Ibid. (1:92-93), 50-51.
124. Ibid. (1:25), 19-20.
125. His observations of Nantucket Island and its legendary origins are quite interesting (1:96-97), 52-53: "Furthermore, on Nantucket Island, situated to the east of Martha's Vineyard, there is a great commerce in whale oil, many ships sailing annually out of that port for whale fishing. Almost all the inhabitants of that otherwise not very productive island subsist on this kind of export. Among them are various Quaker families. The origin

reached Rhode Island, where he was particularly struck by the elegance of Newport's mansions and the loveliness of the women of the city of "Provvidenza":

The ladies enjoy, like those of Newport, the reputation of being among the most beautiful in America; but they are subject to losing their teeth early, like those of Boston; and they are likely to die of consumption at an early age. This terrible disease has become even more common in the last few years, and it appears beyond question that it is communicated from one individual to another in the same family. However, in spite of the annual ravages of this malady, the fair sex is so numerous that about seven marriageable girls are counted for each eligible young man. This disproportion arose from the large number of men employed in navigation and of those who go to Virginia and the other southern states in order to make a living.[126]

He compares the frankness of the inhabitants of Massachusetts and the elegance of the women of Rhode Island to the ignorance of the inhabitants of Vermont where "the sciences are . . . not cultivated at all," and the unscrupulous "licentiousness" of the inhabitants of Connecticut. One of the most original aspects of Castiglioni's *Viaggio* are his remarks on the contradiction between Puritanism and sexual freedom in Connecticut. Here, although "on Sunday the churches are heavily attended and no one stays away except for serious reasons. . . . Abominable vices reduce the strength of amorous emotion in the girls."[127]

Castiglioni dwelt at length on the licentious customs of the people of Connecticut, especially on the popularity of *bundling* ("[the] complete

---

that the Indian inhabitants of these environs ascribed to Nantucket Island is quite curious, and I shall end this section by relating it. At the eastern end of Martha's Vineyard there is a hill made up of earth of various colors known by the name of Gay Head. On its summit can be seen a big hollow that looks like the crater of an ancient volcano, and the evident signs of the now extinct subterranean fire are still there. The Indians used to say that before the arrival of the Europeans a certain deity called by them *Manshop* dwelt there, whose wont it was to walk over the reefs and go down to the sea, where he would catch a whale and bring it back with him, roasting it on the coals of the aforesaid volcano and often inviting the Indians to dine with him, or leaving them what was left over from his dinner. The Indians, to show their gratitude to the god, offered him their whole tobacco crop of the island, which was barely enough to fill his pipe. He then began to smoke, and having used up all the tobacco, threw the ashes into the sea, which created Nantucket Island."
126. Ibid. (2:97-98), 256.
127. Ibid. (2:91, 93), 252, 253.

liberty to spend the night together and even to sleep in the same bed"),[128] which he speculated arose from "the necessity in which the first colonists found themselves to urge young people to marry early in order to increase the population of the colony" or from "imitation of the Indians."[129] In any case, for Castiglioni the term "savage" lost all negative connotation and became synonymous with "ancient inhabitant of America." Indians "although devoid of European education, have a natural talent far superior to what we commonly attribute to them. Very unlike the peoples of Sierra Leone, the Gold Coast, and other African regions, who are brought up in the debasement produced by slavery, the courageous and intelligent American Indians abhor the very name of slavery."[130] In America only blacks were slaves (Mazzei too had made this clear in this *Réponse* to Mably), not the Indians. But, like the slaves, the natives were constantly subjected to abuses on the part of the "Whites." Had this situation been known in Europe, "[it] would serve to give a better idea of the Indians and to reveal the vices and iniquities of those who pretend to belong to a civilized nation."[131]

128. Ibid. (2:93), 253. Castiglioni proceeded to describe this strange custom: "The young lady accordingly takes off all her clothes except her shift and the lad removes his waistcoat and shoes, and everything is allowed that does not lead to consequences—an agreement requested by the girl and which is said to be strictly observed" (253-54). He also recounted a strange episode: "Traveling through Connecticut, I found myself in the company of a young man who spent the night with a girl after having courted her not more than six hours, in which time she let herself be kissed in public without showing either pleasure or embarrassment. The morning after, the young man assured me that the girl was very nice and well behaved. All I said was that the same would not have been believed in Europe. A short time afterward I saw the girl just as unruffled as before, although she was aware that we knew everything; whereupon I was convinced that this is believed there to be a completely innocent matter that casts no shadow upon the character of the girl. It must be said that these two young people had never seen each other before, and that soon thereafter they separated with the moral certitude of never being together again; so the acquiescence of the girl did not have marriage as the object" (ibid., 254).
129. Ibid. (2:94), 254.
130. Ibid. (1:86-87), 48.
131. Ibid. (2:48), 232. Here Castiglioni referred to the wretched conduct of the farmers in the interior parts of Pennsylvania who "are almost always at war with the Indians; and they are the aggressors. They cheat them in contracts, go beyond the boundaries set as limits, steal their canoes, and always bully them whenever they are in greater number" (ibid., 2:47), 232. Furthermore, they "are so given, as I have already said, to strong drinks that they often end up by getting drunk; and when arguments arise among them, they fight with their fists. To this coarse manner of avenging themselves they add customs even more barbaric and ferocious. If two of them challenge each other to fight, they agree between them whether the three following methods of hurting each other are to be permitted: biting, bulking, and

Castiglioni did not mean for this statement to apply to all the Americans in New England; neither did he mean to set forth, as Gerbi claims,[132] a Manichaean opposition: savage/civilized and former colonist/uncivilized. Unlike Carli, who had idealized the Peruvians, Castiglioni objectively judged the Indians from an ethical and sociological point of view, not a naturalistic one (his observations on the Canadian natives, for example, were not always positive). In assessing the culture, the customs, and particularly the dignity of the North American natives compared to the Europeans, he entered into a polemic with those who considered them a race halfway between man and beast, especially Buffon, De Pauw, and Raynal. Castiglioni, who in the course of his voyage would come to know several Indian populations and would be a guest in their villages, appended to the second volume of his *Viaggio* a glossary of Choctaw and Cherokee terms.[133]

Other interesting observations in the *Viaggio* refer to "Nuova York," a city that, because of its commercial traffic on Broadway and Wall Street, creates "more the impression of one of the most flourishing cities than of the capital of a nascent state."[134] Castiglioni favored a moderate constitutional government, neither despotic, nor fully democratic; he admired the sociopolitical structure of the state of New York, where the population is divided into four classes:

> The inhabitants are about 22,000, and although no distinction of rank is permitted in the new legislation, they can be considered as divided into four classes. The first is composed of the owners of manors or *signorie,* who having acquired various privileges under English government, are considered as the nobility of the city, to whom must be added the richest businessmen. This sort of nobility, who did not

---

gouging. The first of these consists in biting fingers and tearing flesh with the teeth; the second is seizing each other by the most delicate parts and trying in this way to destroy the power to reproduce; and the third, finally, consists in grabbing the adversary by the hair and, putting the thumb at the outside corner of the eye, pressing it with full force until it comes out of its socket" (ibid., 2:46-47), 231-32. In a note, Castiglioni added that "traveling through the interior regions of the United States, one often sees persons with fingers and eyes lost in these barbaric duels" (ibid., 318, n. 72).

132. Antonello Gerbi, *The Dispute of the New World,* 276.

133. It would be worthwhile to do a specialized study of these pages as in all probability they are one of the first descriptions which appeared in Italy (and by an Italian) of the Indian languages from the East Coast of the United States.

134. *Viaggio: Travels in the United States of North America* (1:177), 93, 95.

want to associate with the other classes of citizens and among whom prejudiced notions of family antiquity were beginning to take root, lost much of their superiority after the late revolution, when persons of no name were elevated to holding the most conspicuous offices of the new republic. The second includes the less wealthy, or less haughty, businessmen and merchants; the third, the artisans; and the fourth, the people.[135]

In progressing toward the southern states, Castiglioni truly began his American "adventure": in Virginia and in South Carolina he twice risked drowning in river rapids, became lost in a forest, was forced to stay in humble lodgings infested with mice and cockroaches, and finally even found himself in the midst of a smallpox epidemic. The chapter on Virginia opens with emphatic praise of Washington ("produced by nature to free America from European subjection and to create an epoch in the history of human relations"), whose exemplary life Castiglioni hoped would "long serve as an example of virtue and industry for his fellow citizens, as he served as an example to Europe in the victories that consecrated his name to an eternal fame."[136] He writes of the Virginians that they live for "deer hunting, horse racing, fishing, dances and gambling." Their social life is especially active as "the plantations are not far from each other" and "some 20 or more young ladies can be assembled in a short time, often to dance all night to the music of the violin of a negro; and among the other dances they have the jig, which resembles the dance of our peasants."[137]

It is surprising, however, that Castiglioni, who met people from Jefferson's circle in Virginia, makes no mention of Mazzei's political and farming activities. Mazzei had gone to Virginia to introduce the cultivation of the vine, the olive tree and the silkworm; he could not have been unknown to Castiglioni, who traveled to North America in search of decorative and medicinal plants to adapt to the Italian climate. Although his objectives were different from Mazzei's, in the *Botanical Observations* in the second volume of the *Viaggio,* the Tuscan adventurer would reach a similar conclusion about the substantial identity of the nature and climate of of the two hemispheres.

135. Ibid. (1:178-79), 95.
136. Ibid. (1:212, 215), 113.
137. Ibid. (1:377), 196.

After a lengthy description of the natives of the mountains of North Carolina ("if a traveler in answering their questions reveals that he is not a merchant, or a doctor, or that he does not intend to settle in America, they look upon him suspiciously, thinking it impossible that one might travel solely to educate himself"),[138] Castiglioni praised the people of South Carolina for their "hospitality" and their "talents" for "the fine arts, dance, and music."[139] Yet he considered these people doomed to an inevitable physical and moral decay due to dissipation, the climate, and their unhealthy eating habits. His description of the southern "plantators" and of their mistreatment of the slaves is quite effective:

> In addition to the landholders, who live in the capital, there are numerous others who, either for reasons of economy or out of necessity, live all the time in the country on their plantations. The unhealthful location of their plantations has the result that they rarely reach 50 years of age, and they spend their lives in an almost continuous convalescence, in the midst of the sad spectacle of the illnesses of their families. Since they are subject to the bad effects of a bilious humor, they often vent their ill temper on the poor negroes, who, to the shame of mankind, are scarcely reputed to be human beings, and for the slightest failing are exposed to the lash of a slave driver, when the master himself does not take the barbaric pleasure of tormenting them.[140]

Apart from the inhuman treatment inflicted upon the blacks, the issue of the sale of slaves also awakened the traveler's compassion: "Surely it is a matter of surprise and pity for a European to read about the sale of slaves here in the newspapers, and all the more so if these notices are compared with those put out for the sale of horses, from which they differ not a bit."[141]

From Georgia, the last point on his itinerary, Castiglioni returned to Boston in order to go home to Italy with seeds and plants unknown in Europe, including the locust tree, which would spread widely and quickly.[142]

---

138. Ibid. (1:344), 180.
139. Ibid. (1:314), 164.
140. Ibid. (1:315), 164–65.
141. Ibid. (1:182), 97.
142. The results of Castiglioni's voyage are noted first by his contemporaries in the scientific world, then by the cultural world. For the reactions of scientists and naturalists, see

After his long voyage, and having assessed the disastrous consequences of a war and its negative effects on the economy, he was decidedly optimistic in his assessment of the future of the United States:

> However, if the Americans are at present suffering all the disadvantages of a nascent and poor republic and the consequences of a civil war, they have reason to find comfort in the prospect of an improved future situation for themselves. The degree and promptness of future happiness will depend upon how soon a stable and active government is set up, this being the only instrument they still need for achieving it. Their distance from Europe makes them safe from any sudden invasion, and the area and fertility of the land that they own is capable of feeding an immense population, especially in the center of the continent where, as I have already indicated, there are vast plains irrigated by many navigable rivers under a temperate and healthful sky. Motivated by these advantages, the United States will flourish very quickly under the auspices of the new government, and they will arrive more easily at that happy era to which they aspire and in which they can distinguish themselves among the most powerful and civilized nations.[143]

It was definitely not the rhetorical enthusiasm of a Raynal[144] nor the "Machiavellian and Vichian"[145] enthusiasm of a Galiani[146] for a young state that led Castiglioni to predict that the United States would have a successful future. Instead, it was an objective evaluation of the new

---

Antonio Pace's introduction to *Luigi Castiglioni's Viaggio* (Syracuse: Syracuse University Press, 1983), xi–xli. In any case, in 1826 Castiglioni's work would have the merit of being the primary source for a volume titled *Anglo-American United States* in the encyclopedia edited by Giulio Ferrario, *Il costume antico e moderno di tutti i popoli*.

143. *Travels in the United States of North America* (2:167–68), 269.
144. Raynal's *History* ended with a strong prophecy for the future of North America (see Chapter 3, n. 21).
145. See Antonello Gerbi, *The Dispute of the New World*, 142.
146. Ferdinando Galiani (letter of July 26, 1772, to Madame d'Epinay, in *La Signora d'Epinay e l'abate Galiani*, ed. Fausto Nicolini [Bari: Laterza, 1928], 273): "The time has come for the complete fall of Europe and its transmigration to America. Here everything is decaying: religion, law, the arts and sciences, and everything will be newly rebuilt in America. . . . I would wager on behalf of America for the very materialistic reason that genius revolves around the movement of the day and for the past five thousand years, [this] has been going from East to West without deviation."

republic, based on his American experience. Already at the beginning of his journal he stated his intent of objectivity:

> From the quantity of books that speak of this country and its recent revolution, it seems that they should be perfectly informed about it in Europe; but if one considers that the authors were for the most part moved by partisan spirit excessively to exalt or to disparage the Americans, the reader will be glad to have here in brief a general idea of them based upon my own observations and written with that impartiality that I determined to preserve beforehand.[147]

Together with "lack of impartiality," another unforgivable flaw of "enlightened" Americanists, according to Castiglioni, was their view of the United States as an undistinguished whole, which failed to take into account the country's territorial expanse, and therefore the variety in the country's geography and politics. The primary distinguishing characteristic of the new republic lay in its economic, social, and cultural diversity: "There is much argument in Europe about the quality of the climate and fertility of the land in the United States, about their productions, and, above all, about the system of government, and the industry and customs of those inhabitants, as if, in the vast reaches contained within the limits of the Republic, so many different things could be uniform."[148] This was a modern observation, and it marked an important shift in the Italian perception of the New World, insofar as it indicated a progressive "limitation" and "clarification" of the American horizon. The New America could not be perceived through a European perspective: it was truly "another world."

Another point on which Castiglioni disagreed with historians and naturalists of his time was the issue of "American degeneration." As a scientist, he denied Buffon's theory of the deterioration of America and Americans (natives as well as settlers); he included some of his other renowned opponents in this statement: "The theory of the degeneration of animals in America adopted by Count Buffon and exaggerated by Mr. Pauw and other writers has been recognized as false since the fine work of Mr. Jefferson. This author, in his *Notes on Virginia*, demonstrated plainly how little basis there was for such an opinion; and both Mr. Robertson, in his *History of*

---

147. *Travels in the United States of North America* (2:152), 264.
148. Ibid.

America, and Count Carli, in his *Lettere americane,* very clearly proved the same thing."[149] In any case, among the defenders of the American cause, such as Carli and Jefferson, he also surprisingly included Robertson, who sided with De Pauw's naturalistic pessimism and was convinced of the congenital inferiority of the Americans. Although his scientific training led him to pay particular attention to the physical reality of the new country, Castiglioni could not accept that a dialogue about America be limited to its natural aspects. Through a detailed analysis of the various American customs, Castiglioni emphasized that it was essential to discuss "history" and "society," not just "geography" and "nature." And this proposal that historians and philosophers turn to a "sociological" evaluation of the New America came from a botanist.

149. Ibid. (2:155), 265.

5

Epilogue: Nineteenth-Century Developments

1. Lorenzo Da Ponte's America

Along with Filippo Mazzei, Lorenzo Da Ponte undoubtedly occupies a position of note in the history of Italian intellectuals in America. Both Mazzei and Da Ponte felt a sense of mission in the New World: the former as a theoretician and promulgator of revolutionary ideas, the latter as a divulger of Italian language and literature. A Jew who converted to Catholicism, an abbot, the author of opera librettos (including *Le nozze di Figaro*, *Così fan tutte*, and *Don Giovanni*, with music by Mozart) and a passionate bibliophile, Lorenzo Da Ponte (Cèneda 1749–New York 1838) moved from London to the United States in 1805, to escape creditors who were pursuing him as a result of bankruptcy. His thirty-year life experience in Sunbury, Philadelphia, and New York has been the focus of some original critical studies, mainly by American scholars. From the monograph by Livingston, *Lorenzo Da Ponte in America* (1930) to the monograph by

Sheila Hodge, *Lorenzo Da Ponte: The Life and Times of Mozart's Librettist* (1985), the history of Da Ponte's life and the reconstruction of the years he spent in America seem, in fact, to have been the exclusive province of American scholars.[1]

The main document of Da Ponte's American experience are the last two chapters of his *Memoirs*,[2] where he intended to present the history, or rather the "praise" of his mission as promulgator of Italian culture in a foreign country.[3] Here, America as a social, political, and environmental reality is reduced to just a background or, better, to a theater, as the author himself stated:

> Thus, living in America, I could only write about everyday household and city cares, in which I was and still am, if not the protagonist, certainly one of the principal actors of this tragicomedy.[4]

Da Ponte steered every impression on the New World back into a domestic and literary horizon and rarely formulated judgments of a general nature.

His first encounter with America, a somewhat shady and coarse America, had already taken place during his voyage from London to Philadelphia on a New England whaling ship. The voyage was "long, disastrous and full of vexation":

> I fell into the clutches of a rascal from Nantucket, whose accustomed business was whale-fishing and who treated his passengers like the

---

1. We note the following works: Joseph Louis Russo, *Lorenzo Da Ponte: Poet and Adventurer* (New York: Columbia University Press, 1922); Luigi Russo, *Lorenzo Da Ponte*, in *Italy and the Italians in Washington's Time* (New York: Italian Publisher, 1933); Howard Rosario Marraro, "Da Ponte and Foresti: An Introduction of Italian at Columbia. Some Unpublished Documents Translated and Annotated," in *Columbia University Quarterly* (March 1937); Angelina La Piana, *La cultura americana e l'Italia*; April Fitzlyon, *The Libertine Librettist: A Biography of Mozart's Librettist, Lorenzo Da Ponte* (New York: Abelard-Shuman, 1957).

2. *Memorie di Lorenzo da Ponte da Cèneda scritte da esso*, ed. Giovanni Gambarin and Fausto Nicolini (Bari: Laterza, 1918). [Translator's note: published in an abridged edition in English as *Memoirs of Lorenzo da Ponte*, trans. Elisabeth Abbott, ed. and annotated by Arthur Livingston, preface by Thomas G. Bergin (New York: Orion, 1929). There is another translation, also somewhat abridged: *The memoirs of Lorenzo Da Ponte, etc., from the "Antologia of Florence," published in April, May, and June of the year 1928. Translated into English by some of my Italian pupils* (New York: Gray and Bunce, 1929).]

3. See Angelina La Piana, *La cultura americana e l'Italia*, 87.

4. *Memorie di Lorenzo da Ponte*, 2:85.

vilest sailors, whom, in turn, he treated exactly like those monsters of the sea. He had with him only the coarsest provisions and of these he was a very sparing dispenser. My first mistake was to pay him forty-four guineas before setting foot on his ship, without contracts or papers, and without making adequate investigation; asking nothing else of him than to be taken to Philadelphia and fed. At the dinner hour, I began to foresee what my fate was to be. The meal was made ready on the deck aft. A rickety old table of worm-eaten pineboards, a tablecloth blacker than a charcoal-burner's shirt; three plates of nicked china, and three rusty iron knives and forks were the sweet preludes to the approaching feast. Messire the Nantucketer took a seat, invited me to sit down opposite him and in a few minutes the African cook arrived with a great wooden bowl in one hand and a pewter platter in the other, which he silently deposited on the table, and, lowering his head, departed.

"Odoardo," cried my aquatic host in a loud voice, "Odoardo! Come to dinner!"

At the second call "Mr. Odoardo" appeared, emerging from the vessel's cabin where he had been sleeping for some hours. He nodded his head a little and, without speaking to me or looking at me, sat down to the captain's right. His strange appearance did not leave me time to look at what the bowl contained. "Odoardo" was the image of a sleeping Bacchus, save that he was dressed like a miller in working garb, his *quondam* white linen according perfectly with the charcoal-burner's shirt and with the tablecloth of our Typhoïs.[5]

The ship's captain was the first of a long series of "scoundrels" encountered by Da Ponte during his American sojourn, where he would become involved in various "businesses" and activities, not all of which would be successful. After setting himself up as a grocer in New York ("I turned grocer accordingly; and let him who had a grain of sense imagine how I must have laughed at myself every time my poet's hand was called upon to weigh out two ounces of tea").[6] Da Ponte began to "examine whether [he] could somehow make a living along the lines of Italian or Latin letters." From that moment on, the prevailing image in his *Memoirs* is one of an America needing to be "enlightened" by Italian letters. "I learned that as

5. *Memoirs of Lorenzo da Ponte*, 183–84.
6. Ibid., 185.

far as the Italian language and literature were concerned, they were about as well known in this city as Turkish or Chinese,"[7] he stated, referring to "Nuova Jorca" where, thanks to Clement Clarke Moore, the son of the president of Columbia College, he began his career as a teacher of Italian. After a conversation with Moore, whom he had casually met in a bookseller's shop, Da Ponte realized how little known Italian literature was in America, a country considered "enlightened":

> I was almost hopeless of success, when the good genius of Italian literature willed that as I was passing in front of the shop of the late M. Riley, bookseller on Broadway, it occurred to me to enter. I approached his counter and asked him if he had any Italian books in his store.
> "I have a few," he replied, "but no one ever asks for them."
> While we stood chatting, an American gentleman approached and joined our conversation. I was soon aware from his remarks that he was admirably read in a variety of literature. Coming by chance to allude to the language and literature of my country, I took occasion to ask him why they should be so little studied in a country as enlightened as I believed America would be.
> "Oh sir," he replied, "modern Italy is not, unfortunately, the Italy of ancient times. She is not that sovereign queen which gave to the ages and to the world emulators, nay rivals, of the supreme Greeks."[8]

Moore saw no continuity in Italian literature after Tasso; this statement incited Da Ponte to a kind of challenge: "If that be the case, . . . I shall be the fortunate Italian to make known to gentlemen in America the merits of his language, and the number and deserts of his greatest men of letters!"[9] Nevertheless, he was convinced that America was favorably

---

7. Ibid., 187.
8. Ibid.
9. Ibid., 188. In New York, as in Philadelphia, Da Ponte had resolved to endeavor to make Italian known (letter to Michele Colombo of September 24, 1818, in *Memorie di Lorenzo Da Ponte compendiate da Jacopo Bernardi e scritti vari in prosa e poesia* [Florence: Le Monnier, 1871]): "After having spent seven lean years in a small town in Pennsylvania as a merchant, certain events brought me to the decision of settling in Philadelphia, where I want to endeavor to introduce the taste of the Italian language, which is either scarcely known, or not appreciated at all. In the city of New York alone where I taught Italian for four years, there are, at most, one hundred people who speak Italian and have a middling appreciation of our Authors' beauty. Philadelphia is a rich and populated city and I want to try" (180).

disposed toward getting to know and appreciate the "flower of Italian literature" and, as his sonnet *Agli Americani* (1835) would show, toward understanding and welcoming it:

> You welcomed me with courtesy, your affection
> increased my constancy, my enthusiasm;
> My pleasure consisted solely in pleasing you.[10]

Always in search of a "better fortune" in his business, Da Ponte moved in 1811 to Pennsylvania, to the pleasant village of Sunbury, a charming "American Arcadia." His description of the Pennsylvanian countryside echoes bucolic stereotypes from the literary tradition:

> Sunbury is a little town of Pennsylvania, in the County of Northumberland and about one hundred and twenty miles distant from Philadelphia. One arrives at the foot of a mountain thirty-six miles in length.... The flanks of that mountain figure on both sides a theatre of rustic magnificence. Brooks, cascades of water, hillocks, precipices, masses of white rock and multiform clumps of trees stretch away in two broad and deep valleys, which end at other mountains of not dissimilar aspect. Here and there are little cottages, shepherds' cabins, great quarries of coal and limestone, tracts of well-cultivated land, very comfortable inns, and amid no end of deer, wild boars, partridges, pheasants, and all other kinds of game, wolves, foxes, bears and rattlesnakes, which last, though they rarely attack the wayfarer, add nevertheless a certain delightful terror, a certain touch of solemnity, to that majestic solitude. The waters are quite as "Clear, cool, and sweet," as those in which the deified Lauretta "bathed her fair limbs."[11]

---

10. "M'accoglieste cortesi, il vostro affetto / La mia costanza accrebbe l'ardor mio; / Trovai sol nel piacervi il mio diletto." *Agli Americani*, in *Memorie compendiate da Jacopo Bernardi*, 374, lines 5-8. From the beginning, for Da Ponte learning a language was inseparable from learning its literature. During these years he asked his brother Paolo to send him a series of Italian classics for his students: "It was my dear brother, Paolo, by no means rich, and harassed by terrible worries, who sent me the first series of our classics. I distributed them among my pupils, incited them to read and ponder them, and in less than three years I had the pure delight of seeing the libraries and the desks of studious Americans ornamented with the flower of our literature which was making its first appearance in the country" (*Memoirs of Lorenzo da Ponte*, 189).

11. *Memoirs of Lorenzo da Ponte*, 193.

Amid Sunbury's pastoral setting, Da Ponte lived turbulent years studded with intrigues, swindlers, and creditors, which brought him to a business crisis and finally to the door of Philadelphia's prisons. The main cause of all his misadventures was the trust he had placed in a thieving, unfaithful secretary, the "angelic Yankee" Thomas Robins. At his trial, Robins was found by the court to be innocent. After the judge's verdict, Da Ponte came to the conclusion that not only should foreigners—Americans included— not be trusted, but that in Pennsylvania, lawyers were generally corrupt. He thought the roots of the injustice to which he had been subjected should be sought in the lack of enforcement of the laws:

> Are there then no laws in most unhappy Sunbury?
> "Yes", answers Dante, "Laws there are, but who lays hand to them?"
> For if someone were to lay hand to them, not so many crimes, not so many abuses, not so many betrayals would go unpunished! A lawyer of that court would not have dared fraudulently to remit an instrument of sale signed by the grantors, to a wretch who, by that manoeuvre, cheated me out of three thousand *jugeri* of land for less than a quarter part of what they were worth. And another would not have had the boldness to extract three hundred and fifty dollars from me to escape paying himself, constraining me thereby to the harsh necessity of going to law with an assassin, with whom he thereupon joined to cheat me out of it, with the interest of eight years. . . . Yet, these were among others just as many and just as bad, the extortions, abuses, betrayals that I suffered . . . in a town of this blessed America, so much admired for her laws, her justice, and her hospitable brotherly love![12]

After these misadventures, Da Ponte's leave-taking of the idyllic village of Sunbury and arrival in New York were a liberation. He resumed teaching Italian and developed the idea of founding a civic theater[13] as well as an

---

12. Ibid., 207.
13. In the ten-year period from 1820 to 1830, Da Ponte, along with his literary interests, continued to pursue the idea of establishing a civic theater in New York. In 1823 he was able to have the company of Manul Garcia stage *Don Giovanni*. For Da Ponte, the introduction of Italian opera served the purpose of popularizing the knowledge of Italian language and literature (*Memoirs of Lorenzo da Ponte*, 231); "Though, to my joy, I could see the interest in Italian letters increasing daily both in New York and other cities of the Union, I still

Italian library.[14] But the lack of original texts was an unsurmountable obstacle to the dissemination of Italian language and literature; disappointed, he stated:

> In almost every city one finds the wines and the grapes of Sicily, the oil, the olives, and the silks of Florence, the marble of Carrara, the gold chains of Venice, the cheese of Parma, the straw hats of Leghorn, the ropes of Rome and Padua, the *rosolio* of Trieste, the sausages of Bologna, and even the *maccheroni* of Naples and the plaster figurettes of Lucca. Yet, to the shame of our country, there is not, in the whole of America, a bookstore kept by an Italian![15]

The image of an America that favored the ephemeral over books reappears in the final page of the *Memoirs*, where the elderly Da Ponte described how, alone in his bookseller's shop, he had little occasion to "get up from his chair" to attend customers. People preferred to buy "sugar-plums and jam-tarts" from his neighbor, rather than books:

> Five months have already passed since I took up the trade of bookseller. I have no great occasion, in truth, to rise from my chair in the course of a day. My customers are few and far between, but I have, instead, the joy of seeing coaches and carriages drive up at every moment before my door and sometimes the most beautiful faces in the world emerge from them, mistaking my book store for the shop next door, where sweets and cakes are for sale. To make people imagine I have many customers, I am thinking of

---

thought there was another way of making them both more widely spread and more highly esteemed; but, to tell the truth, I did not dare to hope for such a thing. What, therefore, was my delight, when a number of persons assured me that the famous Garzia, with his incomparable daughter [the famous opera singer Malibran] and several other Italian singers, was coming from London to America, and in fact to New York, to establish the Italian opera there—the desideratum of my greatest zeal?" Da Ponte continued:"I knew well the advantages that would derive to our literature, and how much our tongue would become popular due to the attractions of Italian drama, the most noble and attractive of all the amusements which man's genius has invented, in all the cultivated nations of the world, and for whose excellence the most noble arts compete" (ibid).

14. In 1828 Da Ponte composed an ode, *A' miei carissimi allievi per eccitarli allo stabilimento d'una pubblica italiana libreria*, included with *Storia della letteratura italiana in New York* in part 5 of his *Memoirs*.

15. *Memoirs of Lorenzo da Ponte*, 215.

placing a placard in my window with the words: "Italian sweets and pastry for sale." Then if that jest chance to bring some one to my shop, I will show him a Petrarch or some other of our poets, and hold that ours are the sweetest of sweets for such as have teeth to chew them.[16]

Nonetheless, after having been sent "by a beneficent genius, . . . to sound for the first time on the shores of the deserving Hudson the flageolets, lyres and trumpets of modern Italy,"[17] Da Ponte felt somewhat discouraged in the last years of his life. This feeling was especially clear in the poem *Storia americana* (1835),[18] where Da Ponte resumed the theme of the admirable results achieved in his heroic "literary mission" to the shores of the Hudson. This time, however, it was a dream:

> On the shores
> By the waves of the Hudson
> Touched,
> I sound the tongue
> of Alighieri and Boccaccio,
> Its best flowers
> Transplanting,
> And I care for them
> With my hand, water them
> With my sweat,
> And those flowers produced fruits

---

16. *Memoirs of Lorenzo da Ponte*, 255-56. By 1823 he had opened an Italian bookstore, taking on as partner his son Carlo, and had compiled an annotated bibliography, his *Catalogo ragionato dei libri che si trovano attualmente nel negozio di Carlo e Lorenzo Da Ponte* (New York: Gravy and Bunce, 1823).

17. *Memorie di Lorenzo da Ponte*, 2:117.

18. *Storia americana, ossia lamento di Lorenzo Da Ponte al nonagenario Michele Colombo, pubblicato nell'anniversario del suo ottantesimo sesto dì natalizio* (New York: Joseph Desnoues, 1835). In a letter to Michele Colombo, the elderly Da Ponte seemed quite discouraged after the many efforts made to disseminate "the flower of Italian literature" in America (letter to Michele Colombo of August 4, 1828, in *Memorie compendiate da Jacopo Bernardi*): "Up to now I have sung the praises of providence and nature, let me now praise myself. Truly I dare say that no living man has up to now done for the joy of his country, what your friend Lorenzo has done and still does for America. I was ill paid by all, but above all by Americans. They persecuted me here, and they mistreated me in Italy" (187).

Epilogue: Nineteenth-Century Developments   169

And took root
In all the gardens of the New World.[19]

The blooming garden he had dreamed of was merely an illusion; in the New World, the exact sciences were preferred over the study of language and literature:

With praiseworthy preference
All sciences are cultivated,
The numerical especially,
For it America is well known.
But it is not as distinguished
In the study of languages.[20]

Accordingly, Lorenzo Da Ponte's America was not a "new" world insofar as it had to be discovered, but "new" insofar as it needed yet to be educated and enriched by Italian letters. This one-sided perspective led him to disregard the fundamental social and environmental "diversity" that had struck eighteenth-century intellectuals. They were truly the real discoverers of America, although they had never traveled there.

19.   Sulle sponde
    Che dell'Hudson bagnan
    l'onde
    L'idioma suonar faccio
    D'Alighieri e di Boccaccio,
    Ne trapianto i più bei
    fiori,
    Coltivandoli, innaffiandoli
    Di mia man, co' miei
    sudori,
    E que' fior produsser frutti
    Che allignarono per tutti
    I giardin del Nuovo Mondo.
              (Ibid., canto 1)
20.   Con lodevol preferenza
    Si coltiva ogni scienza,
    Soprattutto la numerica,
    In cui celebre è l'America.
    Ma ne' studi delle lingue
    Un po' meno si distingue.
              (Ibid., canto 3)

2. Carlo Botta's *History of the War of the Independence of the United States of America*

In a long oration delivered on the occasion of his seventieth birthday in 1828, the elderly Da Ponte praised, along with several Italian literary luminaries, some historians who were then still living. Among those he had included Carlo Botta, who had written "with elegance, truthfulness and historical method, not only the history of their country, but also the histories of almost the whole world." On the subject of Botta's *History of the War of the Independence of the United States of America*, Da Ponte urged his American guests to "read it . . . but in Italian."[21]

While in the previous century, Botta's histories were read and appreciated, today they are given scant appreciation by historians and scholars; as a case in point, there is no exhaustive critical bibliography on Botta. Over thirty years ago Walter Maturi wrote that "Botta, who enjoyed quite some fame in times past, is known today only to a few scholars."[22] This observation was already applicable to the 1880s, when the historical and literary work of Carlo Botta had interested only a few scholars (the first and last biography is by Dionisotti).[23]

Carlo Botta (San Giorgio Canavese, 1766–Paris, 1837), following an ancient family tradition, received a degree in medicine in Turin when he was only twenty years old. Soon, however, political passion determined a turn in his life. Caught up in ideas from the French Revolution, he took part in the clandestine activities of the first Piedmontese groups against the government of Savoy. Arrested in 1794, he was forced to

---

21. *Memorie di Lorenzo da Ponte*, 370. In the *Annotated Catalogue* Da Ponte wrote, concerning Botta: "The histories of almost all the nations of the World were written better by the Italians than by anyone else. Although this might seem a daring assertion, I would challenge those who might want to deny this merit to Italy, and would summon to my assistance the likes of Siri, Leti, Davila, Sarpi, Strada, Bentivoglio, Beccatini and many others whose names would take too long to mention. A good history of the glorious revolution of North America was lacking, and Botta provided it" (36).

22. Walter Maturi, *Interpretazioni del Risorgimento* (Turin: Einaudi, 1962), 36. On Botta the historian we should always keep in mind Paolo Pavesio, *Carlo Botta e le sue opere storiche: Con appendice di lettere inedite ed un ragguaglio delle opere del Botta* (Florence, 1874); one bibliography was compiled by Carlo Salsotto, *Le opere di Carlo Botta e la loro varia fortuna: Saggi di bibliografia critica con lettere inedite* (Rome: Bocca, 1921). Procacci's pages on the topic are enlightening: Giuliano Procacci, "Rivoluzione americana e storiografia italiana," in *Atti del XXIII Congresso di Storia del Risorgimento Italiano* (Rome, 1954): 395–401.

23. *Vita di Carlo Botta* (Turin: Favale, 1867).

emigrate to Switzerland and from there to France, where he remained until 1798, enlisting in that country's army as a military physician (he served in this capacity for a year with the French occupying forces on the island of Corfu). After having being part of the provisional Piedmontese government, following the abdication of Carlo Emanuele IV and after voting for the annexation of Piedmont to France, Botta again had to seek refuge in Paris in 1799, in the wake of the occupation of Turin by the Russians. In 1800 he took part in Napoleon's Italian campaign and for a year was a member of the Piedmontese government, Piedmont having been annexed to France in 1801. He finally moved to Paris, where his aversion to Napoleon's regime grew. In those years, he devoted himself more to historical-literary work than to political activities. In fact, it was during this period that he wrote his most committed historical works, *History of the War of the Independence of the United States of America* (1809), *Storia d'Italia dal 1789 al 1814* (1824), and *Storia d'Italia continuata da quella del Guicciardini* (1833).

Before examining the history of the American war, it is necessary to elucidate Botta's ideal of history, as well as the position of his work in the historiographical tradition of the eighteenth and nineteenth centuries. Even today, Benedetto Croce's judgment, although peremptory, is a point of departure for a discourse on Botta the historian. In his *Storia della storiografia*, Croce emphasized Botta's complete detachment from eighteenth-century canons, and identified his sole bond with the nineteenth century in his patriotic and moral inspiration. Rejecting a conception of history prevalent during the first half of the nineteenth century, and founded—as Maturi observed—on the fusion of Vico's and Muratori's teachings, a fusion of "philosophy" and "philology,"[24] Botta chose classical and Renaissance historians as his models. This preference for classical and humanistic historians led Croce to state that Botta's works represented an "anachronism" in the nineteenth century, hence "an attempt to restore humanistic historiography in opposition to the preceding century and the new century."[25] This is an arbitrary interpretation, perhaps acceptable from a literary point of view, but not from an ideological or methodological perspective.

For Croce, a return to Roman and humanistic historiography coincided, essentially, with a return to a "historiography of literati"; this conclusion

---
24. See *Interpretazioni del Risorgimento*, 40.
25. Benedetto Croce, *Storia della storiografia italiana* (Bari: Laterza, 1921), 76.

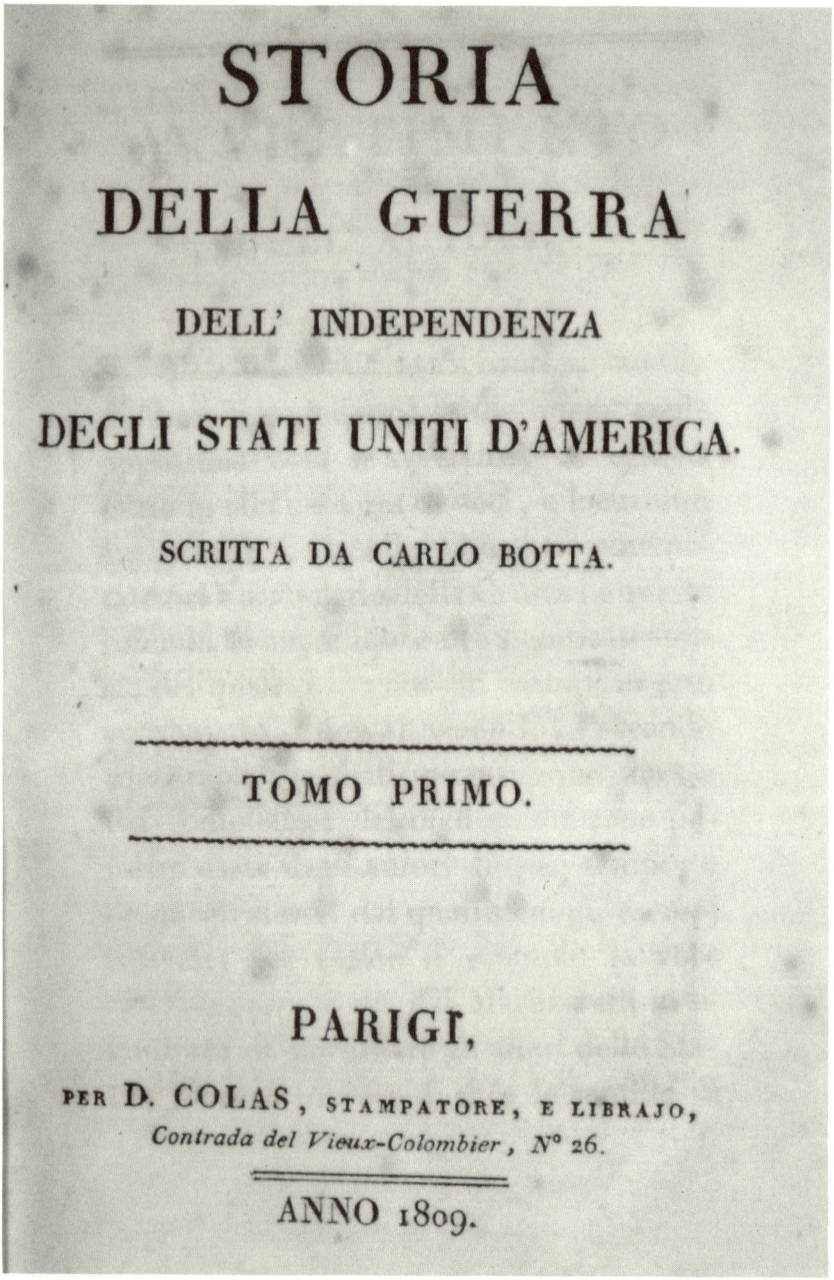

STORIA

DELLA GUERRA

DELL' INDEPENDENZA

DEGLI STATI UNITI D'AMERICA.

SCRITTA DA CARLO BOTTA.

TOMO PRIMO.

PARIGI,

PER D. COLAS, STAMPATORE, E LIBRAJO,
Contrada del Vieux-Colombier, N° 26.

ANNO 1809.

Fig. 18. Title page of Carlo Botta's *Storia della guerra dell'indipendenza degli Stati Uniti d'America*.

led him to observe that all of Botta's historical works had an exclusive literary genesis instead of a critical and scientific origin. He noted this in Botta's search for a pleasing style, in his description of battles, in his often invented orations of illustrious people and in his frequent moral judgments.

Certainly, the genesis of the *History of the War of the Independence of the United States of America*, is literary. Its topic was suggested to Botta by Giulia Beccaria—Manzoni's mother, as Botta himself recalled in his letter to the twenty-three-year-old nephew of General Greene, George Washington Greene:

> About 1806 Madame Beccaria was in Paris. . . . At that time I frequented her house along with many others who enjoyed conversing with a beautiful, virtuous and intelligent woman. One evening the topic of conversation was: which modern theme could be an adequate subject for a heroic poem. After some discussion, finally all agreed that only one modern example could be of use to mankind, and that was the American effort which carried the United States to independence. Returning home that evening, crossing the square then called Revolution Square, and now Concord Square—I mulled thus: *If that event can be a convenient subject for a poem, why not for history?* It seemed to me that it could be so; and so, feeling naturally attracted to history, and having already determined in my soul to write any history, I then resolved to write the history of American independence. I searched in all corners to collect material; then I wrote, and so was born my history of America.[26]

The *History of the War of the Independence of the United States of America*, which an American scholar has called "the most important contribution to the historiography of that war in the first half of the nineteenth century,"[27] was published for the first time in Paris in 1809

---

26. Letter to George Washington Greene of March 20, 1835, in *Lettere inedite di Carlo Botta*, ed. Caterina Maggini (Florence: Le Monnier, 1900), 75–76. Some unpublished letters of Botta to Greene were published in *Archivio storico italiano*, 2d installment (Florence, 1855). For the most part they dealt with literary topics, as Greene cultivated an interest in Italian literature. On another letter by Botta to Greene, kept at the Boston Public Library, see Michele Ricciardelli, "Carlo Botta e George Washington Greene (with an unpublished letter by Botta)," *Symposium* (Fall 1968): 285–88.

27. Jourdan D. Fiore, "Carlo Botta: An Italian Historian of the American Revolution," *Italica* 28 (1951): 158.

at the author's expense; it was then reprinted ten years later in Milan,[28] with some revisions. It enjoyed immediate success with the contemporary public and was soon translated into French and published between 1812 and 1813.

Immediately after its publication it was translated into English by George Alexander Otis and printed in 1820 in Philadelphia (by 1848 there were already ten American editions).[29]

In any case, aside from the episode of the conversation at Beccaria's house, we have yet to determine what motives led Botta to write a history of the American war. On the one hand, there was ethical-political need to show Italians "which means they should utilize to remove themselves from the yoke of despotism and regain national independence"[30]; on the other hand, there were the stimuli from the intellectual climate of contemporary Paris, where American democratic principles had been disseminated by Condorcet and La Fayette.

---

28. Botta's history would be reprinted several times in the nineteenth century: Milan: Ferrario, 1819; Milan: Bettoni, 1820; Florence: Marchini, 1822; Florence: Stamperia Formigli, 1825; Leghorn: Meucci, 1825; Milan: Truffi, 1829-30; Naples: Marotta, 1830; Turin: Vaccarino, 1833; Padua: Tipi della Minerva, 1833-34; Leghorn: Bertani, Antonelli e Co., 1836; Milan: Borroni e Scotti, 1844-45; Florence: Le Monnier, 1856. All reprints subsequent to the Paris edition are based on the 1819 revised edition which, compared to that of 1809, included the Declaration of Independence and the American Constitution. The only variations in the text are of a linguistic nature, as confirmed by Dionisotti (*Vita di Carlo Botta*, 147): "The new Milanese edition was purged of some Gallicisms which the author was accused of having used." In the preface to later editions, Botta stated (Florence: Le Monnier, 1856): "The author of this work thinks it appropriate to warn [the readers] that he used three kinds of voices and expressions: the first are noted in the Dictionary of the Crusca Academy . . . ; the second, although omitted by the compilers of the Crusca Dictionary, were nevertheless in use by the writers of that period, and the examples [the author used] are taken from those same authors; and the third are found neither in the Dictionary nor in writers that the author has used, but are, however, authorized by today's popular usage" (ii-iii). See also *Lettere di Carlo Botta ad un suo amico intorno la lingua e lo stile ch'egli ha usato nella "Storia della guerra dell'indipendenza degli Stati Uniti d'America"* (Milan: Ferrario, 1820).

29. *History of the War of the Independence of the United States of America, written by Charles Botta and translated from the Italian by George Alexander Otis* (Philadelphia: Lydia Bailey, 1820-21). Other American editions are: Boston: H. Gray, 1826; New Haven: N. Whiting, 1834, 1837, and 1838; New Haven: T. Brainard, 1839 and 1840; New Haven: L. Candee, 1842; Cooperstown: H. & I. E. Phinney, 1845, 1847, and 1848; Buffalo: Phinney, 1852 and 1854. Because of the success his *History* met in America, in 1816 Botta was deemed worthy of induction into the Philadelphia Philosophical Society (see Carlo Dionisotti, *Vita di Carlo Botta*, 140).

30. Carlo Dionisotti, *Vita di Carlo Botta*, 138.

As confirmed by the English and French bibliography at the beginning of his *History*, Botta availed himself of a vast repertory of sources and geographical maps. The various English contributors to a history of the New America in the bibliography include the *Journals of the House of Lords*; the *History of the Campaign of 1780 and 1781 in the Southern Provinces of America* by Tarleton (1787); and *The Life of George Washington* by John Marshall (1804–7).[31] Among the French entries are works by well-known "Americanists" of the eighteenth century, such as *La révolution de l'Amérique* by Raynal; the *Voyage de M. le Marquis de Chastelux dans l'Amérique septentrionale, pendant les années 1780–1781 et 1782*; the *Recherches* by Mazzei; and the *Mémoires historiques et pièces authentiquées sur M. de la Fayette*. In addition to these sources, Botta reported that he had also consulted "a large number of pamphlets which at the time of the American revolution were printed and published almost daily in England as well as in America and France."[32]

The *History of the War of the Independence of the United States of America* is composed of fourteen books and divided into three parts. The first part includes the first four books and consists of a synthesis of American events from the arrival of the Pilgrim Fathers up to the first beginnings of the conflict between the colonies and their motherland; the second part, from the fifth through the tenth book, analyzes the final phase of the Revolution after the Declaration of Independence of July 4, 1776; finally, the third part, which includes the last four books, deals with the outcome of the war.

The first book is truly a historical and anthropological introduction. Here Botta depicts the distinctive traits of colonial philosophy and customs, beginning with a portrayal of the first English settlements in New England and a forceful description of the Pilgrims' heroic undertaking:

America, and especially some parts of it, having been discovered by the genius and intrepidity of Italians, received, at various times,

---

31. Among other bibliographical entries, we note: John Clarke, *An Impartial and Authentic Narrative of the Battle Fought on the 17 June, on Bunker's Hill* (1775); John Andrews, *History of the War with America, France, Spain, and Holland Commencing in 1775, and Ending in 1783* (1783); William Gordon, *The History of Rise, Progress, and Establishment of the Independence of the United States of America* (1788); and David Ramsay, *The Life of Washington* (1807).

32. *Storia della guerra dell'indipendenza degli Stati Uniti d'America* (Paris: Colé, 1809), xi.

as into a place of asylum, the men whom political or religious disturbances had driven from their own countries in Europe. The security which these distant and desert regions presented to their minds, appeared to them preferable even to the endearments of country and of their natal air.

Here they exerted themselves with admirable industry and fortitude, according to the custom of those whom the fervor of opinion agitates and stimulates, in subduing the wild beasts, dispersing or destroying pernicious or importunate animals, repressing or subjecting the barbarous and savage nations that inhabited this New World, draining the marshes, controlling the course of rivers, clearing the forests, furrowing a virgin soil, and committing to its bosom new and unaccustomed seeds; and thus prepared themselves a climate less rude and hostile to human nature, more secure and more commodious habitations, more salubrious food, and a part of the conveniences and enjoyments proper to civilized life.[33]

Religious intolerance and the political and ideological incompatibilities forced the Pilgrim Fathers to cross the ocean and to travel to the most remote and inhospitable regions in order to profess their faith. Botta borrowed from the eighteenth century the tendency to represent, in exaggerated fashion, an American nature totally hostile to man; this was a fundamental belief of naturalists such as Buffon, and De Pauw, and of historians such as Robertson and Raynal. The insistence on an inhospitable environment permitted Botta to emphasize the exemplary courage of the colonists in their struggle for survival in a wild land:

> And what toils, what fatigues, what perils, had they not encountered, upon these unknown and savage shores? All had opposed them; their bodies had not been accustomed to the extremes of cold in winter, and of heat in summer, both intolerable in the climate of America; the land chiefly covered with forests, and little of it habitable, the soil reluctant, the air pestilential; an untimely death had carried off most of the first founders of the colony: those who had resisted the climate, and survived the famine, to secure

33. *History of the War of the Independence of the United States of America by Charles Botta, translated from the Italian by George Alexander Otis, Esq., edition*, 2 vols., revised and corrected (New Haven: T. Brainard, 1840), 1:1.

their infant establishment, had been forced to combat the natives, a ferocious race, and become still more ferocious at seeing a foreign people, even whose existence they had never heard of, come to appropriate the country of which they had so long been the sole occupants and masters.[34]

According to Botta, the need to face together the hardships of the natural environment and the fierceness of the Indians led the colonists to found a society based on solidarity and equality: "It should not be omitted, that even the composition of society in the English colonies, rendered the inhabitants averse to every species of superiority, and inclined them to liberty. Here was but one class of men."[35] From its very first beginning, America did not exhibit rigid social roles, as Mazzei had already submitted to the pedant Abbot Mably, and the settler could be at the same time "steward," lord, and laborer on his own lands. Life in the "colonies" therefore had all the blessings of a new golden age:

Each might hunt, fowl and fish, at his pleasure, without fear of possible injury to others; poachers were consequently unknown in America. Their parks and reservoirs were boundless forests, vast

---

34. Ibid., 1:15. Again, Botta wrote: "If liberty is the due of those who have sense enough to know the value of it, and courage enough to expose themselves to every danger and fatigue to acquire it, the American colonists are better entitled to possess it than even their brethren of Great Britain; since they not only renounced their native soil, the love of which is so congenial with the human mind, and all those tender charities inseparable from it, but exposed themselves to all the risks and hardships unavoidable in a long voyage; and, after escaping the danger of being swallowed up by the waves, encountered, upon those uninhabited and barbarous shores, the more cruel danger of perishing by a slow famine; which having combated, and surmounted, with infinite patience and constancy, they have, as if by a miracle of Divine Providence, at length arrived at this vigorous and prosperous state, so eminently profitable to those from whom they derive their origin" (1:45-46).

35. Ibid., 1:16. Botta also stressed the religiosity of the New England settlers: "The religious zeal, or rather enthusiasm, which prevailed among the colonists, and chiefly among the inhabitants of New England, maintained the purity of their manners. Frugality, temperance, and chastity, were virtues peculiar to this people. There were no examples, among them, of wives devoted to luxury, husbands to debauch, and children to the haunts of pleasure. The ministers of a severe religion were respected and revered; for they gave themselves the example of the virtues they preached. Their time was divided between rural occupations, domestic parties, prayers, and thanksgivings, addressed to that God by whose bounty the seasons were made propitious, and the earth to smile on their labors with beauty and abundance, and who showered upon them so many blessings and so many treasures" (1:19).

and numerous lakes, immense rivers, and a sea unrestricted, inexhaustible in fish of every species. As they lived dispersed in the country, mutual affection was increased between the members of the same family; and finding happiness in the domestic circle, they had no temptation to seek diversion in the resorts of idleness, where men too often contract the vices which terminate in dependence and habits of servility.[36]

The insistence on the three features of "equality," "rural life," and "liberty" of the first American society confirms Botta's bonds—which Croce had denied—with other "American" historians of the Enlightenment, such as the Burkes and Raynal. This explains also the "canonization" of Penn as founder of an egalitarian, free, and essentially farming community.

Concerning slavery, which, for the majority of progressive intellectuals, represented a contradiction in a country that aspired toward freedom, Botta wrote:

In these provinces also, the slavery of the blacks, which was in use, seemed, however strange the assertion may appear, to have increased the love of liberty among the white population. Having continually before their eyes, the living picture of the miserable condition of man reduced to slavery, they could better appreciate the liberty they enjoyed. This liberty they considered not merely as a right, but as a franchise and privilege.[37]

Here Botta reached a unique, and in a certain sense paradoxical, conclusion with respect to other contemporary opinions held on the issue of blacks: in America slaves fulfilled a psychological function, in addition to a practical one, insofar as their presence assisted colonists in acquiring a consciousness of liberty and of its value.

The leading theme of the first pages of Botta's *History* is the certainty that liberty had always marked American society, from the very first settlements up to their definitive separation from England; thus it was inevitable that, with the passing of generations, "love for the sovereign and the ancient motherland" would diminish and finally become extinguished in the souls of the colonists:

36. Ibid., 1:16.
37. Ibid., 1:18.

The love of the sovereign, and their ancient country, which the first colonists might have retained in their new establishment, gradually diminished in the hearts of their descendants, as successive generations removed them further from their original stock; and when the revolution commenced, of which we purpose [sic] to write the history, the inhabitants of the English colonies were, in general, but the third, fourth, and even the fifth generation from the original colonists, who had left England to establish themselves in the new regions of America. At such a distance, the affections of consanguinity became feeble, or extinct; and the remembrances of their ancestors lived more in their memories, than in their hearts. . . . The greater part of the colonists had heard nothing of Great Britain, excepting that it was a distant kingdom, from which their ancestors had been barbarously expelled, or hunted away, as they had been forced to take refuge in the deserts and forests of wild America, inhabited only by savage men, and prowling beasts, or venomous and horrible serpents.[38]

When England became a "far away" land, the separation of the colonies became imminent, and in the second book the historian recalls the first rebellions subsequent to the Stamp Act of 1765. He dwelt upon the first uprisings in Massachusetts, and in particular on the people's attack on the homes of the English authorities in Boston:

> The people followed, stamping, and shouting from all quarters, "Liberty and property forever—no stamp." Having passed through the town house, they proceeded with their pageantry down King street, and into Kilby street; when arrived in front of a house owned by one Oliver, which they supposed was designed for a stamp office, they halted, and without further ceremony, demolished it to the foundation. Bearing off, as it were in triumph, the wood of the ruined house, with continually increasing shouts and tumult, they proceeded to the dwelling of Oliver himself, and there having beheaded his effigy, broke all his windows in an instant. . . . A particular whistle was heard from several quarters, which was followed by innumerable cries of "Sirrah! Sirrah!" At this signal advanced a long train of persons disguised, armed with clubs and bludgeons, who

38. Ibid., 1:17.

proceeded to invest the house of Paxton, marshal of the court of admiralty, and superintendent of the port. . . .

Their repeated libations having renewed their frenzy, they sallied forth, and assaulted the house of William Story, register of the vice-admiralty, opposite the court-house, the lower part of which, being his office, they broke open, seized and committed to the flames the files and public records of that court, and then destroyed the furniture of the house. . . .

They renewed their potations, in the cellar; and what they were unable to drink, they wasted; they searched every corner, and carried off about thirty pounds sterling in money. They are joined by fresh bands. In a state bordering on madness, they proceed to the residence of Hutchinson, the lieutenant-governor, about ten o'clock at night; they invest it, and employ every means to enter it by violence.[39]

In Botta's stylistic virtuosity, we can identify a humanistic historiographical model. However, as Maturi noted[40]—in a partial criticism of Croce's interpretation, which emphasized a clear split between Botta and the eighteenth century—several sections of the history echo quite a few Enlightenment topics and conventions. Like most eighteenth-century historians, for example, Botta was reluctant to identify "glory" with military conquest ("The rulers of nations," he wrote, "invented the bestial name of glory: glory for he who cherishes man, not for he who kills man: William Penn, Bartolomeo Las Casas and Fénelon are worthier of praise and admiration than a thousand Alexanders, a thousand Napoleons and so many similar armoured Attilas.");[41] to warriors and conquistadors he opposed "apostles of liberty" such as Penn, Franklin, and Washington. However, although he stressed the guiding role of the "heroes" of the Revolution, one of the more original aspects of the *History of the War of the Independence* is the attention given to the masses and their reactions. The "people's voice" returns frequently, as evidenced by the following passage where the famous massacre that occurred in Boston on March 5, 1770, is remembered:

They [the rioters] approached the sentinel, crying, "*Kill him! kill him!*" . . . The maledictions, the imprecations, the execrations of

39. Ibid., 1:65, 66, 67.
40. See *Interpretazioni del Risorgimento*, 43.
41. Quoted in ibid.

the multitude, were horrible. In the midst of a torrent of invectives from every quarter, the military was challenged to fire. The detachment was surrounded; and the populace advanced to the points of their bayonets. The soldiers appeared like statues; the cries, the howlings, the menaces, the violent din of bells, still sounding the alarm, increased the confusion and the horrors of these moments.[42]

The people's choruses, almost certainly invented, are flanked by several speeches by the most illustrious personalities of the Revolution.[43] Most of them were modeled after the originals as we read in Botta's introduction to this *History*:

> There will be found, in the course of this history, several discourses of a certain length. Those I have put in the mouth of the different speakers have really been pronounced by them, and upon those very occasions which are treated of in the work. I should, however, mention that I have sometimes made a single orator say what has been said in substance by others of the same party. Sometimes, also, but rarely, using the liberty granted in all times to historians, I have ventured to add a small number of phrases, which appeared to me to coincide perfectly with the sense of the orator, and proper to enforce his opinion; this has appeared especially in the two discourses pronounced before congress, for and against independence, by Richard Henry Lee and John Dickinson.[44]

In general, in Botta's *History* these long speeches preceded a battle and were given on the occasion of political meetings. Here we quote also the concluding and most emphatic part of a speech given by Lee in support of independence, during the assembly that took place in Virginia on June 8, 1776:

> Let us hail the favorable omen, and fight not for the sake of knowing on what terms we are to be the slaves of England, but to secure

---

42. *History of the War of the Independence*, 113.
43. Benedetto Croce, *Storia della storiografia*, 81.
44. *History of the War of the Independence*, author's preface, introductory page. Botta goes on to note: "It will not escape attentive readers, that in some of these discourses are found predictions which time has accomplished. I affirm that these remarkable passages belong entirely to the authors cited. In order that these might not resemble those of the poets, always made after the fact, I have been so scrupulous as to translate them, word for word, from the original language."

to ourselves a free existence, to found a just and independent government. Animated by liberty, the Greeks repulsed the innumerable army of Persians; sustained by the love of independence, the Swiss and the Dutch humbled the power of Austria by memorable defeats, and conquered a rank among nations. But the sun of America also shines upon the heads of the brave; the point of our weapons is no less formidable than theirs; here also the same union prevails, the same concept of dangers and of death in asserting the cause of country.

Why then do we longer delay, why still deliberate? Let this most happy day give birth to the American republic. Let her arise, not to devastate and conquer, but to re-establish the reign of peace and of the laws.[45]

Thus for Botta, the American Revolution embodied the ideal of a war fought not for "glory" or "conquest," but exclusively in defense of free human rights and the establishment of a peaceful republic. A positive hero who eminently represented this American libertarian ideal was Washington, whom Botta polemically compared to Napoleon, the "liberticide" and the "anti-hero" of the *Storia d'Italia continuata da quella del Guicciardini*: "An unanimous voice pronounced him [Washington] the savior of his country; all extolled him as equal to the most celebrated commanders of antiquity; all proclaimed him the Fabius of America. His name was in the mouth of all; he was celebrated by the pens of the most distinguished writers."[46] In 1834, in a letter to George Washington Greene, Botta would praise Washington again as the "faithful custodian of American liberty":

I adore Washington, whom many in this ugly Europe discuss and few imitate. I feel like an honest man because I ardently love that great American: he died at the plow; he did not chirp on benches so that the world would speak of him.[47]

---

45. Ibid., 1:349.
46. Ibid., 1:429.
47. Letter to George Washington Greene, in *Lettere inedite di Carlo Botta*, 77. In another letter to Greene of January 29, 1836 (p. 80), Botta sent the following verses to Greene's wife:

> Here wrote a man, who was a friend of liberty;
> Here wrote a man, who sounded the bugle for Washington;
> Here wrote a man, who was dear to Jefferson,

"Dying at the plow" after fighting for independence, Washington became the perfect embodiment of the three ideals of "liberty," "equality," and "rural life" that eighteenth-century Europe had indicated as being the distinctive features of the New America.

Nonetheless, the true propagandist of revolutionary ideology was Paine, whose pamphlets were starting to circulate when "the desire of Independence insinuated itself little by little into the minds of all. In public, particularly, the harangues had no other object; the general attention was fixed upon events."[48] Paine, by pointing to the defense of the rights of man as moral justification for the Revolution, endeavored to make people conscious of the need for autonomy.[49] The simple ideas and the passionate appeal for the defense of human rights set forth in *Common Sense* (1776) and in other writings which found a general consensus among the urban masses as well as the farmers. It may be affirmed, in effect, that this work (*Common Sense*) was one of the most powerful instruments of American independence. Botta observed: "The success of this writing of Paine cannot be described. The vehemence of opinion redoubled in the minds of all; even loyalists were seen to declare for liberty; an unanimous cry arose for independence."[50]

        Here wrote a man who cried for Venilia;
        Here wrote a man who in sorrow and pain
        Wept for the fate of Italy enslaved.

        ("Qui scrisse un uomo di libertade amico;
        Qui scrisse un uomo che a Washington fu tromba;
        Qui scrisse un uom che a Jefferson fu caro,
        Qui scrisse un uom che di Venilia pianse;
        Qui scrisse un uom che della serva Italia
        Pien di sdegno e dolor le sorti pianse.")

48. *History of the War of the Independence*, 1:343.

49. "The author endeavored, with very plausible arguments, to demonstrate that the opposition of parties, the diversity of interest, the arrogance of the British government, and its ardent thirst of vengeance, rendered all reconciliation impossible. On the other hand, he enlarged upon the necessity, utility, and possibility of independence.

He omitted not to sprinkle his pamphlet with declamations calculated to render monarchy odious to the people, and to inspire them with the desire of a republic. The excellency of the English constitution had never till then been called in question; Paine criticized it very freely in the part which relates to the royal power, but praised its other institutions. . . . He congratulated the Americans that Heaven had placed it their power to create a constitution that should embrace all the excellencies of England without any of its defects; and thus, again, he intimated the exclusion of royalty" (ibid., 1:343-44).

50. Ibid.

The Declaration of Independence of July 4 came at a moment when public opinion was ready and generally favorable to a separation from the motherland.

From the seventh to the twelfth book, Botta analyzed the final phase of the American riots, which "grew without obstacle, till at length, swollen like an overflowing river, they acquired such an impetuosity as to sweep before them the impotent dikes with which it was attempted too late to oppose them."[51] With the outburst of the conflict, Botta proceeded along two themes: one theme, the military, which was devoted to the dynamics of the war and a careful description of the various battles; the other, the political theme, which allowed him to judge that "neither so many advantages, nor even the retired situation of these unfortunate colonists, could exempt them from the baneful influence of party spirit."[52] He compared the admirable military conduct of the rebels to the uncertainty of the English soldiers:

> The Americans were always constant in their resolution, the English always versatile, uncertain, and wavering. Hence it is not at all surprising that [the former] found new friends, and that [the latter] not only lost theirs, but also made enemies of them at the very moment when they could do them the least harm, and might receive the most from them.[53]

As he had already pointed out in book 2, the historian did not believe that France's help could have been a disinterested gesture. As a matter of fact, France was "ever bearing in mind the wounds received in the war of Canada, . . . always jealous of the power of England"[54] and hoped to extract economic benefits from its participation in the American war. Later, shifting his attention from the complex dynamics of alliances to the American predicament, Botta identified in internal political disagreements and in the prevailing of private interests over the public interest, a serious danger for the rebels' victory.[55]

51. Ibid., 1:360.
52. Ibid., 2:158.
53. Ibid., 2:129.
54. Ibid., 2:88.
55. "Nor was avarice the extent of the evil; the contagion of the pestiferous passion attacked the very source of every virtue. Private interest every where carried it against the interests of the public. A greater number than it is easy to believe, looked upon the love

Epilogue: Nineteenth-Century Developments   185

The books on the most intense phase of the war are certainly anecdotal and colorful, at times horrid in their description of battles and natural calamities. For example, summarizing the stages of the English-French conflict in the Antilles, Botta describes a violent tropical storm on the island of Barbados:

> The thickness of the darkness, and the lurid fire of the lightning, the continual peal of the thunder, the horrible whistling of the winds and rain, the doleful cries of the dying, the despondent moans of those who were unable to succor them, the shrieks and wailings of women and children, all seemed to announce the destruction of the world. But the return of day presented to the view of the survivors a spectacle which the imagination scarcely dares to depict. This island, lately so rich, so flourishing, so covered with enchanting landscapes, appeared all of a sudden transformed into one of those polar regions where an eternal winter reigns. Not an edifice left standing; wrecks and ruins every where; every tree subverted; not an animal alive; the earth strewn with their remains, intermingled with those of human beings; the very surface of the soil appeared no longer the same.[56]

Botta's penchant for describing frightful scenes suffused with romantic, gloomy accents is again present in his recounting of the destruction of the happy colony of "Viomino" [Translator's Note: Wyoming, in northeastern Pennsylvania] founded by the "Connecticutese" on the eastern shores of the Susquehanna river at the extreme border of Pennsylvania. Botta wrote: "The mildness of the climate answered to the fertility of the soil. . . . All lived in a happy mediocrity, frugal of their own, and coveting nothing from others. Incessantly occupied in rural toils, they avoided idleness,

---

of country as a mere illusion, which held out no better prospect than ruin and desolation. Nobody would enlist without exorbitant bounty; nobody would contract to furnish the public supplies, none would supply the contractors, without enormous profits first lodged in their hands; none would accept of an office or magistracy without perfect assurance of a scandalous salary and illicit perquisites. The disorder, the depravation, were pushed to such a point, that perhaps never was the ancient adage more deplorably confirmed, that *there is no halting-place on the road of corruption*.

To the insatiable thirst of gold was joined the rage of party spirit [so that] even the members of congress could not escape its vortex. Hence they too often disputed among themselves about their personal affairs, instead of discussing the grave and important interests of the state" (ibid., 2:215-16).

56. Ibid., 2:271.

and all the vices of which it is the source. In a word, this little country presented in reality the image of those fabulous times which the poets have described under the name of the *Golden Age*."[57] However, this idyllic state of happiness was destined to vanish after a barbaric attack by the Indians, who had allied themselves with the English:

> The Americans immediately break, the savages leap in among the ranks, and a horrible carnage ensues. The fugitives fall by missiles, the resisting by clubs and tomahawks. The wounded overturn those that are not, the dead and the dying are heaped together promiscuously. Happy those who expire the soonest! The savages reserve the living for tortures! and the infuriate tories, if other arms fail them, mangle their prisoners with their nails! . . . But who will believe that their fury, not yet satisfied upon human creatures, was also wreaked upon the very beasts? That they cut out the tongues of the horses and cattle, and left them to wander in the midst of those fields lately so luxuriant, and now in desolation, seeming to enjoy the torments of their lingering death?[58]

After dwelling on the fury of battles and in great detail on the Indians' barbarian exploits, Botta was careful to stress: "We have long hesitated whether we ought to relate particular instances of this demoniac cruelty; the bare remembrance of them makes us shudder. But on reflecting that these examples may deter good princes from war, and citizens from civil discord, we have deemed it useful to record them."[59] The educational intent ("ethical rhetoric" according to Croce) of his histories was so declaired along with his inclination to formulate what Botta himself called "moralità" (moral observations of a general nature), so criticized by Gino Capponi:

> Concerning "moralità," Count Velo and Marquis Capponi may talk, but certainly I will never restrict myself to being a mere narrator, as historians of our time are wont to be: another, higher duty is

57. Ibid., 2:157-58.
58. Ibid., 2:160-61. Botta censored the English for manipulating the Indians and the slaves against the Americans: "Why do they continue to embitter the minds of the savages against you? Surely, this is not the way to conciliate the affections of America. Be not, therefore, deceived. Your foreign alliances . . . cannot secure your country from desolation" (2:125).
59. Ibid., 2:161.

incumbent on the historian; and were he not to praise virtue and chastise vice, it would be better from him to be silent, nor would he deserve to be called a historian. If someone wants a news-sheet from me, I know not how to write it. I want to write as much as I can like Tacitus, not like some modern, middling writer.[60]

Recalling Tacitus, thus an ethical and political historiographic ideal, Botta intended to differentiate himself from "modern middling writers" and to recover the moral meaning of historical events. Writing history does not consist, therefore, in recording the events, but rather in exploring their causes and effects. This conception is reflected in the last book of the *History of the War of the Independence* where, in giving an overall evaluation of the Revolution, he reviewed the causes of American victory. We attempt to summarize them here as follows:

1. Alliance with other nations: "[The Americans gained independence because] in the first place, they had the good fortune not to encounter opposition from foreign nations, and even to find among them benevolence, countenance, and succors."[61]

2. Continuity, not rupture, with the old English order: "One of the most powerful causes of the success of the American Revolution, should, doubtless, be sought in the little difference that existed between the form of government they abandoned, and the one they wished to establish. It was not from absolute, but from limited monarchy, that they passed to the freedom of an elective government. Moral things, with men, are subject to the same laws as physical; *the laws of all nature*. Total and sudden changes cannot take place without causing disasters or death."[62]

3. Unity and perseverance in achieving objectives: "Another material cause of the happy issue of this grand enterprise, will be seen in the

---

60. Letter to Count Littardi dated September 27, 1822, in *Lettere inedite di Carlo Botta*, 112. His ideal of history, far from a philosophical-type reconstruction or an erudite account, is enunciated in the preface to the later Italian editions of the *Storia della guerra dell'indipendenza degli Stati Uniti d'America*: "The ancients were content with narrating changes in government, the facts of war, the biographies of the powerful and a few unusual and outstanding events; they derived their material from tradition or memory, collected and put together coarsely, and their explanation of effects was limited, so to speak, to the alpha and the omega, their immediate causes and the vaguest generalizations about nature. Today we need to look at the widest and most varied surface of facts, so as to include all the classes and all the intellectual and material efforts of men, their economic conditions, the relations among nations, and so many details which may seem boring at first, but which give connection and color, that is to say, truth to the [historical] representation" (iii).
61. *History of the War of the Independence*, 2:459-60.
62. Ibid., 2:460.

circumspect and moderate conduct invariably pursued by that considerate and persevering people by whom it was achieved."[63]

4. Homogenous character of the war, with no division of roles: "They presented not the afflicting spectacle of friends dissolving their ancient intimacies, and even declaring a sudden war upon each other, because one was arrived at the helm of state without calling the other to it. With them patriotism triumphed over ambition. There existed royalists and republicans; but not republicans of different sects, rending with their dissensions the bosom of their country. . . . An ever memorable proof that if precipitate resolutions cause the failure of political enterprises, temper and perseverance conduct them to a glorious issue."[64]

From these reflections, we conclude that Botta interpreted the American war not as a "revolution" (a term that seldom recurs in his "history"), but as a "transformation" that did not set for itself impossible goals (contrary to what would happen in France because of the "anachronistic" pretense of wanting to move from a despotic regime to a republic). Therefore, unlike Alfieri who praised the destruction of the old order and the revolutionary phase, Botta appreciated the "conservative" character of the young republic. As Maturi noted, Botta favored the "quietest" and conservative aspect over the creative and progressive aspect of the eighteenth century: "In Botta we no longer see the belligerent eighteenth-century illuminist, but rather the conservative illuminist of the Restoration: no longer Voltaire's enlightenment, but Metternich's."[65] Thus it is in this perspective that we ought to understand his agreement with the maintenance of ancient institutions and the establishment "in the New World of a Republic, happy within by its constitution, pacific by its character, respected and courted abroad for the abundance of its resources."[66]

Although its basis is literary, as pointed out by Croce, Botta's work has a place in the historiography of the last two centuries. Because of both the originality of its viewpoints and the careful selection of its sources it will be the point of departure for subsequent studies on the American Revolution. Unfortunately, after the extensive national and international success reaped in the nineteenth century, the *History of the War of the*

63. Ibid., 1:461.
64. Ibid., 2:461–62.
65. *Interpretazioni del Risorgimento*, 45.
66. *History of the War of the Independence*, 2:452.

Independence of the United States of America fell into oblivion; we hope a new edition will rescue it.

3. Giacomo Leopardi and the New World

Recalling the opinions of the classical authors on the existence of antipodes in his *Saggio sopra gli errori popolari degli antichi*, Leopardi noted that "there are nevertheless those who think that the ancients had some notions about the American peoples. Count Gianrinaldo Carli argued this opinion in his famous *Lettere americane*."[67] Taking his cue from the letters in which the well-known Istrian intellectual discussed Atlantis, Leopardi divided those who "considered this island allegorical" from those who "recognized in the same [island] clear indications that it is America."[68] But Leopardi was skeptical about identifying the sunken lands with the New World and concluded his thought by quoting Aristotle:

> But putting aside these fables and ill-founded conjectures, we can almost certainly say that the ancients . . . knew of the existence of the lands and populations of the other hemisphere, only through reasoning, in the same way in which Aristotle knew as probable that there existed other countries not yet discovered, in addition to the countries that were known in his times.[69]

Again, in the chapter on pigmies and giants, referring to the existence of "tiny men," he stated that "this tale has always been held to be true, from Homer up to the scientific Renaissance, and all scholars thought it was a factual truth, just like the existence of America."[70]

Once discovered and thus accepted as a "factual truth," America provoked a psychological trauma in humankind that had always believed in the myth of a continent situated in the middle of the ocean, as borne out by the remote origins of the Atlantis legend. Thus, Columbus's discovery of "an unknown, immense land" destroyed humanity's "fair dreams," as we read in Leopardi's canzone "Ad Angelo Mai":

67. *Saggio sopra gli errori popolari degli antichi*, in *Tutte le opere*, 1:830.
68. Ibid.
69. Ibid., 289.
70. Ibid., 831.

> Nature's obstacles having all been tamed,
> An unknown, immense land to your voyage
> Gave glory, and to your return
> Risks. Ah, but having known it, the world
> Does not grow, it shrinks instead, and much vaster
> The resounding air, the noble earth, the sea
> To the child appear, than to the wise old man.
> Where have our fair dreams gone
> Of an unknown haven
> To unknown dwellers, of the daily
> Refuge of stars, and the far-away bed
> Of young Aurora, and the nightly
> Hidden sleep of the greatest planet?[71]

Thus the "embodiment" of a dream opens wider geographic horizons; but at the same time, it inevitably shrinks the horizons of myth.

In addition to Carli's *Lettere americane*, undoubtedly the best known late eighteenth-century Italian work on an American topic, Leopardi read other eighteenth-century texts that were fundamental to a knowledge of the new continent. A review of the *Zibaldone*, however, shows that Leopardi's perspective was substantially "Hispanocentric" insofar as his attention was focused on the Iberian possessions in America.[72] Among his readings were *Chronica del Perú* by Cieça de Leon, the *History of America* by Robertson, the *Histoire naturelle* by Buffon and Algarotti's essays.

---

71. E rotto di natura ogni contrasto,
Ignota immensa terra al tuo viaggio
Fu gloria, e del ritorno
Ai rischi. Ahi Ahi, ma conosciuto il mondo
Non cresce, anzi si scema, e assai più vasto
L'etra sonante e l'alma terra e il mare
Al fanciullin, che non al saggio, appare.
    Nostri sogni leggiadri ove sono giti
Dell'ignoto ricetto
D'ignoti abitatori, o del diurno
Degli astri albergo, e del rimoto letto
Della giovane Aurora, e del notturno
Occulto sonno del maggior pianeta?
    "Ad Angelo Mai," 1:7-8, lines 84-96.

72. In his *Memorie e disegni letterari*, Leopardi wrote: "The history of the Mexican people before the Spaniards, adapted from Clavigero's, as the history of Oracles" (1:371). However, we do not know whether this was a research project or a reading plan.

Epilogue: Nineteenth-Century Developments   191

His attention to the physical aspect of the Americas and the anthropological and somatic characteristics of the natives confirms that Leopardi was aware of the main arguments on which historians and naturalists relied to "denigrate" the Americas. Ideas about "drunkenness," which drove Americans to deadly wars, about beardless Indians,[73] about the "custom of wrapping children's heads with bandages and other tight wraps,"[74] and about the usage of "burying men and women alive together with their dead masters,"[75] were supplemented by other anthropological observations about the social order of the American Indians and their sacrificial and man-eating practices. On the subject of cannibalism, Leopardi wrote:

> What could be more contrary to nature than an animal species that serves as its own nourishment and food? . . . Nature fated many animal species to be food and nourishment to other species, but did not fate that an animal eat of its like, and not even because of an extraordinary hunger, but regularly, and that it prefers its like to other foods; this incredible absurdity is only found in the human species. Entire nations of almost primitive customs, united in informal societies, customarily practice or for many centuries practiced this custom, not only towards their enemies, but towards their friends, their elders, their parents, wives and children. . . .
>
> Superstitions, human victims of the same nations and among friends, sacrificed not out of hate, but out of fear, as we wrote elsewhere, and also out of custom; further, the enemies sacrificed most cruelly to the gods without any passion, but only out of custom; torture, self-mutilation, etc. done out of vanity, superstition, or custom; wives freely setting fire to themselves at the death of their husbands; burying of live men and women, along with their dead masters, as was the custom in many countries of South America, etc. are all well known facts.[76]

73. See *Zibaldone di pensieri*, 2:1102.
74. Ibid., 1008.
75. Ibid., 951.
76. Ibid. On cannibalism Leopardi quoted the following passages from the *Correspondance du Prince Royal de Prusse* by Voltaire: "I saw four savages from Louisiana who had been brought to France in 1723. Among them was a woman with a very sweet disposition. Through an interpreter, I asked her if she had sometimes eaten her enemies' flesh and if she had found pleasure in it; she replied yes; I asked her if she would have willingly killed or had someone kill one of her compatriots so as to eat him; she replied by shaking; she was visibly terrified by such a crime" (840).

Leopardi was convinced that cannibalistic practices, "possibly common to all American barbarous and savage peoples, both in the South as well as in the North," were abolished by the Incas and the Mexicans, who were "somewhat cultivated" populations of the New World. But although he recognized the higher level of progress reached by the ancient Pre-Columbian societies, he judged them to be merely "somewhat cultivated" (in fact, he could not believe that the Incas had reached the summit of civilization without knowing how to write),[77] and ignored the traditional Enlightenment praise of the Incas and Aztecs that had inspired Parini's verses and the works of Algarotti and Carli. The reason for this attitude must be found in the very definition of "civilization" that in Leopardi's thought, takes on a negative connotation of "corruption." The distinction between "pure savage state" and "barbarianism," as a "principle of civilization," is useful in understanding Leopardi's conception:

> We rightfully consider all primitive, early societies to be barbarian societies; they are generally so called, and the closer they are to their principles, the more barbarous they are. There has never been found, nor will there ever be found, a society of so-called savages, that is, a primitive society, which is not truly barbarous and unnatural. . . . The first steps man has taken or is taking toward a closed society lead him by leaps to a place which is so far from nature, and a state which is so contrary to it, that only in the course of a very long time, and with the aid of many circumstances and infinite casual incidents (which happen very rarely) can man be led back to a state which is not contrary to nature.[78]

The golden age, therefore, coincided with a pre-social stage of man on earth, when all traces of any kind of order, including tribal order,

---

77. "In all of America, which most certainly has been inhabited since the most remote times, as there is no history or memory of when it was first settled, no alphabet of any kind was found, nor is there any kind of alphabet now, nor anything similar to it. And this, notwithstanding the abundant and wonderful culture, arts, manufacturing, admirable buildings, fine politics and legislation, and other large elements of civilization that were found in the lands subjected to the kingdom of the Incas, which began three centuries before the discovery and conquest of that country (that is to say, in the thirteenth century); and even more in Mexico, whose civilization is, I believe, even more ancient" (ibid., 1008).
78. Ibid., 1008. See Ibid. 998: "Yet, the travels and the histories of all ancient nations show that the closer a society is or was to its beginnings, the farther the life of individuals and of peoples is or was from nature, and contrary to it."

were unknown ("Primitive does not mean barbarian. The barbarian is already decaying; the primitive is not yet ripe"). At this point Leopardi's distance from Rousseauian naturalism is clear; for Rousseau, the ideal state of mankind coincided exactly midway between the bestiality of the first beginnings and the most advanced phases of a debased society; for Leopardi the midpoint—as Sozzi pointed out in a careful analysis of this Leopardian utopia—"is no longer a summit between two low points but an intermediate time, between the summits of the beginnings and the barbarians' darkness. It is a silver age midway between the unreachable splendor of the initial golden age, and the base metal of the age of decay."[79]

After the "leap" that distanced them from nature, Peruvians and Mexicans must also be considered among the "civilizations" tending to a conscious recovery of their original innocence. Leopardi further noted:

> Undoubtedly, civilized man is closer to nature than savage, social man. What does this mean? Society corrupts. During the course of time, circumstances and understanding, man tries to get closer to that nature from which he had distanced himself, through the only force and means provided by society. Therefore, civilization takes us closer again to nature.[80]

In another page of the *Zibaldone* Leopardi again clarified his concept of a conscious return to nature after an "excess of civilization":

> Man was corrupted, that is, as I have shown, reason had overtaken nature: therefore, man had become social: hence, he had become unhappy, because reason prevailing, his primitive nature had been altered and tainted, and he had fallen from his primordial perfection, which consisted solely in his own primordial essence or condition. Experience teaches us that man cannot revert from this state of corruption unless there is a miracle: this is also proven by reason,

---

79. Lionello Sozzi, "Le californie selve: un'utopia leopardiana," in *Annali della Scuola Normale* 11 (1985): 194. "Reason is the source of barbarianism (it is itself barbarian), an excess of reason being so always; but nature is never so, because, finally, only what is against nature is barbarian . . . therefore nature and barbarianism are contradictory, and nature's essence cannot be barbarian" (*Zibaldone*, 135). On the relationship between Leopardi and Rousseau, see Ferdinando Neri, *Il pensiero del Rousseau nelle prime chiose dello "Zibaldone,"* in *Letteratura e leggende* (Turin: Chiantore, 1951).
80. *Zibaldone*, 1000.

because what is learned cannot be forgotten. In fact, human history shows only a continuous passage from one degree of civilization to another, then to an excess of civilization, and finally to barbarianism, whence it starts all over again. We mean by barbarianism, corruption, not an absolute, natural state, since the latter would not be barbarianism.[81]

Coming back to the Americans, Leopardi wrote that when the Europeans discovered Peru, "whenever they found a trace or sign of civilization and sophistication, they found the cult of the sun. . . . Generally, the temples to the sun were a sign of civilization, and the boundaries of the cult of the sun were also the boundaries of civilization." Thus the Incas civilized a large part of South America "as compared to the extreme barbarian state of the peoples of those lands who were not subjected to their dominion, and of the peoples bordering them, and the barbarian state of the peoples who had been subjected before."[82] At this point we ought to review the connotation Leopardi gave to "barbarianism," understood as a precivilized state which is no longer a state of "nature" insofar as "barbarians," having just come out of their "savage" state, were also the founders of the first social nuclei or of the so-called "closed societies." One condition that characterized these societies was the spirit of vengeance, which made anger and hate everlasting: "Now this spirit, inevitable in every closed human society, was unknown to primitive man, just as it is unknown to other animals; in them, anger lasts momentarily, like any other passion, and so does the memory of the insult received."[83] Thus, vengeance was at the source of the American peoples' barbaric wars:

> The savage tribes of America, who reciprocally destroy themselves in deathly wars, and also destroy themselves on account of their drunkenness, do not engage in these actions because they are savage, but because they are in an initial stage of civilization, a most imperfect, coarse beginning; because they have started to become civilized, and are therefore barbarian. The state of nature does not teach this; and in this state they are not. Their evils proceed from an initial stage of civilization.[84]

81. Ibid., 149.
82. Ibid., 964.
83. Ibid., 995.
84. Ibid., 1101.

Epilogue: Nineteenth-Century Developments   195

However, among Americans, now turned barbarians because they have been corrupted by civilization or the beginnings of civilization, only the natives of California (*Californii*) still lived in a "pure savage state." For Leopardi, they became a symbol of that residuum of humanity not yet absorbed by civilization, but which was, in any case, destined to be so absorbed:

> In the vast Californian forests
> A blessed offspring is born, whose bosom is not
> torn by care, whose limbs
> are not tamed by wild plague; and the woods are food,
> the secluded cliffs are nests, the drained valley
> serves, and unexpected the day
> of dark death looms. Oh against our
> wicked daring the helpless kingdoms
> of wise nature! The shores, caves,
> the quiet forests our undefeated
> frenzy; it educates violated
> people to foreign worry,
> to unknown desires; and fleeting, naked
> truth presses on the low-lying sun.[85]

The miracle of the "Californii" allowed Leopardi to reinforce and objectify his reflections on nature and on society that recur in *Zibaldone*, especially between 1822, the year in which *Inno ai patriarchi* was

85.   Tal fra le vaste californie selve
       Nasce beata prole, a cui non sugge
       Pallida cura il petto, a cui le membra
       Fera tabe non doma; e vitto il bosco
       Nidi l'intima rupe, onde ministra
       L'irrigua valle, inopinato il giorno
       Dell'atra morte incombe. Oh contra il nostro
       Scellerato ardimento inermi regni
       Della saggia natura! I lidi e gli antri
       E le quiete selve apre l'invitto
       Nostro furor; le violate genti
       Al peregrino affanno, agl'ignorati
       Desiri educa; e la fugace, ignuda
       Felicità per l'imo sole incalza.
(*Inno ai patriarchi o de' principi del genere umano*, in *Tutte le opere*, 1:14, lines 104-17).

composed, and 1824. The "Californii," like the "coarsest" Patagonians of Vico, represented the last traces of a primordial humanity; they were

> a people with possibly a unique life, since there is almost no society among them, excepting what other animals have, and not the most social among them (such as bees, etc.), only what is necessary to procreate the species, etc. and I believe, they either have no language or a most imperfect kind of language, or tongue, they are savages but not barbarians, that is, they do nothing against nature (at least by custom), neither toward themselves, nor toward their fellow men, nor towards anyone.[86]

Here Leopardi conceived a hierarchy of American peoples:

Pure Savage State	*Barbarians*	*Civilized*
"Californii"	American tribal societies	Incas
		Aztec

Leopardi drew from numerous sources for news about the "Californii"; his draft version in prose of the *Inno ai patriarchi* provides useful cues for their identification:

> Even today in the forests of California, amidst cliffs, near brooks, etc. lives a people who ignores the name of civilization, and is more than any other people averse (as travelers have observed) to that miserable corruption that we call culture. Happy people, whose food are roots and herbs and animals reached by running, tamed only by their own arm, and the brook's waters are their drink, and the trees and caves provide a roof to them against rain, storms and hurricanes.[87]

The description of a Californian paradise, although inhabited by "devils" still prey to "unbridled freedom" and to "gentile vices and customs," recalls Lodovico Antonio Muratori's *Il Cristianesimo felice* and Francesco Maria Piccolo's *Sopra lo stato delle missioni stabilite di fresco nella California*. Muratori wrote:

86. *Zibaldone*, 1000.
87. *Notes, prefaces, drafts*, in *Tutte le opere*, 1:75.

Here [in California] we see spacious plains, considerable mountains, very pleasant valleys and views, abundant springs and rivers, whose shores are especially crowned by very tall willow trees and reeds. The air is sweet and healthy; they do not know snow and there is never excessive cold or heat. . . . Usually dew is so abundant that it can substitute for rain. Hills are especially most pleasing, because here more than anywhere else nature has provided a great variety of trees, especially prickly pear trees.[88]

However, these natural resources were unfortunately destined to remain uncultivated insofar as "in barbarian countries, such as California, one is satisfied with what nature itself yields."[89] Muratori's description recalls the report *Sopra lo stato delle missioni stabilite di fresco nella California*, by the Franciscan Francesco Maria Piccolo, who in 1697 had begun his missionary activity in the Californian peninsula:

One finds in California, as in the most beautiful countries of the world, vast plains and pleasant valleys, and excellent pastures in every season for large and small cattle, and delicious running water springs; brooks and rivers, whose shores are covered with willow trees, reeds and wild vines. . . . Truly we can say that California is a most fertile land. . . . Here the seashore is covered with sea shells, much larger than mother-of-pearl shells. Salt is not extracted from the sea: there are salt works where the salt is white, shiny like crystal. Nature has been most generous with the "Californici" and the earth effortlessly yields fruits, which in other lands it yields only through much effort and work. Nevertheless, they do not care about the abundance or wealth of their fields; satisfied with the necessities of life, they care not about the rest.[90]

88. *Il Cristianesimo felice*, 2:172-73.
89. Ibid., 174.
90. Francesco Maria Piccolo, *Sopra lo stato delle missioni stability di fresco nella California*, in *Lettere edificanti e curiose, scritte dalle missioni straniere d'alcuni missionari della Compagnia di Gesù*, (Venice: Antonio Mora, 1752), 50. One should also read California's description in the appendix to the *Three English Volumes in Folio of Morery's Great Historical, Geographical, Geneological and Poetical Dictionary*, "California": "The country affords a great deal of excellent pasture, the water is very good, and the rivers are stored with fish: the fruit-trees are very fine, and all the pulse and grain sown there yields a plentiful product: they have two sorts of willd [*sic*] cattle, unknown in Europe, which are delicate meat. Almost all the fowls seen in Spain and Mexico may be found in California.

In the *American Gazetteer* and in the majority of eighteenth-century sources, the distinctive traits of the "Californians" were marked by "stupidity and insensibility, want of knowledge and reflexion, a total indocility, excessive sloth, pusillanimity, love of trifles."[91] Also, in nineteenth-century texts such as *Il costume antico e moderno di tutti i popoli*, we read: "The natives of ancient California were, at the time of the Missionaries' arrival, in an extreme state of stupidity; they would spend entire days lying face down in the sand like animals, and like them, spurred by hunger, they would run to hunt so as to satisfy that moment's need."[92]

Leopardi believed that the "Californii," as they still lived in accordance with pure instinct, could not think: "Thus, he who does not reason, or, as the French say, he who does not think, is most wise. Therefore, before wisdom and reasoning about things were born, men were at their wisest: just as most wise is the child, and the savage from California who does not know what *thinking* is."[93] In fact, reflection, from which sadness and ennui come, implies a "leap" from the "pure savage" state to "civilization":

> From the heights of their mountains the *Californii* freely contemplate, free of desire or fear, the vault and breadth of the sky and the open fields unencumbered by cities or towers. They listen, without impediment, to the sound of the rivers, the echo of the valleys, the song of the birds, like them free, unburdened, and masters of the earth and the air . . . there is neither sadness nor ennui among them. The uniformity of their lives does not bore them: nature has so many resources in itself, if only it were obeyed and followed. . . . They see death (or deaths, rather) but do not prevent it. A storm may trouble them for a moment: they escape into caves: the supervening calm comforts and gladdens them.[94]

Plus, the "Californii" did not know fire:[95]

They have likewise salt-pits, affording good salt, both for colour and hardness. . . . The Californians have no houses, the shades of trees skreen [*sic*] them from the sun in day-time, and they get heaps of leaves for shelter and softness in the night. During the winter they keep close in caves, where a great many lodge together. The men go stark-naked. . . . The Californians are under no form of government, or regulated worship."

91. *American Gazetteer*, vol. 1, s.v. "California."
92. *Il costume antico e moderno di tutti i popoli*, 2:335.
93. *Zibaldone*, 1020.
94. Ibid.
95. See Lionello Sozzi, *Le californie selve*, 218.

Epilogue: Nineteenth-Century Developments 199

That in hot climates the human species has no need of fire to live and to live well according to nature (not according to society, as social life cannot exist without it), we can readily see, for instance, in the *Californii* who, as far as I know, in no way use fire, as they live in a very hot climate for which they have no need of it, nor of clothes.[96]

Furthermore, Leopardi wrote that the "Californii" were lacking in any "perfected tongue, or language";[97] however, this is not documented in any other sources. In fact, the Jesuits confirmed that California natives spoke several dialects, very similar to each other (Gilij even theorized a common root of the "Californiese" and "Muscovite" languages; see Chapter 3, note 41). This is probably an invention, possibly confirmed by a passage in *Zibaldone*:

The use of language is necessary to society. The discovery of speech is truly extraordinary. Nevertheless, all people have speech. As soon as men started to form a society, they started to babble a language. Up to a certain point, nature itself teaches it not only to men, but to the other animals as well; more to men, since nature has made them more sociable. With the growth of society and of the custom of exchange among men, it reached and went beyond the boundaries intended and prescribed by nature, and language of necessity grew and became more powerful than nature had intended.[98]

The "Californii" thus could not know any "perfected language," which is the product of civilization; and since they had "no society," they could not yet "babble."

96. The issue of the nakedness of the "Californii" gave Leopardi a reason for stressing how the use of clothing had introduced in our society the sense of the forbidden: "Humankind is naturally naked and, following nature, at least in many parts of the globe, man would have never used clothes, as clothing is completely unknown for example, to the Californii. Neither man, nor youth would have even seen or imagined anything hidden in women (and the same could be said of women with respect to men). And neither seeing, nor desiring or hoping to see anything hidden, and well knowing from the beginning the nudity and form of the other sex, man would have never felt for woman any other effect or feeling or desire, than what animals desire with respect to their females. . . . Such would have man been with respect to woman, and woman with respect to man. But the use of clothing having been introduced . . . man and woman have become almost mysterious beings to each other" (*Zibaldone*, 914).
97. *Zibaldone*, 952.
98. Ibid., 917.

Leopardi pointed out that the natives of California were "very strong" and that they "ignored disease, the deadly gift of civilization."[99] Insisting on the theme of disease, he added that

> civilization introduced mankind to a thousand kinds of disease which it did not know before, and which would not have existed without it. . . . We see, in fact, how few and mild are the spontaneous diseases of other animals, especially wild animals, that is, animals that man has not corrupted; and similarly among the savages, especially the most natural among them, such as the *Californii*.[100]

There are several texts confirming that the savages of California were among the "most natural" tribes in America.[101] Leopardi used the same sources for an opposite purpose, to praise those features of savagery that travelers and missionaries had denigrated because they were insurmountable obstacles to the path of the "Californii" from the *state of nature* to civilization. We must, however, recognize that the blessed thoughtlessness of the California Indians was from the beginning purely temporary, insofar as was fated to vanish with the "wicked daring" of the civilizers, as stated in Leopardi's conclusion to *Inno ai patriarchi*.

At the time that Leopardi composed the poem he still believed in the resources of a beneficent nature and in the happiness of the pure savage state: civilized, cultivated man is unhappy when compared to natural, ignorant man. However, in the *Moral Tales* Leopardi's conception reached a crossroads. He no longer came to impute human unhappiness to a historical cause such as man's conversion to civilization, but to a natural,

---

99. Ibid.
100. Ibid., 853. "Those who wish to see the effect of civilization on bodily strength, should compare civilized man to peasants or savages. . . . They should note what the human body is capable of, seeing our complete incapability at doing what the least robust of the peasants can do; the dangers to which we would expose ourselves if we were to bear any of their misery; the shameful daily custom of fleeing the air, the sun etc., of wondering how such and such could have faced [the elements] in this or that circumstance; the diseases which we daily catch for the least excess of work or mental exertion, and then we should say whether indeed civilization strengthens man, raises his capacity and power" (457-78). "It is thus proven without argument, that the perfection of man involves, not by accident but of necessity, the corresponding and proportional deterioration and, should we say, decrease in perfection of a small part of man, i.e. his body: so that the more man advances toward perfection, the more his body's imperfection grows; and when man will be fully perfect he will find, generally speaking, that he is in the worst state he ever found himself" (796).
101. See Lionello Sozzi, *Le californie selve*, 207.

unfathomable mechanism that is hostile to humanity. At this point, even a life lived according to nature, such as California's Indians lived, could no longer guarantee happiness. The last reference to the miracle of the "Californii" is in the "History of the Human Race" where Leopardi fancied that Jupiter put an end to the golden age:

> And to eradicate the sloth of the past, he kindled in the human race a craving and appetite for new foods and drinks, which could not be obtained without a great deal of toil; whereas until the flood men had quenched their thirst with water only, and fed on herbs and fruits which the earth and trees provided for them of their own accord, and other nourishments both modest and easy to gather, as even today some peoples do, and especially those of California.[102]

The survival of the "Californii" seemingly confirmed by Leopardi's use of the present tense remained however an unresolved issue, as Leopardi would not revert to this theme in his later works.

However, in the *Moral Tales* other American themes may be noted. For example, in "The Wager of Prometheus" two divinities, Momos and Prometheus, descend from Olympus to Earth to determine whether humankind in all the five continents could be considered "the best work of any of the immortals to have appeared in the world."[103] Prometheus bets with Momos, the god of mockery, that everywhere in the world there will be proof of mankind's superiority with respect to any other divine creation. But one of the confirmations that man is not the most perfect creature of the universe is the encounter with a tribe of American cannibals in the land of Popaian in Colombia:

> The two Celestials approached, taking on human form; and Prometheus, after greeting everyone politely, turned to the one who seemed to be the chief, and asked: What are you doing?

---

102. "History of the Human Race," in *Moral Tales*, trans. Patrick Creagh, in *Works of Giacomo Leopardi* (Manchester: Carcanet New Press, 1983–), 1:38. The reference to the happy "Hyperboareans" is also interesting: "A people unknown but famous; whom one cannot reach either by land or by water; rich in all possessions, but especially in fine asses, which they are accustomed to make hecatombs of; who if I am not mistaken could be immortal, as they have no infirmities or labours or wars or quarrels or famines or vices or faults" ("The Dialogue of a Physicist and a Metaphysician, in *Moral Tales*, 87).

103. "The Wager of Prometheus," in *Moral Tales*, 79.

Savage: Eating, as you can see.
Promet.: What do you have in the way of good food?
Savage: This scrap of meat.
Promet.: Is it game, or domestic meat?
Savage: Domestic. In fact it's my son.
Promet.: Do you have a calf for a son, like Pasiphaë?
Savage: Not a calf but a man, like everyone else.
Promet.: Are you speaking in earnest? Do you eat your own flesh and blood?
Savage: Nor my own, but his: for that's the only reason I brought him into the world, and took the trouble to feed him.
Promet.: You mean, to eat him?
Savage: What's so surprising? And then his mother, as she can't be good for childbearing any more, I'm thinking of eating her too pretty soon.
Momos: As one eats a hen after eating her eggs.
Savage: And my other women too, as soon as they become useless for childbearing, I shall eat them in the same way. And as for these slaves of mine that you see here, do you think I would keep them alive if I couldn't have their children to eat from time to time? But when they get old I shall eat them one after the other, if I live.[104]

This was undoubtedly a contact with a "closed society," therefore with a people already "barbarous" in the Leopardian conception, insofar as cannibalism has a ritualistic character and presupposes a pre-social order.

The last tale to reflect an American theme is the "Dialogue of Christopher Columbus and Pedro Gutierrez," although here the New World is completely absent. Gutierrez, taken by ennui during an endless voyage, asks Columbus if he is really convinced he will discover the Indies:

Columbus: A beautiful night, my friend.
Gutierr.: Beautiful indeed: and I think that seen from dry land it would be more beautiful still.
Columbus: Very good: so you too are tired of sailing.
Gutierr.: Not of sailing in general; but this voyage is proving longer than I had thought, and is beginning to weary

---

104. Ibid., 80-81.

me. All the same you must not think that I am complaining about you, as the others are. Indeed you may count on it, that whatever decision you may come to about this voyage, I will always back you up, as I have in the past, with all the means in my power. But, by way of conversation, I would be glad if you were to tell me exactly, and in all sincerity, if you are still as sure as you were at first, of being likely to find land in this part of the world; or whether, after so long a time and so much experience to the contrary, you are not beginning to have some doubts.[105]

Columbus replies that he is starting to have doubts, although logically it is absurd that the Indies do not exist:

Columbus: To speak plainly, as one can to a close friend, I confess that I have begun to wonder; all the more so because during the voyage a number of signs that had given me great hopes then proved vain. . . . So that I am thinking, that as these predictions deceived me, even though they seemed virtually certain; so also my chief prediction might prove false, that is, of discovering land on the other side of the Ocean. It is true that it has such foundations, that if it be false, it appears to me on the one hand that one could have no faith in any human judgment, unless it consisted entirely of things that one can see and touch at the moment.[106]

After Gutierrez points out that for a simple hypothesis Columbus risked his life and that of his companions, the famous navigator replies: "Even if we gain no other benefit from this voyage, it seems to me that it is most profitable to us, in that for a while it keeps us free of boredom, renders life dear to us, and makes us value many things that we would not otherwise take into account."[107] The hope of reaching a destination becomes secondary to the voyage itself, which has the function of providing an escape.

105. "Dialogue of Christopher Columbus and Pedro Gutierrez," in *Moral Tales*, 158–59.
106. Ibid., 159.
107. Ibid., 161.

The theme of the tale was suggested to Leopardi from Robertson's *History of America*, especially by the chapters on the oceanic expeditions of Columbus. Robertson, after quoting the sailors' discouragement from the long voyage, wrote:

> He promised solemnly to his men that he would comply with their request, provided they would accompany him. . . .
> Enraged as the sailors were, and impatient to turn their faces again towards their native country, this proposition did not appear to them unreasonable. . . . The presages of discovering land were now so numerous and promising, that he deemed them infallible. For some days the sounding-line reached the bottom, and the soil which it brought up indicated land to be at no great distance. The flocks of birds increased, and were composed not only of sea-fowl, but of such land birds as could not be supposed to fly far from the shore.[108]

Leopardi took very little from the description of the solemn night of discovery, and only at the conclusion would his tale evoke Robertson's description:

> For some days now the lead, as you know, has touched bottom; and the kind of stuff that comes up with it seems to me a good sign. Toward evening the clouds around the sun impress me as of a different shape and colour from those of the previous days. The air, as you can feel, has become a little milder and warmer than before. The wind is no longer blowing as forcefully as it was, or as straight, or as ceaselessly; but on the contrary, uncertainly and changeably, as if it were blocked by some obstacle. Add to this the cane seen floating on the surface, that seemed to have been recently cut; and that little branch with its fresh red berries. Even the flocks of birds, though they have deceived me on other occasions, nevertheless now pass in such great numbers, and of such a size; and increase so greatly from day to day; that I think it likely we may make some landfall; especially as we see among them certain birds that from their shape do not seem to be seabirds.[109]

---

108. William Robertson, *History of America*, 1:122.
109. "Dialogue between Christopher Columbus and Pedro Gutierrez," in *Moral Tales*, 162.

Leopardi refused to give any rhetorical praise to Columbus's discovery; he "emptied" the traditional myth of its substance: a voyage to the New World had the sole function of providing an escape to monotony.

After the *Moral Tales*, America was no longer present in Leopardi's works, neither as anthropological and geographical reality, nor as the myth of the noble savage embodied in the "Californii." In any case, in canto 4 of *The War of the Mice and Crabs*, although no reference is made to the American natives, Leopardi returned to the question of the "savage" in his criticism of the theory of the theological and aprioristic school (De Bonald, De Maistre, and Lamennais). According to this, God could not have created perfect men, and mankind had fallen from a primitive state of perfection down to the state of nature:

> Consequently it is believed that the rough and savage life is corruption, not the natural state, and that insulting his destiny man falls here from a great height, I mean from the civilized level, where divine wisdom was careful to place him: because if we don't want to outrage heaven, he is born civilized and later on becomes savage.[110]

The perspective shifts and the savage now becomes the "living witness of the indifference of nature for her children who, instead of being gratified with providential support, are by nature left to struggle with the laborious, burdensome conquest of civilization."[111]

This last reference to the savage world does not seem to evoke implicit references to the "Californii"; the only reference to the New World in *The War of the Mice and the Crabs* is to Washington, whom Leopardi places next to Timoleon the Corinthian and Andrea Doria, among the heroes who did not thirst after power:

> Worthy therefore of eternal praise was he, to whom ancient and modern history has no one equal or even to compare, as far as I can now recall, apart from three of illustrious and immortal fame,

---

110. *The War of the Mice and the Crabs*, trans., intro., and annotated by Ernesto G. Caserta, University of North Carolina at Chapel Hill, Department of Romance Languages, Texts, Textual Studies and Translations, no. 4 (Chapel Hill: University of North Carolina, 1976), 62.

111. Gennaro Savarese, *Saggio sui "Paralipomeni" di Giacomo Leopardi* (Florence: La Nuova Italia, 1967), 135.

Timoleon the Corinthian and Andrea Doria on this side of the ocean, and Washington on the American side.[112]

References to the New America seldom appear in Leopardi's works. In *Zibaldone*, apart from the two brief references to Franklin and to his *Observations sur les sauvages de l'Amérique du Nord* (Leopardi ignored the Italian version of 1785), the conditions of United States prisons is discussed, and nothing else.[113]

The Revolution, birth, and growth of the young American republic did not prevent Leopardi from continuing to think of the New World as barbaric and enigmatic. With his concept of a savage America where the blessed "Californii" still lived beholden only to the dictates of nature, Leopardi represented an exception within the Italian antiprimitivistic tradition.

---

112. *The War of the Mice and the Crabs*, 55.
113. "In the United States of America no disgrace is attached to punishment, and the guilty man who was punished and reenters society is freer of shame than the one who, unpunished, circulates in society, insofar as: 1. it is considered that by the punishment to which he was subjected the guilty man has atoned for his offence, repaired the wrong he committed, satisfied society and paid his debt thereof; 2. it is considered, as it usually happens, that the punishment, which is there considered and called penance (prisons are called houses of penance), and the treatment given during the time served specifically to cure, physically as well as morally, the guilty man's morality, have so corrected and reformed his character, customs, inclinations, principles, and led him again on an honest course. Rightfully and factually he becomes again the complete equal of other citizens and foreigners. See the account on New York's prisons in *Antologia di Firenze*, No. 37, January, 1824 and in particular, page 54" (*Zibaldone*, 1045).

Select Bibliography

Sixteenth- and Seventeenth-Century Texts

Gemelli Careri, Francesco. *Giro del mondo*. 9 vols. Venice: Sebastiano Coletti, 1719.
Guicciardini, Francesco. *Storia d'Italia*. Bari: Laterza, 1981.
Hennepin, Louis. *Descrizione della Luigiana: Paese nuovamente scoperto*. Bologna: Giacomo Monti, 1686.
Montaigne, Michel de. *Essais*. Paris: Gallimard, 1962.
Moscardo, Ludovico. *Note ovvero memorie del Museo di L. M. nobile veronese*. Padua: Paolo Frambotto, 1656.
Tonti, Henri. *Dernières découvertes dans l'Amérique septentrionale de M. de La Sale*. Paris: Jean Guignard, 1697.
Zani, Valerio Degli Anzi Aurelio. *Il genio vagante: Biblioteca curiosa di cento, e più relazioni di viaggi stranieri de' nostri tempi*. Parma: Giuseppe Dall'Oglio e Ippolito Rosati, 1691-93.

Eighteenth- and Nineteenth-Century Texts

Alfieri, Vittorio. *L'America libera*. Asti: Kehl, 1784.
———. *Opere di V.A. ristampate nel primo centenario della morte*. Turin: Paravia, 1903.
———. *Scritti politici e morali*. Edited by Piero Cazzani. Asti: Casa dell'Alfieri, 1951.
Algarotti, Francesco. *Opere*. Venice, 1792.

———. *Saggi*. Edited by Giovanni Da Pozzo. Bari: Laterza, 1963.
Angiolini, Luigi. *Lettere sopra l'Inghilterra, la Scozia e l'Olanda*. In *Letterati, memorialisti e viaggiatori del Settecento*, edited by Ettore Bonora. Milan: Ricciardi, 1951.
Baretti, Giuseppe Antonio. *Epistolario*. In *Opere*, edited by Franco Fido. Milan: Rizzoli, 1967.
———. *La scelta delle lettere*. Edited by Leone Piccioni. Bari: Laterza, 1912.
Boccage, Marie Anne Le Page Fiquet du. *La Colombiade*. Milan: Marelli, 1771.
Botta, Carlo. *Lettere inedite di C.B.* Edited by Caterina Maggini. Florence: Le Monnier, 1900.
———. *Storia della guerra dell'indipendenza degli Stati Uniti d'America*. Milan: Oliva, 1850.
Boturini Benaduci, Lorenzo. *Idea de una nueva historia general de la America septentrional*. Madrid: Juan de Zuñiga, 1746.
Bougainville, Louis Antoine de. *Voyage autour du monde en 1766, 1767, 1768 et 1769*. 2 vols. Neuchâtel: La Société Typographique, 1772.
Burke, William, and Edmund Burke. *Storia degli stabilimenti europei in America*. 2 vols. Venice: Giambattista Novelli, 1763.
Carli, Gian Rinaldo. *Delle lettere americane*. 2 vols. Florence: Cosmopoli, 1780.
———. *Delle lettere americane*. Con selezione, studio introduttivo e note di Aldo Albonico. Rome: Bulzoni, 1988.
———. *Le lettere americane. Nuova edizione corretta ed ampliata con l'aggiunta della parte III, ora per la prima volta impressa*. 3 vols. Cremona: Manini, 1781-83.
Castiglioni, Luigi. *Viaggio negli Stati Uniti dell'America settentrionale fatto nel 1785, 1786 e 1787*. 2 vols. Milan: Giuseppe Marelli, 1790.
Cerlone, Francesco. *Gl'Inglesi in America, o sia il selvaggio*. Naples: Ruffo, 1770.
Chiari, Pietro. *L'Americana raminga cioè memorie di Donna Innez di Quebrada scritte da lei stessa ed ora pubblicate da M.G. di S. sua confidente amica*. Naples: Vincenzo Flauto, 1764.
———. *La corsara francese della guerra presente*. In *Trattenimenti dello spirito umano sopra le cose passate presenti e possibili ad avvenire*. Brescia: Berlendis, 1781.
———. *La donna che non si trova o sia le avventure di Madama Delingh scritte da lei medesima e pubblicate dall'abate Pietro Chiari*. Venice: Pasinelli, 1768.
———. *L'uomo d'un altro mondo, o sia memorie d'un solitario senza nome, scritte da lui medesimo in due linguaggi, chinese e russiano, e pubblicate nella nostra lingua dall'abate Pietro Chiari*. Parma: Carmignani, 1760.
———. *I privilegi dell'ignoranza. Lettere di un'Americana ad un letterato d'Europa*. Venice: Bassaglia, 1784.
Clavigero, Francesco Saverio. *Storia della California*. Venice: Modesto Fenzo, 1789.
Colden, Cadwallader. *The History of the Five Nations of Canada*. London: Locker Davis, 1755.
Cook, James. *Storia de' viaggi intrapresi per ordine di S.M. Britannica dal Capitano Giacomo Cook*. 10 vols. Naples: La Nuova Società Letteraria e Tipografica, 1784.
Coronelli, Vincenzo. *Biblioteca universale sacro-profana o sia gran dizionario*. Venice: Tivani, 1703.
Da Ponte, Lorenzo. *Catalogo ragionato dei libri che si trovano attualmente nel negozio di Carlo e Lorenzo Da Ponte*. New York: Gravy and Bunce, 1823.

Select Bibliography

———. *Memorie di Lorenzo Da Ponte compendiate da Jacopo Bernardi e scritti vari in prosa e poesia*. Florence: Le Monnier, 1871.
———. *Memorie di Lorenzo Da Ponte da Cèneda scritte da esso*. 2 vols. Edited by Giovanni Gambarin and Fausto Nicolini. Bari: Laterza, 1918.
Fantoni, Giovanni. *Poesie*. Bari: Laterza, 1913.
Ferrario, Giulio, ed. *Il costume antico e moderno di tutti i popoli*. Florence: Batelli, 1826-28.
Franklin, Benjamin. *Osservazione a chiunque desideri passare in America; e riflessioni circa i selvaggi dell'America settentrionale*. Padua: Conzatti, 1785.
———. *Il povero Ricciardo e la Costituzione di Pensilvania, italianizzati per uso della Democratica Veneta Restaurazione*. Venice, 1787.
———. *Scelta di lettere e di opuscoli del Signor Beniamino Franklin*. Milan: Marelli, 1774.
Galiani, Ferdinando. *La Signora d'Epinay e l'abate Galiani*. Edited by Fausto Nicolini. Bari: Laterza, 1929.
Il gazzettiere americano. Leghorn: Coltellini, 1763.
Genovesi, Antonio. *Autobiografia, lettere ed altri scritti*. Edited by Gennaro Savarese. Milan: Feltrinelli, 1962.
———. *Lezioni di commercio ed economia civile*. In *Economisti Italiani Classici*. Milan: De Stefani, 1803.
Gilij, Filippo Salvatore. *Saggio di storia americana o sia naturale, civile, e sacra de' regni, e delle province spagnuole di terra-ferma nell'America meridionale*. 4 vols. Rome: Luigi Perego erede Salvioni, 1780.
Goldoni, Carlo. *Tutte le opere di Carlo Goldoni*. 14 vols. Edited by Giuseppe Ortolani. Milan: Mondadori, 1945-59.
Gozzi, Gasparo, ed. *La Gazzetta Veneta*. Edited by A. Zardo. Florence: Sansoni, 1905.
Graffigny, Françoise de. *Lettres d'une Péruvienne*. Paris: Migneret, 1797.
Grimaldi, Francescantonio. *Discorso sull'ineguaglianza tra gli uomini*. In *Illuministi Italiani*, edited by Franco Venturi, vol. 5. Milan: Ricciardi, 1962.
Gumilla, Joseph. *Histoire naturelle, civile et géographique de l'Orénoque*. Marseille: La Veuve de F. Girard, 1758.
Joubert de la Rue, Hector. *Letters d'un sauvage dépaysé, contenant une critique des moeurs du siècle, et des réflexions sur les matières de religion et de politique*. Amsterdam: Jean François Jolly, 1738.
Kino, Eusebio Francisco. *Passage per terre à la Californie découvert par le Rev. Père Eusebe-François Kino Jésuite depuis 1698 jusqu'à 1701*. Paris: Nicolas Le Clerc, 1705.
La Condamine, Charles Marie de. *Relation abrégée d'un voyage fait dans l'intérieur de l'Amérique méridionale*. Paris: La Veuve Pissot, 1745.
Lafitau, Joseph-François. *Moeurs des sauvages amériquains comparées aux moeurs des premiers temps*. 2 vols. Paris: Saugrain Ainé, 1724.
Lahontan de Lom D'arce, Louis Armand. *Nouveaux voyages dans l'Amérique septentrionale*. La Haye: Frères l'Honoré, 1703.
Leopardi, Giacomo. *Tutte le opere*. 2 vols. Edited by Walter Binni. Milan: Sansoni, 1969.
Lettres édifiantes et curieuses, écrites des missions étrangères par quelques missionnaires de la Compagnie de Jésus. 34 vols. Paris: Nicolas Le Clerc, 1702-76.
Marmontel, Jean-François. *Les Incas ou la destruction de l'empire du Perou*. Lyon: Chez Amable Leroy, 1810.
Martinelli, Vincenzio. *Istoria del governo d'Inghilterra e delle sue colonie in India, e nell'America settentrionale*. Florence: Cambiagi, 1776.

Mazzei, Filippo. *Memorie della vita e delle peregrinazioni del fiorentino Filippo Mazzei.* 2 vols. Edited by Alberto Aquarone. Milan: Marzorati, 1970.
———. *Philip Mazzei: Selected Writings and Correspondence.* 3 vols. Edited by Margherita Marchione. Prato: Cassa di Risparmi e Depositi di Prato, Edizioni del Palazzo, 1983.
———. *Recherches historiques et politiques sur les Etats-Unis de l'Amérique septentrionale.* 4 vols. Paris: Froullé, 1788.
Metastasio, Pietro. *Opere.* Edited by Bruno Brunelli. 5 vols. Milan: Mondadori, 1947–56.
Montesquieu, Charles Louis de Secondat, baron de. *Lettres Persanes.* In *Oeuvres complètes.* 2 vols. Paris: Gallimard, 1949.
Monti, Vincenzo. *Opere.* Edited by Manara Valgimigli e Carlo Muscetta. Milan: Ricciardi, 1953.
Moreri, Louis. *Le grand dictionnaire historique, de le mélange curieux de l'histoire sacrée et profane.* Amsterdam: Les Libraires Associés, 1740.
Muratori, Ludovico Antonio. *Il Cristianesimo felice nelle Missioni dei Padri della Compagnia di Gesù nel Paraguai.* 2 vols. Venice: Pasquali, 1743.
Obizzi, Ferdinando degli. *Il filosofo e il pazzo: Commedia per la villa.* Padua: Conzatti, 1766.
Occhiolini, Giambattista. *Memorie storiche sopra l'uso della cioccolata in tempo di digiuno.* Venice: Occhi, 1748.
Parini, Giuseppe. *Opere.* Edited by Ettore Bonora. 2 vols. Milan: Editoriale Vita, 1967.
———, ed. *La Gazzetta di Milano.* 2 vols. Milan: Ricciardi, 1981.
Pernety, Antoine Joseph. *Dissertation sur l'Amérique et les Américains contre les "Recherches philosophiques" de M. de Pauw.* Berlin: Decker, 1769.
———. *Histoire d'un voyage aux Iles Malouines, avec des observations sur le détroit de Magellan et sur les Patagons.* Paris: Saillant et Nyon, 1770.
Piccolo, Francesco Maria. *Sopra lo stato delle missioni stabilite di fresco nella California.* In *Lettere edificanti e curiose, scritte dalle missioni straniere d'alcuni missionari della compagnia di Gesù.* Venice: Antonio Mora, 1752.
Prévost, Antoine-François. *Histoire générale des voyages.* 24 vols. Paris: Didot, 1746.
Raynal, Guillaume-Thomas. *Histoire philosophique et politique des établissements et du commerce des Européens dans les deux Indes.* 6 vols. Geneva: Libraires Associés, 1775.
———. *La révolution de l'Amérique.* London: Locker Davis, 1781.
———. *Storia dell'America settentrionale.* 2 vols. Venice: Zatta, 1778.
Roberti, Giambattista. *Le perle.* Bologna: Stamperia di Lelio della Volpe, 1763.
Robertson, William. *Storia d'America.* 4 vols. Venice: Gatti, 1778.
Rousseau, Jean-Jacques. *Correspondance complète de Jean-Jacques Rousseau.* Edited and critically annotated by R. A. Leigh. Geneva: Institut et Musée Voltaire, 1966.
———. *Discours sur l'origine et les fondements de l'inégalité parmi les hommes.* In *Du contrat social et autres ouevres politiques.* Paris: Garnier Frères, 1975.
Sangro di San Severo, Raimondo de. *Lettera apologetica dell'Esercitato accademico della Crusca contenente la difesa del libro intitolato "Lettere d'una Peruana" per rispetto alla supposizione de' Quipu.* Naples, 1750.
Savioli Fontana, Ludovico. *Poesie.* In *Lirici del Settecento,* edited by Bruno Maier. Milan: Ricciardi, 1959.
Soave, Francesco. *Novelle morali.* 2 vols. Naples: Marotta, 1796.
Verri, Alessandro. *Dissertazione sugli orologi.* In *Il Caffè ossia brevi e vari discorsi distribuiti in fogli periodici (dal giugno 1764 a tutto il maggio 1765),* edited by Sergio Romagnoli. Milan: Feltrinelli, 1960.

―――. *Ragionamento di un pedante e di un Ottentotto*. In *Il Caffè ossia brevi e vari discorsi distribuiti in fogli periodici (dal giugno 1764 a tutto il maggio 1765)*.

―――. *Lo spirito di società*. In *Il Caffè ossia brevi e vari discorsi distribuiti in fogli periodici (dal giugno 1764 a tutto il maggio 1765)*.

Verri, Pietro, and Alessandro Verri. *Carteggio di*[. . .]. Edited by Francesco Novati and Emanuale Greppi. Milan: Cogliati, 1910.

Vico, Giambattista. *Principi di una scienza nuova d'intorno alla comune natura delle nazioni*. In *Tutte le Opere*, edited by Francesco Flora. Milan: Mondadori, 1957.

Voltaire [François-Marie Arouet]. *Candide*. In *Romans et contes*. Paris: Gallimard, 1954.

―――. *Essai sur les moeurs et l'esprit des nations*. Paris: Garnier Frères, 1963.

―――. *L'ingénu, histoire véritable tirée des manuscrits du Père Quesnel*. In *Romans et contes*. Paris: Gallimard, 1954.

―――. *Lettres philosophiques ou lettres anglaises*. Paris: Gallimard, 1986.

Critical Literature

Acutis, Cesare, and Angelo Marino. *L'America dei Lumi*. Turin: La Rosa, 1989.

Adams, D. J. "The *Lettres d'une Peruvienne*: Nature and Propaganda." *Forum for Modern Language Studies* 28, no. 2 (April 1992): 121-29.

Ambrosini, Federica. *Paesi e mari ignoti: America e colonialismo europeo nella cultura veneziana (secoli XVI-XVII)*. Venice: Deputazione Editrice, 1982.

Le Americhe. Storie di viaggiatori Italiani. Milan: Electa Spa, 1987.

Annali d'Italianistica. Special issue, "Images of America and Columbus in Italian Literature." Vol. 10 (1992).

Axtell, James. "Europeans, Indians, and the Age of Discovery in American History Textbooks." *American History Review* 92, no. 3 (June 1987): 621-32.

Bairati, Pietro. *Alfieri e la rivoluziona americana*. In *Italia e America dal Settecento all'età dell'imperialismo*. Venice: Marsilio, 1976.

Balmas, Enea. *Il Buon Selvaggio nella cultura francese del Settecento*. Milan: Cisalpino-Golia, 1980.

Beale Polk, Dora. *The Island of California: A History of the Myth*. Spokane: Arthur H. Clark, 1991.

Berengo, Marino, ed. *Giornali veneziani del Settecento*. Milan: Feltrinelli, 1962.

Berthiaume, Pierre. *Approche de l'hétérologie au siècle des Lumières; Proceedings of the Canadian Society for Eighteenth Century Studies/Actes de la Société Canadienne d'Etudes du Dix-Huitième Siècle*. In *Man and Nature: L'homme et la nature, 2*, edited by Marie-Laure Girou-Swiderski and John Hare. 2 vols. Edmonton: Academic Printing, 1988.

Bloom, Harold. *The Anxiety of Influence: A Theory of Poetry*. London: Oxford University Press, 1975.

Blow, Robert, ed. *Abroad in America: Literary Discoverers of the New World from the Past 500 Years*. New York: Continuum, 1990.

Boelhower, William. "New World Topology and Types in the Novels of Abbot Pietro Chiari." *Early American Literature* 19 (1984): 153-72.

Brandon, William. *New Worlds for Old: Reports from the New World and their Effect on the Development of Social Thoughts in Europe, 1500-1800*. Athens: Ohio University Press, 1986.
Cachey, Theodore J., Jr. "The Literary Response of Renaissance Italy to the New World Encounter." *Claudel Studies* 15, no. 2 (1988): 66-75.
Caracciolo Aricò, Angela, ed. *L'impatto della scoperta dell'America nella cultura veneziana*. Rome: Bulzoni, 1990.
Chiappelli, Fredi, ed. *First Images of America: The Impact of the New World on the Old*. Berkeley and Los Angeles: University of California Press, 1976.
Chinard, Gilbert. *L'Amérique et le rêve exotique dans la littérature française au XVIIe et au XVIIIe siècle*. Paris: E. Droz, 1934.
Cocchiara, Giuseppe. *Il mito del buon selvaggio: Introduzione alla storia delle teorie etnologiche*. Messina: D'Anna, 1948.
Collo, Paolo, and Pierluigi Crovetto, eds. *Nuovo Mondo: gli Italiani*. Turin: Einaudi, 1991.
Costa, Gustavo. *La leggenda dei secoli d'oro nella letteratura italiana*. Bari: Laterza, 1972.
Cro, Stelio. "Muratori, Charlevoix, Montesquieu, and Voltaire: Four Views of the Holy Guarani Republic." *Dieciocho: Hispanic Enlightenment, Aesthetics, and Literary Theory* 14, nos. 1-2 (spring-fall 1991): 113-23.
―――. *The Noble Savage: Allegory of Freedom*. Waterloo: Wilfrid Laurier University Press, 1990.
Croce, Benedetto. *Storia della storiografia italiana*. Bari: Laterza, 1921.
―――. *I teatri di Napoli*. Bari: Laterza, 1926.
Dazzi, Manlio. *Carlo Goldoni e la sua poetica sociale*. Turin: Einaudi, 1957.
De Martino, Ernesto. *Il mondo magico: Prolegomeni a una storia del magismo*. Turin: Boringhieri, 1981.
Del Beccaro, Felice. "L'esperienza 'esotica' del Goldoni." In *Studi goldoniani*, 62-101. Turin: Einaudi, 1957.
Del Negro, Piero. *Il mito americano nella Venezia del Settecento*. Padua: Liviana, 1986.
Devèze, Michel. *L'Europe et le monde à la fin du XVIIIe siècle*. Paris: Albin Michel, 1970.
Donazzolo, Pietro. *I viaggiatori veneti minori*. Rome: Alla Sede della Società, 1928.
Douthwaite, Julia V. "Relocating the Exotic Other in Graffigny's *Lettres d'une Peruvienne*." *Romanic Review* 82, no. 4 (November 1991): 456-74.
Duchet, Michèle. *Anthropologie et histoire au siècle des lumières*. Paris: François Maspero, 1971.
Echeverria, Durand. *Mirage in the West: An Image of the French History of American Society to 1815*. Princeton: Princeton University Press, 1957.
Fairchild, Hoxie Neale. *The Noble Savage: A Study in Romantic Naturalism*. New York: Columbia University Press, 1928.
Falco, Giorgio, and Fiorenzo Forti, eds. *Dal Muratori al Baretti*. Milan: Ricciardi, 1967.
Fido, Franco. "A proposito di un manoscritto dell'America libera'." *Giornale Storico della Letteratura Italiana* 149 (1972): 469-74.
―――. *Il paradiso dei buoni compagni*. Padua: Antenore, 1988.
―――. "I romanzi: temi, ideologia, scrittura." In *Pietro Chiari e il teatro europeo del settecento: Atti del convegno "Un rivale di Carlo Goldoni. Pietro Chiari e il teatro europeo del Settecento," Venice, 1-3 March 1985*, edited by Carmelo Alberti, 281-301. Vicenza: Neri Pozza, 1986.

Fiore, Jourdan D. "Carlo Botta: An Italian Historian of the American Revolution." *Italica* 28 (1951): 154-71.
Fubini, Mario. *Ritratto dell'Alfieri*. Florence: La Nuova Italia, 1967.
Garlik, Richard Cecil. *Philip Mazzei, Friend of Jefferson: His Life and Letters*. Baltimore: Johns Hopkins University Press, 1955.
Gerbi, Antonello. *La disputa del Nuovo Mondo: Storia di una polemica (1750-1900)*. Milan: Ricciardi, 1955.
———. *Il mito del Perù*. Milan: Angeli, 1988.
———. *La Natura delle Indie Nove. Da Cristoforo Colombo a Gonzalo Fernandez de Oviedo*. Milan: Ricciardi, 1975.
Glass, John B. *The Boturini Collection: The Legal Proceedings and the Basic Inventories (1742-44)*. Lincoln Center, Mass.: Conemex Associates, 1981.
Gliozzi, Giuliano. *Adamo e il Nuovo Mondo. La nascita dell' antropologia come ideologia coloniale: dalle genealogie bibliche alle teorie razziali (1500-1700)*. Florence: La Nuova Italia, 1977.
———. "Tre studi sulla scoperta culturale del Nuovo Mondo." *Rivista storica italiana* 98 (1985): 161-80.
Gonnard, René. *La légende du bon sauvage: Contribution à l'étude des origines du socialisme*. Paris: Les Libraires de Médicis, 1946.
Grafton, Anthony, April Shelfard, and Nancy Siraisi. *New Worlds, Ancient Texts: The Power of Tradition and the Shock of Discovery*. Cambridge: Harvard University Press, 1992.
Greenblatt, Stephen. *Marvelous Possessions: The Wonder of the New World*. Chicago: Chicago University Press, 1991.
———, ed. *New World Encounters*. Berkeley and Los Angeles: University of California Press, 1993.
Guglielminetti, Marziano, ed. *Viaggiatori del Seicento*. Turin: Utet, 1967.
Hazard, Paul. *La crisi della coscienza europea (1680-1715)*. Milan: Il Saggiatore, 1983.
Hodge, Sheila. *Lorenzo Da Ponte: The Life and Times of Mozart's Librettist*. New York: Universe Books, 1985.
Hugh, Honour. *The New Golden Land: European Images of America from the Discoveries to the Present Time*. New York: Pantheon Books, 1975.
The Italians and the Creation of America: An Exhibition at the John Carter Brown Library, prepared by Samuel J. Hough. Providence: Brown University, 1980.
Italica. Special issue, "Discoveries: The Columbian Quincentennial." Vol. 69, no. 3 (autumn 1992).
Jacobson, Timothy C. *Discovering America: Journeys in Search of the New World*. Toronto: Key Porter Books, 1991.
Jantz, Harold. "The Myths about America: Origins and Extensions." *Jahrbuch für Amerikastudien* 15 (1962): 6-18.
Jehlen, Myra. "The Civilizations of the New World and the State of Nature." *Revue Française d'Études Américaines* 16, nos. 48-49 (April-June 1991): 117-24.
Kraus, Michael. *The Atlantic Civilization: Eighteenth-Century Origins*. New York: Russel and Russel, 1961.
Landucci, Sergio. *I filosofi e i selvaggi (1580-1780)*. Bari: Laterza, 1972.
La Piana, Angelina. *La cultura americana e l'Italia*. Turin: Einaudi, 1938.
Le Duc-Fayette, Denise. *Jean-Jacques Rousseau et le mythe de l'Antiquité*. Paris: J. Vrin, 1974.

Levenson, Jaya, ed. *Circa 1492: Art in the Age of Exploration.* New Haven: Yale University Press, 1992.
Levin, Harry. *The Myth of the Golden Age in the Renaissance.* Bloomington: Indiana University Press, 1969.
Mancini, Albert N. "Nuovo e Vecchio Mondo." *Esperienze letterarie* 17, no. 1 (1992): 3-15.
Marchesi, Giambattista. *Studi e ricerche intorno ai nostri romanzieri e romanzi del Settecento.* Bergamo: Istituto di Arti Grafiche, 1903.
Marraro, Howard Rosario. *Philip Mazzei, Virginia's Agent in Europe: The Story of His Mission as Related in His Own Dispatches and Other Documents.* New York: New York Public Library, 1935.
Mason, Peter. "Exoticism in the Enlightenment." *Anthropos: International Review of Ethnology and Linguistics* 86, nos. 1-3 (1991): 167-74.
Massara, Giuseppe. *Americani. L'immagine letteraria degli Stati Uniti in Italia.* Palermo: Sellerio, 1984.
Maturi, Walter. *Interpretazioni del Risorgimento.* Turin: Einaudi, 1962.
Mauzi, Robert. *L'idée du bonheur dans la littérature et la pensée française au XVIIIe siècle.* Paris: Armand Colin, 1967.
McGregor, Gaile. *The Noble Savage in the New World Garden: Notes Toward a Syntactics of Place.* Toronto: University of Toronto Press, © 1988.
Meek, Ronald L. *Social Science and the Ignoble Savage.* Cambridge: Cambridge University Press, 1976.
Moravia, Sergio. *La scienza dell'uomo nel Settecento.* Bari: Laterza, 1951.
Morison, Samuel Elliot. *The European Discovery of America: The Southern Voyages, 1492-1616.* New York: Oxford University Press, 1974.
Neri, Ferdinando. *Letteratura e leggende.* Turin: Chiantore, 1951.
O'Gorman, Edmundo. *The Invention of America: An Inquiry into the Historical Nature of the New World and the Meaning of its History.* Bloomington: Indiana University Press, 1961.
Ortolani, Giuseppe. *Nota Storica a "La Bella Selvaggia."* In *Opere Complete di Carlo Goldoni.* Vol. 24: 583-96. Venice: Edizioni del Municipio di Venezia, 1907-60.
Pace, Antonio. *Benjamin Franklin and Italy.* Philadelphia: American Philosophical Society, 1958.
Pagden, Antony. *The Fall of Natural Man: The American Indian and the Origin of Comparative Ethnology.* Cambridge: Harvard University Press, 1982.
Parkman, Francis. *Jesuits in North America.* Boston: Little, Brown, 1967.
Pavesio, Paolo. *Carlo Botta e le sue opere storiche: Con appendice di lettere inedite e di un ragguaglio delle opere del Botta.* Florence, 1874.
Phelan, John Leddy. *The Millenial Kingdom of the Franciscans in the New World.* 2d rev. ed. Berkeley and Los Angeles: University of California Press, 1970.
Pranzetti, Luisa. "Il Perù di Antonello Gerbi." *Il Veltro: Rivista della Civiltà Italiana* 36, nos. 1-2 (January-April 1992): 157-70.
Pratt, T. M. "Of Exploration and Exploitation: The New World in Later Enlightenment Epic." *Studies on Voltaire and the Eighteenth Century* 267 (1989): 291-319.
Procacci, Giuliano. "Rivoluzione americana e storiografia italiana." In *Atti del XXIII Congresso di Storia del Risorgimento Italiano,* 395-401. Rome, 1954.
Radcliff-Umstead, Douglas. "The Noble Savage: A Review Article." *Modern Language Review* 87, no. 2 (April 1992): 330-34.
Ricciardelli, Michele. "Carlo Botta e George Washington Greene (con una lettera inedita del Botta)." *Symposium* (fall 1968): 285-88.

Romeo, Rosario. *Le scoperte americane nella coscienza italiana del Cinquecento.* Preface by Rosario Villari. Bari: Laterza, 1989.
Rousseau, G. S., and Roy Porter, eds. *Exoticism in the Enlightenment.* Manchester: Manchester University Press, 1990.
Russo, Joseph Louis. *Lorenzo Da Ponte: Poet and Adventurer.* New York: Columbia University Press, 1922.
Sale, Kirkpatrick. *The Conquest of Paradise: Christopher Columbus and the Columbian Legacy.* New York: Plume Books, 1992.
Salsotto, Carlo. *Le opere di Carlo Botta e la loro varia fortuna: Saggio di bibliografia critica con lettere inedite.* Rome: Bocca, 1921.
Savarese, Gennaro. *Saggio sui "Paralipomeni" di Giacomo Leopardi.* Florence: La Nuova Italia, 1967.
Schiavo, Giovanni. *The Italians in America before the Civil War.* New York: Vigo, 1934.
Sestan, Ernesto. *Europa settecentesca e altri saggi.* Milan: Ricciardi, 1951.
Sozzi, Lionello. "Il buon selvaggio e le lettere italiane." *Studi di letteratura francese* 7 (1981): 7-27.
―――. "Le californie selve: un'utopia leopardiana." *Annali della Scuola Normale* 15 (1985): 191-97.
Stannard, David E. *American Holocaust: Columbus and the Conquest of the New World.* New York: Oxford University Press, 1992.
Starobinski, Jean. *La scoperta della libertà (1700-1789).* Milan: Skira-Fabbri, 1965.
Todorov, Tzvetan. *La conquista dell'America: Il problema dell'"altro."* Turin: Einaudi, 1984.
―――. *On Human Diversity: Nationalism, Racism, and Exoticism in French Thought.* Translated by Catherine Porter. Cambridge: Harvard University Press, 1993.
Tortarolo, Edoardo. "Filippo Mazzei e la rivoluzione americana. Alcuni documenti inediti." *Rivista storica italiana* 93 (1981): 186-200.
―――. *Illuminismo e rivoluzioni: Biografia politica di Filippo Mazzei.* Milan: Angeli, 1985.
Turchi, Roberta. *La commedia italiana del Settecento.* Florence: Sansoni, 1985.
Van Keuren, Luise. "The American Indian as Humorist Colonial Literature." In *A Mixed Race Ethnicity in Early America,* edited by Frank Shuffelton, 77-91. New York: Oxford University Press, 1993.
Venturi, Franco. *Settecento riformatore.* 5 vols. Turin: Einaudi, 1969.
―――. "Un vichiano tra Messico e Spagna: Lorenzo Boturini Benaduci." *Rivista storica italiana* 87 (1975): 770-83.
Vincenti, Lionello, ed. *Viaggiatori del Settecento.* Turin: Ricciardi, 1981.
Viola, Herman J., and Carolyn Margolis, eds. *Seeds of Change.* Washington: Smithsonian Institution Press, 1991.
Wissler, Clark. *The American Indian: An Introduction to the Anthropology of the New World.* 3d ed. Gloucester, Mass: P. Smith, 1957.
Wright, Ronald. *Stolen Continents: The New World through Indian Eyes.* Boston: Houghton Mifflin, 1992.
Zaboklicki, Krysztof. "Le commedie 'esotiche' di Carlo Goldoni: rassegna della critica novecentesca." In *L'interpretazione goldoniana, critica e messinscena,* 158-73. Rome: Officina, 1982.
―――. "Il mito del buon selvaggio nel teatro goldoniano." *Kwartalnik Neofilologiczny* 28 (1981): 283-92.

Supplementary Texts used in the English Edition

Alfieri, Vittorio. *The Life of Vittorio Alfieri, Written by Himself.* Translated by Sir Henry McAnally. Lawrence: University of Kansas Press, 1953.
———. *Of Tyranny.* Translated, edited, and with an introduction by Julius Molinari and Beatrice Corrigan. Toronto: University of Toronto Press, 1961.
———. *The Prince and Letters.* Translated by Beatrice Corrigan and Julius Molinari. Introduction and notes by Beatrice Corrigan. Toronto: University of Toronto Press, 1972.
The American Gazetteer. 3 vols. London: A. Millar and J. & R. Tonson, 1762.
Botta, Charles. *History of the War of Independence of the United States of America.* 2 vols. Translated by George Alexander Otis. 2d ed., revised and corrected. Boston: T. Brainard, 1840.
Bougainville, Lewis de. *Voyage round the World, Performed by Order of His Most Christian Majesty, in the years 1766, 1767, 1768, and 1769.* Translated by John Reinhold Forster. London: J. Nourse, 1772.
Burke, William, and Edward Burke. *An Account of the European Settlements in America.* 2 vols. (reprint of the 2d ed., London, 1758). New York: Research Reprints, 1970.
Castiglioni, Luigi. *Viaggio: Travels in the United States of North America, 1785-87. With Natural History Commentary and Botanical Observations.* Translated and edited by Antonio Pace. Syracuse: Syracuse University Press, 1983.
Clavigero, Don Francisco Javier, S.J. *The History of [Lower] California.* Translated and edited by Sara E. Lake and A. A. Gray. Stanford: Stanford University Press; London: Humphrey Milford, Oxford University Press, 1937.
Da Ponte, Lorenzo. *Memoirs of Lorenzo Da Ponte.* Translated by Elizabeth Abbott. Edited and annotated by Arthur Livingston. Preface by Thomas G. Bergin. New York: Orion, 1929.
Franklin, Benjamin. *A Benjamin Franklin Reader.* Edited by Nathan G. Goodman. New York: Crowell, 1945.
———. *Writings from Poor Richard's Almanac, 1733-1758.* New York: Library of America, 1987.
Garlick, Richard Cecil, Jr. *Philip Mazzei, Friend of Jefferson: His Life and Letters.* Baltimore: Johns Hopkins University Press; London: Humphrey Milford, Oxford University Press; Paris: Société d'Edition "Les Belles Lettres," 1933.
Gemelli Careri, Francis. *A Voyage Round the World.* Vol. 4 (1745) of *A Collection of Voyages and Travels,* compiled by Awnsham Churchill and John Churchill. 3d ed. 6 vols. London: H. Lintot and J. Osborn, 1744-46.
Gerbi, Antonello. *The Dispute of the New World: The History of a Polemic, 1750-1900.* Revised and enlarged edition. Translated by Jeremy Moyle. Pittsburgh: University of Pittsburgh Press, 1973.
Graffigny, Françoise de. *Letters of a Peruvian Princess, with the Sequel.* Translated by Francis Ashworth. In *Novelist's Magazine,* vol. 9. London: Harrison, 1782.
Guicciardini, Francesco. *The Historie of Guicciardin: containing the warres of Italie and other parts, continued for manie yeares vnder sundrie kings and princes. . . .* Reduced into English by Geffray Fenton. 3d ed. London: R. Field, 1618.
Hennepin, Father Louis. *Description of Louisiana.* Translated from the edition of 1683 by John Gilmary Shea. New York: John G. Shea, 1880.

Lafitau, Joseph-François. *Customs of the American Indians Compared with the Customs of Primitive Times*. Edited and translated by William N. Fenton and Elizabeth Moore. 2 vols. Toronto: the Champlain Society, 1974.

Leopardi, Giacomo. *The War of the Mice and the Crabs*. Translated, introduced, and annotated by Ernesto G. Caserta. University of North Carolina at Chapel Hill, Department of Romance Languages, Text, Textual Studies and Translations, no. 4. Chapel Hill: University of North Carolina at Chapel Hill, 1976.

Mazzei, Philip. *Memoirs of the Life and Peregrinations of the Florentine Philip Mazzei, 1730-1816*. Translated by Howard R. Marraro. New York: Columbia University Press, 1942.

———. *Philip Mazzei, Researches on the United States*. Translated and edited by Constance D. Sherman. Charlottesville: University Press of Virginia, 1976.

Montaigne, Michel de. *Of the Caniballes*. Vol. 1 of *Montaigne's Essays*. 2 vols. Translated by John Florio. Edited by J. M. Stewart. London: Nonesuch, 1931.

Moreri, Louis. *Appendix to the Three English Volumes in Folio of Morery's Great Historical, Geographical Genealogical and Poetical Dictionary*. London: Jer. Collier, 1721.

———. *The Great Historical, Geographical, Genealogical and Poetical Dictionary*. 2d ed. 2 vols. London: Jer. Collier for Henry Rhodes, 1701.

Muratori, Ludovico Antonio. *A Relation of the Missions of Paraguay. Wrote Originally in Italian, by Mr. Muratori, and Now Done into English from the French Translation*. London: J. Marmaduke, 1759.

Pace, Antonio. *Benjamin Franklin and Italy*. Philadelphia: American Philosophical Society, 1958.

Raynal, Guillaume-Thomas. *A Philosophical and Political History of the British Settlements and Trade in North America, from the French of Abbé Raynal*. 2 vols. Edinburgh: C. MacFarquhar, 1776.

———. *A Philosophical and Political History of the Settlements and Trade of the Europeans in the East and West Indies*. 6 vols. Revised, augmented, and published in ten volumes by the Abbé Raynal. Translated by J. O. Justamond. Dublin: John Exshaw and Luke White, 1784.

Robertson, William. *The History of America*. 4 vols. (reprint of the 1st ed., 2 vols., London, J. Strahan, 1777). London: Sharpe and Son, 1820.

Rousseau, Jean-Jacques. *Basic Political Writings*. Translated and edited by Donald A. Cress. Introduction by Peter Gay. Indianapolis: Hackett, 1987.

Todorov, Tzvetan. *The Conquest of America: The Question of the Other*. Translated by Richard Howard. 1st ed. New York: Harper and Row, 1984.

Tonti, Enrico. *An Account of Monsieur de La Salle's Last Expedition and Discoveries in North America*. Vol. 2 of *Collections of the New York Historical Society, 1814*. New York: Van Winkle and Wiley, 1814.

Venturi, Franco. *The End of the Old Regime in Europe, 1768-1776*. Vol. 3, *The First Crisis*. Translated by R. Burr Litchfield. Princeton: Princeton University Press, 1979.

Vico, Giambattista. *The New Science of Giambattista Vico*. 2 vols. Edited and translated by Thomas G. Bergin and Max H. Fisch. Revised translation of the 3d ed. (1744). Ithaca: Cornell University Press, 1968.

Voltaire, [François-Marie Arouet]. *Candide; or Optimism*. Translated by John Butt. Harmondsworth: Penguin, 1947.

———. *The Works of Voltaire, A Contemporary Version*. 22 vols. Vol 19. Notes by Tobias Smollett. Revised and modernized new translation by William F. Fleming.

Introduction by Oliver H. G. Leigh. Critique and biography by the Rt. Hon. John Morley. Akron: St. Hubert Guild, 1901-3.

———. *The Works of Voltaire, A Contemporary Version*. 42 vols. Vol. 39. Notes by Tobias Smollett. Revised and modernized new translation by William F. Fleming. Introduction by Oliver H. G. Leigh. Critique and biography by the Rt. Hon. John Morley. Akron: Werner, 1905.

———. *Zadig. L'ingénu*. Translated and with an introduction by John Butt. Baltimore: Penguin, 1964.

Index

Abbot, Elizabeth, 161 n. 2, 216
Abraham, 36 n. 84
Acosta, José de, 30 n. 75, 37 n. 89
Acutis, Cesare, 211
Adams, David J., 211
Adams, Thomas, 138, 139 n. 89
Africa, Africans, 40, 42, 65, 82
Albonico, Aldo, 76 n. 101, 208
Alfieri, Vittorio, xiv, 119, 123, 126-36, 151, 188, 207, 216
Algarotti, Francesco, xiii, 50, 71, 72, 75 n. 99, 77, 81, 118, 190, 192, 207, 208
Amazon River, 17, 53
Ambrosini, Federica, 3 n. 8, 211
Andrews, John, 175 n. 31
Angiolini, Luigi, 109 n. 7, 208
Anzi (degli), Aurelio, 15, 207
Apih, Elio, 81 n. 114
Appalachians, 75
Aquarone, Alberto, 136 n. 84, 210
Aristotle, 189
Ashworth, Francis, 69 n. 84, 216
Atlantis, 20, 76 n. 101, 81, 82, 83, 189
Austria, 182

Axtell, James, 211
Azores, 82
Aztecs, xii, 19, 20, 37, 73 n. 93, 192

Bailly, Jean Silvain, 76 n. 101
Bairati, Pietro, 130 n. 68, 211
Balmas, Enea, 211
Barbados, 185
Baretti, Giuseppe Antonio, 124-26, 208
Beale Polk, Dora, 211
Beccaria, Cesare, 74
Beccaria, Giambattista, 120 n. 39
Beccaria, Giulia, 173, 174
Bellesteros y Gambrios, Manuel, 37
Bellini, Lorenzo, 74 n. 96
Bentivoglio, Guido, 171
Berengo, Marino, 44 n. 15, 211
Bergin, Thomas G., 30 n. 78, 162 n. 2, 216
Bertati, Giovanni, 111
Berthiaume, Pierre, 211
Bianchi, Isidoro, 77 n. 103, 122
Binni, Walter, 73 n. 93, 209
Bloom, Harold, 37 n. 90, 211
Blow, Robert, 211

Boccage, Marie-Anne Lepage du, 73 n. 93, 208
Boelhower, William, 63 n. 65, 211
Bologna, Italy, 167
Bonora, Ettore, 18 n. 46, 109 n. 7, 208, 210
Bossi, Luigi, 119
Boston, 124 n. 49, 126, 150, 151, 153, 157, 179, 180
Botta, Carlo, iv, 131, 142, 170-89, 208
Bottoni, Mario Saverio, 35 n. 83
Boturini Benaduci, Lorenzo, 31-38, 208
Bougainville, Louis-Antoine de, xii, 10, 31 n. 80, 46 n. 19, 54 n. 39, 208, 216
Branca, Vittore, 58 n. 49
Brandon, William, 212
Brunelli, Bruno, 52 n. 33, 210
Bruni, Arnaldo, 49 n. 25
Buccini, Stefania, xiii, xiv, xv
Buenos Aires, 9
Buffon, Georges-Louis Leclerc de, 46, 70 n. 101, 78 n. 105, 98, 148, 155, 159, 176, 190
Burkes, Edmund, 47, 48 n. 22, 54 n. 39, 63, 64, 86-90, 92, 101, 107, 178, 208
Burkes, William, 47, 48 n. 22, 54 n. 39, 63, 64, 86-90, 92, 101, 107, 178, 208
Butt, John, 46 n. 20, 76 n. 100, 217, 218

Cachey, Theodore J., Jr., 212
Cadiz, Spain, 49 n. 25
California, Californians, "Californii," xiv, 10, 21, 22, 75, 104 n. 40, 195-206
Cambridge, Massachussetts, 151 n. 122
Canada, Canadians, xii, 14, 24, 27, 28, 42, 49, 50, 59, 64, 66, 75, 94, 96, 97, 126, 151, 155, 184
Canaries, 82
Cannibalism, xi, xiii, 5, 191, 192, 201, 202
Cape Cod, 151
Cape of Good Hope, 64
Capponi, Gino, 137, 186
Caracciolo Aricó, Angela, 212
Carcano, Francesco, 126
Caribs, 15, 75
Carli, Gian Rinaldo, xiii, xv, 76-83, 122, 160, 189, 190, 192, 208
Carmignani, Giovanni, 137 n. 86
Carrara, Italy, 167
Caserta, Ernesto G., 205 n. 110, 217

Castiglioni, Luigi, xv, 97, 108 n. 5, 110 n. 10, 114, 117, 121, 122, 131, 149-60, 208, 216
Cataraquí, 96
Cattaneo, Giuseppe, 8
Cazzani, Piero, 207
Cèneda, Italy, 161
Cerlone, Francesco, xv, 58, 59, 61, 208
Chamfort, Nicolas-Sébastien Roch, 56
Chamier, Antonio, 139
Chiappelli, Fredi, 4 n. 12, 212
Chiari, Pietro, 48, 52 n. 33, 54 n. 40, 58, 59, 61, 63-67, 76, 83, 86, 112, 126, 208
Chile, 42, 75 n. 98
China, 18
Churchill, Awnsham, 18 n. 48, 216
Churchill, John, 18 n. 48, 216
Cieça de León, Pedro, xiii, 190
Chinard, Gilbert, 212
Clarke, John, 175 n. 31
Clavigero, Francesco Saverio, 21 n. 58, 208
Cocchiara, Giuseppe, 4 n. 12, 212
Cocoa, 21, 74 n. 96
Colden, Cadwallader, 50 n. 28, 208
Collo, Paolo, 212
Colombia, 201
Colombo, Michele, 164 n. 9, 168 n.18
Columbia College, 164
Columbus, Christopher, xii, 1, 11, 15, 189
Compagnoni, Giuseppe, 119
Condillac, Etienne-Bonnot de, 71
Condorcet, Marie-Jean-Antoine de, 144, 173
Connecticut River, 151 n. 122
Connecticut, 153, 154, 185
Contuccio, Contucci, 7
Cook, James, xii, 46 n. 19, 150, 208
Cordova, Tucuman, 9, 10
Corfu, Greece, 171
Coronelli, Vincenzo, 2 n. 4, 208
Corrigan, Beatrice, 127 n. 61, 129 n. 64, 216
Cortés, Hernan, 37, 73 n. 93
Costa, Gustavo, 72 n. 91, 212
Cowan, Robert Ernest, 22 n. 61
Creagh, Patrick, 201 n. 102
Cress, Donald A., 11 n. 27, 217
Crèvecoeur, Michel-Guillaume-Jean Saint John de, 122, 131
Cro, Stelio, 212

Index

Croce, Benedetto, 171, 178, 180, 186, 188, 212

D'Alessandro, Domenico, 71 n. 87
Da Ponte, Lorenzo, xv, 161-69, 170, 208, 209, 216
Da Pozzo, Giovanni, 50 n. 28, 208
Dartmouth College, 151 n. 122
Davila, Enrico Caterino, 171
Dazzi, Manlio, 57 n. 46, 212
De Bonald, Louis-Gabriel, 205
De La Rue, Joubert, 66, 67 n. 77, 209
De La Vega, Garcilaso, 76 n. 100
De Laët, Jean, 30 n. 75, 36 n. 84
De Maistre, Joseph de, 205
De Martino, Ernesto, 3 n. 7, 212
Deal, England, 150
Defoe, Daniel, 63
Del Beccaro, Felice, 56 n. 43, 212
Del Negro, Piero, xiii, 5 n. 13, 22 n. 60, 86 n. 4, 65, 110, 111 n. 15, 112, 116, 120 n. 37, 126 n. 59, 212
Delaware, "Delawari," 49 n. 25
Devèze, Michel, 46 n. 19, 212
Diderot, Denis de, 71
Dionisotti, Carlo, 170, 174 n. 28
Donazzolo, Pietro, 212
Doria, Andrea, 205
Douthwaite, Julia, 212
Duchet, Michele, 3 n. 10, 28, 31 n. 78, 212
Dumézil, Georges, xiii
Dutch. *See* Holland

Echeverria, Durand, 108, 212
Egypt, Egyptians, 20, 32, 36, 37, 82
El Dorado, 75, 76, 105
Engelhardt, Zephyrin, 22 n. 63
England, English, xii, xiv, 2, 49, 59, 85, 86, 90, 100, 107, 109, 113, 116, 118, 120, 123, 124, 125, 126, 127, 128, 129, 130, 132, 135, 138, 139, 140, 141 n. 95, 143, 144, 148, 149, 175, 177, 178, 179, 181, 183 n. 49, 184, 186
Esprit de Lourmel, Felix, 8 n. 19
Evangelization, 10, 22 n. 62, 103

Fabbroni, Giovanni, 137 n. 86
Fairchild, Oxie Neale, 212
Falco, Giorgio, 212
Fantoni, Giovanni, 119, 134 n. 78, 209

Fenélon, François de Salignac de la Mothe, 180
Fenton, Geffray, 7 n. 16, 216
Fenton, William N., 24 n. 65, 217
Fernandez, Father, 54
Ferrario, Giulio, 7 n. 17, 158 n. 142, 209
Fido, Franco, 45, 63, 123 n. 49, 133 n. 76, 126, 208, 212
Fiore, Jourdan D., 173 n. 27, 213
Fisch, Max H., 30 n. 78
Fisher, Lillian E., 23 n. 63
Fitzlyon, April, 161 n. 1
Fleming, Wiliam F., 40 n. 1, 108 n. 2, 217, 218
Flora, Francesco, 29 n. 71, 211
Florence, Italy, 98, 143, 167
Florio, John, 5 n. 13, 217
Forster, John Reinhold, 216
Forti, Fiorenzo, 212
France, French, xii, 46, 68, 69, 86, 108, 109, 125, 132, 171, 175, 184, 185, 188, 191 n. 76
Franklin, Benjamin, xiv, 5 n. 13, 14, 48 n. 23, 77 n. 103, 118-23, 133, 127, 180, 206, 209
Fubini, Mario, 135, 213

Galiani, Ferdinando, 158, 209
Gambarin, Giovanni, 162 n. 2
Garappa, Orsola, 41 n. 5
Garcia, Manuel, 166 n. 13
Garlik, Richard Cecil, 136 n. 85, 213, 216
Gatti, Giovanni, 98
Gay, Peter, 11 n. 27, 217
Geiger, Maynard J., 23 n. 63
Gemelli Careri, Giovani Francesco, 18-21, 50 n. 28, 74 n. 96, 207, 216
Genovesi, Antonio, 31, 41, 42, 44, 67, 73, 75 n. 98, 109, 113, 209
Georgia, 151, 157
Gerbi, Antonello, xiii, 2, 3 n. 8, 31 n. 79, 37 n. 89, 42, 68, 73 n. 94, 78 n. 105, 79, 94, 98 n. 21, 100, 148, 155 n. 132, 158 n. 145, 213, 216
Germany, 129 n. 64
Gervasoni, Angelino, 9
Gervasoni, Father, 9
Gilij, Filippo Salvatore, 2, 9 n. 21, 11, 32 n. 81, 100-105, 199, 209
Glass, John B., 32 n. 81, 213

Gliozzi, Giuliano, 1 n. 1, 4 n. 12, 13 n. 22, 213
Gold, 21 n. 58, 53, 72, 73 n. 94, 74, 75, 76 n. 100, 78 n. 105
Goldoni, Carlo, 51-58, 59, 61, 68, 109, 110, 209
Gómara, Lopez Francisco de, 101
Gonnard, René, 213
Goodman, Nathan G., 216
Gordon, William, 175 n. 31
Gospel, 5, 9, 10, 11, 14, 22 n. 62, 37, 103, 114
Gozzi, Carlo, 45, 59, 209
Gozzi, Gasparo, 44, 46, 209
Graffigny, Françoise de, 68-69, 71, 209, 216
Grafton, Anthony, 213
Gravisi, Girolamo, 81
Gray, A. A., 21 n. 58, 216
Great Britain. *See* England
Greeks, 36, 71, 182
Greenblatt, Stephen, 213
Greenland, 150
Grégoire, Henri, 102
Greppi, Emaunele, 40 n. 1, 74 n. 97, 211
Grimaldi, Francescantonio, 43-44, 209
Guerrieri, Giosef-Antonio, 19
Guglielminetti, Marziano, 18 n. 47, 213
Guicciardini, Francesco, xii, 7 n. 16, 207, 216
Gumilla, Joseph, 36 n. 84, 209
Guyana, 51, 52, 54

Harvard College, 151
Hazard, Paul, 213
Hebrews. *See* Jews
Hennepin, Louis, ix, 12-14, 41, 47 n. 21, 56 n. 42, 207, 216
Hodge, Sheila, 162, 213
Holland, 129 n. 64, 182
Homer, 28, 189
Honour, Hugh, 213
Hottentots, 42, 74
Howard, Richard, 1 n. 1, 217
Hudson, 168
Hurons, 46, 47, 48, 50

Inca, Incas, 8, 69, 71, 76, 72, 78, 79, 81, 192, 194
Independence War. *See* Revolution

India, 18
Indian languages, 105, 199, 155
Indians, American Indians, 2, 3, 8, 10, 11, 12, 13, 14, 17, 20, 21, 24, 29, 30, 35, 36, 51, 54, 55, 64, 65, 73 n. 93, 75, 87, 94, 99 n. 24, 100, 103, 111, 145, 151 n. 122, 153 n. 125, 154, 155, 177, 186, 191
Inquisition, 32
Iroquois, 14, 17, 26, 28, 42, 47, 50

Jacobson, Timothy C., 213
Jantz, Harold, 2 n. 3, 85
Jefferson, Thomas, xiv, 121, 140, 142, 144, 159, 160
Jehlen, Myra, 213
Jesuits, 4, 7, 8, 10, 21, 22, 42, 50 n. 28, 54, 72, 100, 102, 104, 105, 199
Jews, 13, 42, 102 n. 34
Justamond, John O., 217

Kalcas, 42
Kino, Francisco Eusebio, 22-23, 209
Kraus, Michael, 87 n. 6, 213

La Condamine, Charles-Marie de, 75, 78 n. 105, 209
La Duc-Fayette, Denise, 213
La Fayette, Marie-Joseph-Paul de, 133, 174
La Piana, Angelina, 136 n. 85, 162 n. 1, 213
La Salle, René-Robert de, 12
Labrador, 49 n. 25
Lafitau, Joseph-François, xiii, 24-27, 28, 29, 50 n. 28, 63, 87, 209, 217
Lahontan, Louis-Armand de Lom d'Arce de, 209
Lake, Sara E., 21 n. 58, 216
Lamennais, Félicité-Robert de, 205
Landucci, Sergio xiii, 29, 213
Lapps, 42
Las Casas, Bartolomé, 5, 180
Lavoisier, Antoine-Laurent, 144
Leghorn, Italy, 87, 90, 167
Leigh, Oliver H. C., 40 n. 1, 108 n. 2, 210, 218
Leon-Portilla, Miguel, 32 n. 81
Leopardi, Giacomo, xiii, xiv, 73 n. 93, 189-206, 209, 217
Leopold of Tuscany, 143
Leti, Gregorio, 37 n. 89
Levenson, Jaya, 214

Levin, Harry, 214
Lincoln, Abraham, 121
Lipsius, Joost Lips, 37 n. 89
Litchfield, R. Burr, 86 n. 13, 217
Littardi, Count, 187
Livingston, Arthur, 161, 162 n. 2, 216
London, 109, 123, 124 n. 49, 138, 162, 167
Lousiana, 14, 191 n. 76
Lucca, Italy, 167
Lugano, Switzerland, 137

Mably, Gabriel-Bonnot de, 144, 145, 147, 149, 177
Machiavelli, Niccolò, 83
Madagascar, 31
Madison, James, 121, 141, 149
Maffei, Scipione, 75 n. 95
Magellan, Ferdinand, 32 n. 80
Maggini, Caterina, 173 n. 26, 208
Maggini, Francesco, 123 n. 48
Maier, Bruno, 74 n. 96, 210
Malaspina, Marcello, 74 n. 96
Mancini, Albert N., 214
Manco Capac, 69
Manzoni, Alessandro, 173
Marañon River, 75
Marchesi, Giambattista, 63 n. 67, 66, 214
Marchione, Margherita, 139 n. 89, 141 n. 98, 143, 210
Marshall, John, 175
Marino, Angelo, 211
Mariscotti, Giacomo, 118
Marivaux, Pierre-Carlet de Chamblain de, 3 n. 67
Marmontel, Jean-François, 56, 77, 92, 144, 146, 209
Marraro, Howard R., 1 n. 1, 137 n. 87, 162 n. 1, 136 n. 85, 214, 217
Martha's Vineyard, 152 n. 125
Martinelli, Vincenzio, 41, 109, 113, 115, 118, 127, 209
Mason, James, 142
Mason, Peter, 214
Massachusetts, 150, 151, 152, 153, 179
Massara, Giuseppe, 111, 214
Maturi, Walter, 170, 171, 180, 214
Mauzi, Robert, 131 n. 71, 214
Maya, xii
Mazzei, Filippo, 115, 116, 131, 136-49, 156, 161, 175, 177, 210, 217

McAnally, Sir Henry, 135 n. 80, 216
McGregor, Gaile, 214
Medes, 36 n. 84
Meek, Ronald L., 214
Metastasio, Pietro, 52 n. 33, 210
Metternich-Winneburg, Klemens Wengel Lothar Furst von, 188
Mexico, Mexicans, xii, 2, 11, 18, 19, 20, 21 n. 58, 22, 32-38, 66, 67, 71 n. 89, 73, 74 n. 96, 76 n. 100, 79, 190 n. 72, 192, 193, 197 n. 90
Milan, Italy, 120, 150, 174
Mississippi River, 12
Molinari, Julius A., 127 n. 61, 129 n. 64, 216
Momigliano, Attilio, 56, 58
Montagioli, Cassiodoro, 7, 8 n. 18
Montaigne, Michel Eyquem de, xii, 5, 11, 207, 217
Montalboddo, Fracanzano da, 15
Montesquieu, Charles-Louis de Secondat, 127, 210
Montezuma, 32
Monti, Vincenzo, 119 n. 135, 210
Moore, Clement Clarke, 164
Moore, Elizabeth, 24 n. 65, 217
Moravia, Sergio, 214
Morellet, André, 144, 145
Moreri, Louis, 21, 110, 210, 217
Morison, Samuel Elliot, 214
Morley, John, 40 n. 1, 218
Moscardo, Ludovico, 35 n. 83, 207
Moyle, Jeremy, 2 n. 2, 216
Mozart, Wolfgang Amadeus, 161
Muratori, Ludovico Antonio, xv, 5-10, 14, 19, 21 n. 59, 22, 54, 105, 171, 196, 197, 210, 217
Muscetta, Carlo, 119 n. 35, 210

Nantucket, 152, 162
Naples, Italy, 59, 167
Neri, Ferdinando, 193, 214
New England, 151, 152, 155, 175, 177
New France. *See* Canada
New Hampshire, 151 n. 122
New Spain. *See* Mexico
New York City, 116, 155, 161, 163, 164, 166, 167, 206
Newport, Rhode Island, 153
Nicolini, Fausto, 158 n. 146, 162 n. 2, 209

Noble Savage, xiii, 2, 4 n. 12, 40, 46, 51, 65, 67, 68, 79, 86, 101, 205
North Carolina, 156, 157
Novati, Francesco, 40 n. 1, 74 n. 97, 211

O'Gorman, Edmundo, 214
Obizzi, Ferdinando degli, 61-63, 210
Occhiolini, Giambattista, 74 n. 96, 210
Orinoco, Orinochese, 9 n. 10, 36 n. 84, 75, 76, 100, 103, 104, 105
Ortolani, Giuseppe, 52 n. 31, 56, 58, 209, 214
Otis, George Alexander, 131 n. 72, 174, 216
Otomite, Indians, 20
Oviedo, Gonzalo Fernandez de, 37 n. 89, 101

Pace, Antonio, 2 n. 2, 119 n. 35, 118 n. 33, 122, 158 n. 142, 214, 216, 217
Padua, Italy, 167
Pagden, Anthony, 3 n. 8, 214
Paine, Thomas, 183
Palestine, 18
Paradise, John, 173 n. 76
Paraguay, 4, 5, 7, 8, 10, 54, 72
Parechi, Indians, 103, 104
Parini, Giuseppe, xiii, 18, 21, 73, 81, 123 n. 49, 192, 210
Paris, France, 144, 145, 149, 170, 171, 173, 174
Parkman, Francis, 22 n. 63, 214
Patagonia, Patagons, xiii, 30, 31, 32, 42
Pauw, Cornelius de, 73 n. 93, 77, 78, 92, 98, 121, 148, 155, 159, 160, 176
Pavesio, Paolo, 170 n. 22, 214
Pearls of California, 21
Peking, China, 49
Penn, William, 73, 107, 108, 111, 113, 114, 180
Pennsylvania, 87, 97, 107, 111-17, 118, 119, 121, 154 n. 131, 164 n. 9, 165, 166, 185
Pernety, Antoine-Joseph, 32 n. 80, 78 n. 105, 210
Perocco, Daria, 12 n. 29
Persians, 36 n. 84, 182
Peru, Peruvians, 2, 11, 52, 66, 67, 68-83, 155, 193, 194
Phelan, John Leddy, 214

Philadelphia, 87, 113 n. 18, 115, 116, 117, 118, 122, 126, 161, 162, 163, 164 n. 9, 165, 166, 174
Philippines, 18
Piccioni, Leone, 126 n. 56, 208
Piccolo, Francesco Maria, 196, 197, 210
Pisa, Italy, 137
Pizarro, Francisco, 73 n. 93
Plato, 20 n. 53, 76 n. 101, 82
Poggio a Cajano, Italy, 137
Poland, 137, 149
Porta, Nunziato, 111
Porter, Roy, 215
Portugal, Portuguese, xii, 53, 74 n. 96
Potomac River, 149
Pranzetti, Luisa, 214
Pratt, T. M., 214
Prévost, Antoine-François, 50 n. 28, 52, 54, 57, 58, 63, 210
Prietley, Herbert I., 23 n. 63
Princeton College, 151 n. 122
Procacci, Giuliano, 170 n. 22, 214
Providence College, 151 n. 122
Pyramids, 20, 75 n. 99

Quakers, xiv, 107-10, 111, 112, 113, 114, 115, 116, 117, 152 n. 125
Quipos, Quipu, 69

Rabany, Charles-Guillaume, 56
Radcliff-Umstead, Douglas, 214
Ramsay, David, 175 n. 31
Ramusio, Giovanni Battista, 15
Raynal, Guillaume-Thomas, 77, 78, 92, 94, 96, 97, 113, 114 n. 21, 115, 127, 144, 145, 147, 148, 149, 155, 158 n. 144, 175, 176, 178, 210, 217
Reconquista, 13
Reinhold, John, 10 n. 21
Revolution, American Revolution, xiv, 113 n. 20, 114, 115, 117 n. 31. 119, 123-36, 140-44, 145, 148, 149, 150, 180, 181, 182, 183, 187, 188
Rhode Island, 153
Ricciardelli, Michele, 173 n. 26, 214
Roberti, Giambattista, 21 n. 57, 115, 210
Robertson, William, xiii, 21 n. 58, 43 n. 13, 47, 64 n. 69, 67, 72 n. 92, 78, 79, 92, 98-100, 159, 176, 190, 204, 210, 217
Rochefoucauld, François de la, 144

Index

Roggeween, Jacob, 31 n. 78
Romagnoli, Sergio, 48 n. 25, 210
Rome, Romans, xii, 36, 71, 128, 133, 167
Romeo, Rosario, xiii, 3, 215
Rousseau George S., 215
Rousseau, Jean Jacques, xiii, 5, 11, 12, 39, 40, 41 n. 3, 42, 43, 44, 45, 56, 57, 61, 64, 66, 67, 71, 79, 86, 98, 193, 210, 217
Rum, 74
Russia, 151, 171
Russo, Luigi, 162 n. 1
Russo, Joseph Louis, 162 n. 1, 215

Sale, Kirkpatrick, 215
Salsotto, Carlo, 170 n. 22, 215
Salvaterra, Father, 10, 21 n. 59
San Giorgio Canavese, Italy, 170
Sangro di San Severo, Raimondo de, 69–71, 81 n. 115, 108, 210
Sarpi, Paolo, 170
Savarese, Gennaro, 31 n. 79, 205 n. 11, 209, 215
Savioli Fontana, Ludovico, 74 n. 96, 210
Schiavo, Giovanni, 17 n. 44, 22 n. 61, 215
Scotland, "Scotilandi," 42 n. 8
Senegal, 75
Sestan, Ernesto, xiii, 57, 81 n. 114, 215
Shea, John G., 12 n. 30, 216
Shelfard, April, 213
Sherman, Constance, 113 n. 19, 145 n. 105, 217
Siberia, 104 n. 40
Sicily, 167
Siena, Italy, 92
Sierra Leone, 154
Silhouette, Etienne de, 71
Sinaloa Mission, 10, 22
Siraisi, Nancy, 213
Siri, Vittorio, 170
Slavery, Slaves, 102 n. 34, 103, 115, 124 n. 49, 142, 143 n. 99, 145, 147 n. 112, 154, 178, 186
Smollet, Tobias, 108 n. 2, 217, 218
Soave, Francesco, 59 n. 52, 111, 210
Sonora Mission, 10, 22
Sorrento, Italy, 42 n. 11
South Carolina, 157
Spain, Spaniards, Spanish, xii, 2, 5, 8, 10, 20, 21, 32, 52, 53, 72, 74, 81, 85, 92, 99, 100, 103, 109, 125, 129, 130, 138, 190 n. 72, 197 n. 90
Stannard, David E., 215
Starobinski, Jean, 51, 215
Sterlich, Romualdo, 42 n. 11
Stewart, James M., 5 n. 13, 217
Strada, Famiano, 171
Sunbury, Pennsylvania, 161, 165, 166
Susquehanna River, 185
Swift, Bernard C., 51 n. 30
Swift, Oliver, 63 n. 67
Switzerland, Swiss, 171, 182

Tacitus, Publius Cornelius, 87
Tahiti, 46
Tamanachi Indians, 104, 105
Tarleton, Banastre, 175
Tasso, Torquato, 164
Terranova, 100
Tertre, Jean-Baptiste du, 15
Tiber, 36 n. 84
Timoleon the Corynthian, 205
Tobacco, 74
Tocqueville, Alexis-Charles-Henri-Maurice Clérel de, xv
Todorov, Tzvetan, xiii, 1, 11, 215
Tonti, Henri, 17, 207, 217
Tortarolo, Edoardo, 136 n. 85, 146 n. 109, 149 n. 116, 215
Trieste, Italy, 167
Tucuman, 9
Turchi, Roberta, 215
Turin, Italy, 170
Turkey, 138

Ulloa Calá, Gerolamo, 77
Ulmecos Indians, 20 n. 53

Valgimigli, Manara, 119 n. 35, 210
Van Keuren, Luise, 215
Venice, 22 n. 60, 86, 92, 98, 111, 135, 167
Venturi, Franco, 37 n. 89, 42 n. 9, 43 n. 13, 44 n. 15, 71, 83, 86 n. 3, 215
Vermont, 153
Verri, Alessandro, 48, 50, 149, 210, 211
Verri, Pietro, 40 n. 1, 149, 211
Vico Equense, Italy, 42
Vico, Giambattista, xiii, 24, 28–30, 31 n. 78, 35, 36, 37, 41, 71, 74 n. 95, 79, 211, 217
Vincenti, Lionello, 215

Viola, Herman J., 215
Viomino (Wyoming), Pennsylvania, 185
Virginia, 111, 112, 138, 139, 140, 143, 145, 147, 148, 149, 153, 156, 181
Vissler, Clark, 215
Voltaire, François-Marie Arouet de, xiv, 10 n. 21, 40, 41, 46, 48, 50, 52, 57, 75, 76 n. 100, 94, 98, 107, 108, 188, 191, 211, 217, 218

Warburton, William, 71
Warsaw, Poland, 157

Washington Greene, George, 73, 182
Washington, George, xiv, 133, 140, 156, 180, 182, 183, 205
West, Benjamin, 87
White, Hayden, 4 n. 12
Williamsburg, Pennsylvania, 140
Wright, Donald, 215

Zaboklicki, Krzysztof, 56 n. 43, 215
Zambi, Indians, 102
Zardo, Antonio, 45 n. 16, 209